Zenescope Entertainment Presents:

Grimm Fairy Tales

Volume 15

Grimm
Fairy

GRIMM FAIRY TALES

CREATED AND STORY BY
JOE BRUSHA
RALPH TEDESCO

WRITTEN BY
JOE BRUSHA
TROY BROWNFIELD
DAN WICKLINE

ART DIRECTOR
ANTHONY SPAY

TRADE DESIGN BY
CHRISTOPHER COTE
STEPHEN SCHAFFER

TRADE EDITED BY
NICOLE GLADE

THIS VOLUME REPRINTS THE
COMIC SERIES GRIMM FAIRY
TALES ISSUES #89-93 PUBLISHED BY
ZENESCOPE ENTERTAINMENT

FIRST EDITION, MARCH 2014
ISBN: 978-1-939683-51-9

WWW.ZENESCOPE.COM
FACEBOOK.COM/ZENESCOPE

ZENESCOPE ENTERTAINMENT, INC.
Joe Brusha • President & Chief Creative Officer
Ralph Tedesco • Editor-in-Chief
Jennifer Bermel • Director of Licensing & Business Development
Raven Gregory • Executive Editor
Anthony Spay • Art Director
Christopher Cote • Senior Designer & Production Manager
Dave Franchini • Direct Market Sales & Customer Service

Grimm Fairy Tales: Volume 15 Trade Paperback, March 2014.
First Printing. Published by Zenescope Entertainment Inc., 433
Caredean Drive, Ste. C, Horsham, Pennsylvania 19044. Zenescope
and its logos are ® and © 2014 Zenescope Entertainment Inc.
All rights reserved. Grimm Fairy Tales, its logo and all characters
and their likeness are © and ™ 2014 Zenescope Entertainment.
Any similarities to persons (living or dead), events, institutions, or
locales are purely coincidental. No portion of this publication may
be reproduced or transmitted, in any form or by any means, without
the express written permission of Zenescope Entertainment Inc.
except for artwork used for review purposes. Printed in Canada.

Zenescope Entertainment presents:

Grimm Fairy Tales

Volume 15

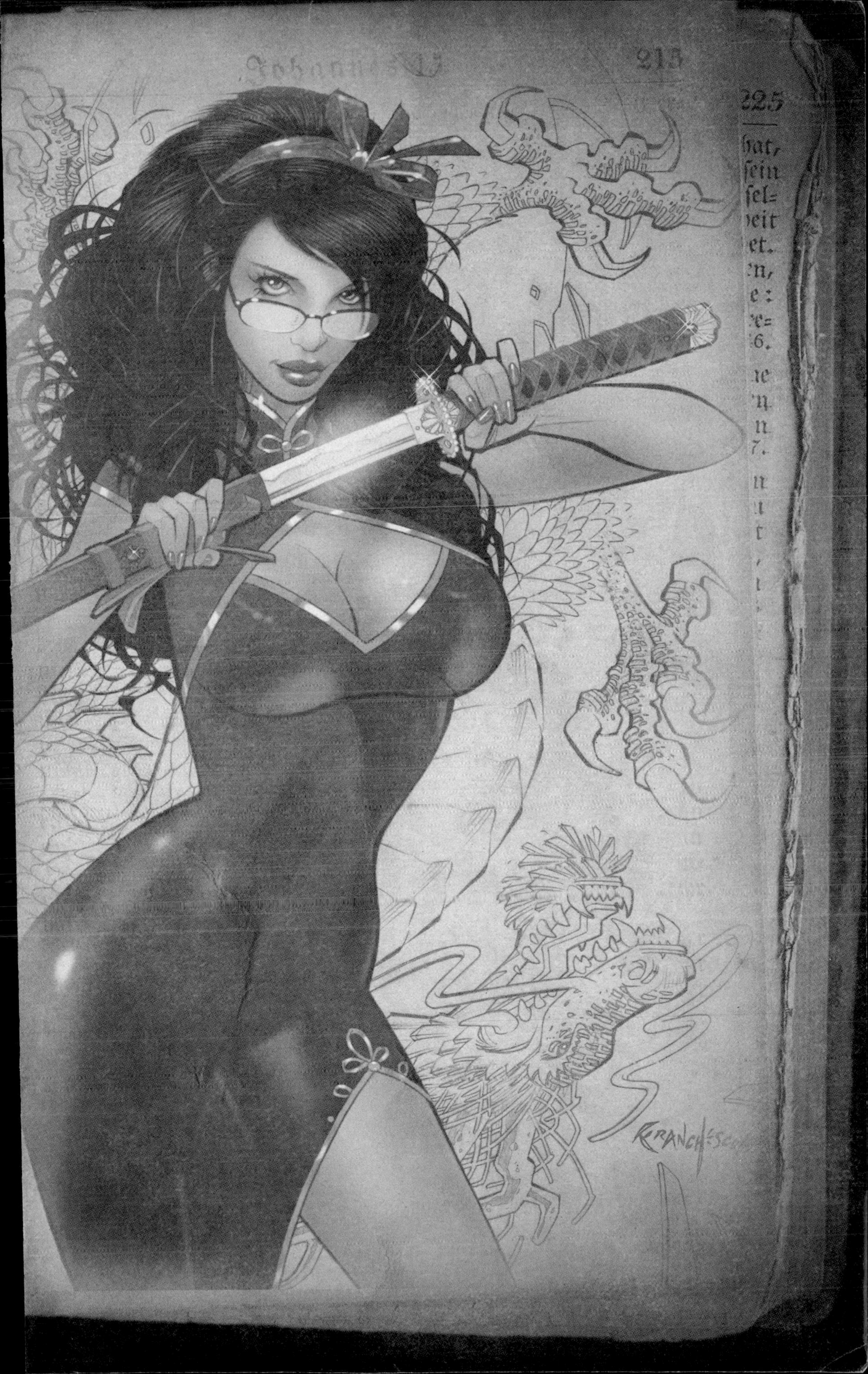
213
225

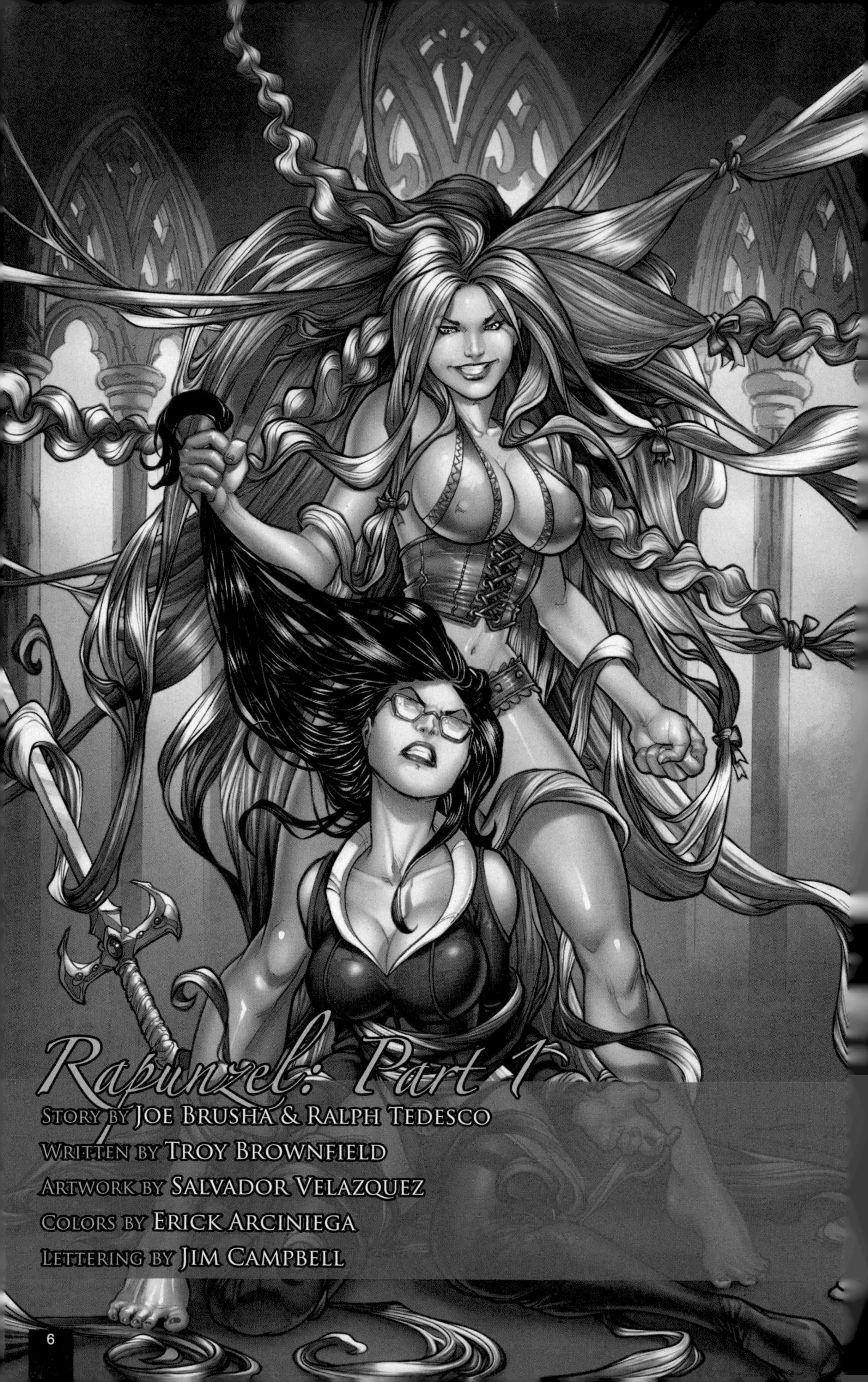
Rapunzel: Part 1
Story by Joe Brusha & Ralph Tedesco
Written by Troy Brownfield
Artwork by Salvador Velazquez
Colors by Erick Arciniega
Lettering by Jim Campbell

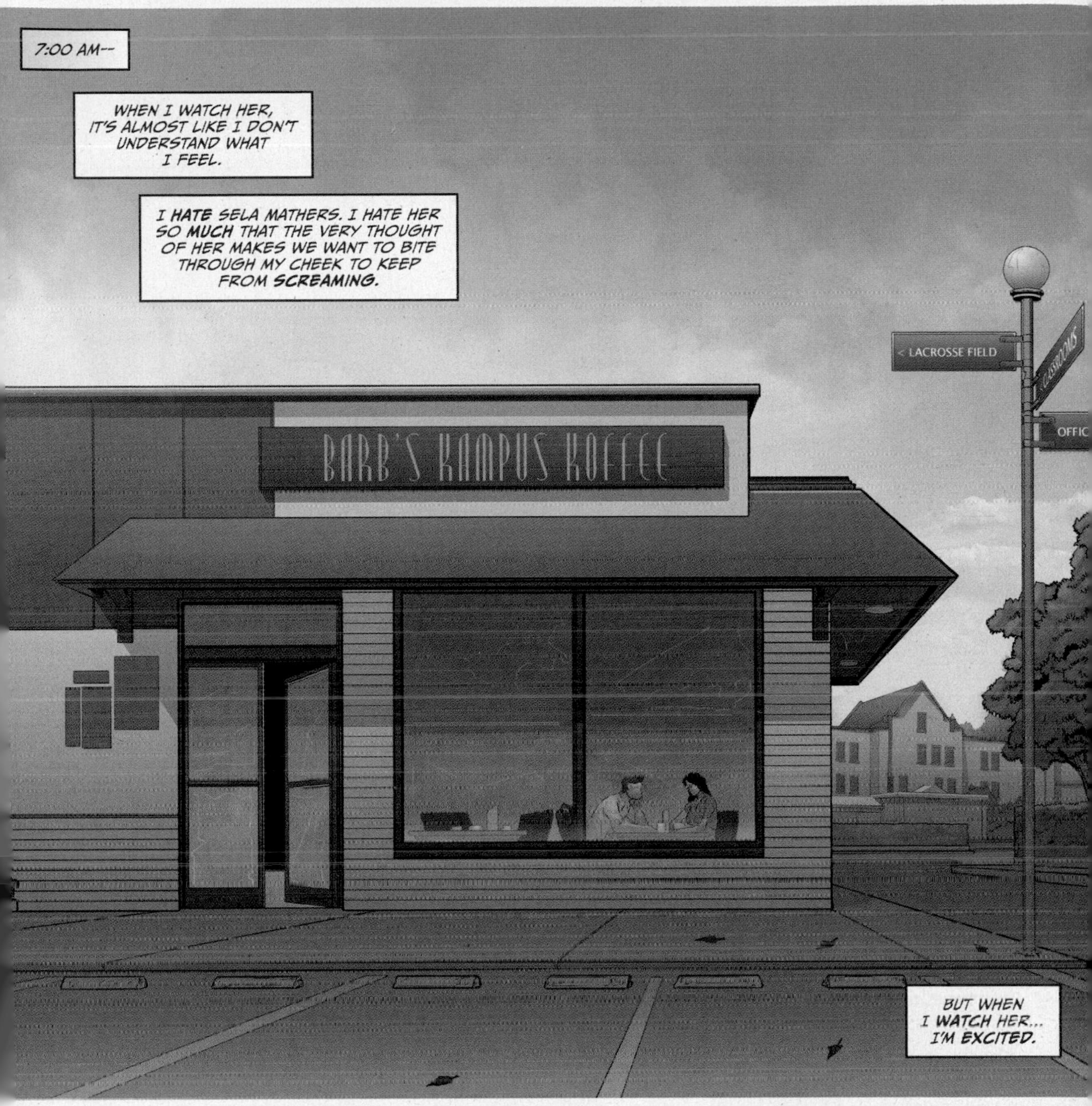
7:00 AM--
WHEN I WATCH HER, IT'S ALMOST LIKE I DON'T UNDERSTAND WHAT I FEEL.
I **HATE** SELA MATHERS. I HATE HER SO **MUCH** THAT THE VERY THOUGHT OF HER MAKES WE WANT TO BITE THROUGH MY CHEEK TO KEEP FROM **SCREAMING.**
< LACROSSE FIELD
OFFIC
BARB'S KAMPUS KOFFEE
BUT WHEN I **WATCH** HER... I'M **EXCITED.**

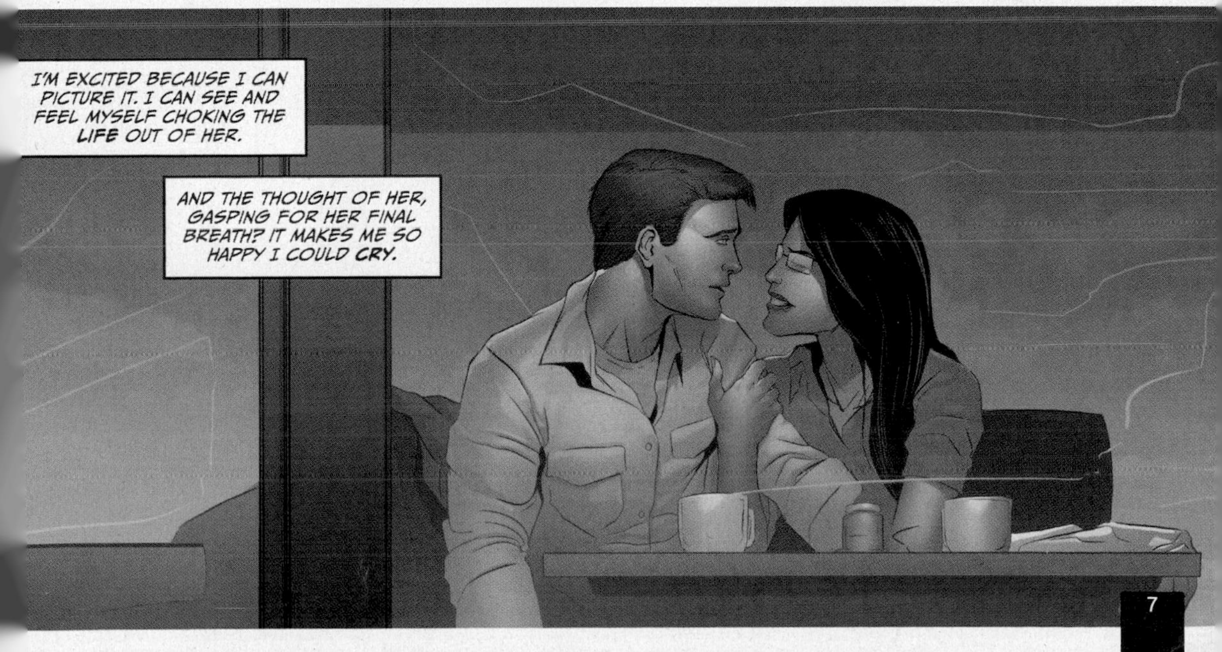
I'M EXCITED BECAUSE I CAN PICTURE IT. I CAN SEE AND FEEL MYSELF CHOKING THE **LIFE** OUT OF HER.
AND THE THOUGHT OF HER, GASPING FOR HER FINAL BREATH? IT MAKES ME SO HAPPY I COULD **CRY.**

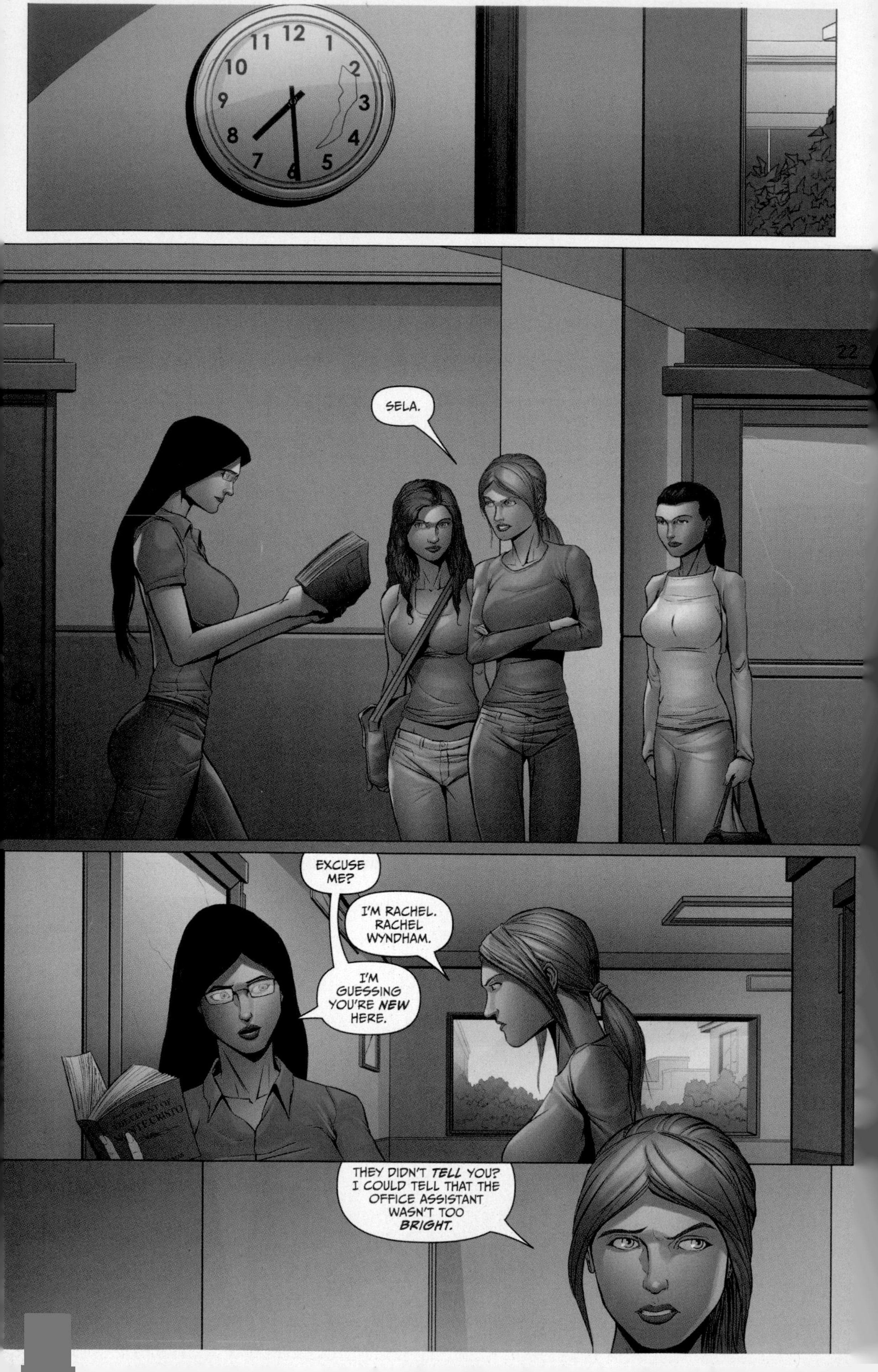
SELA.
EXCUSE ME?
I'M RACHEL. RACHEL WYNDHAM.
I'M GUESSING YOU'RE NEW HERE.
THEY DIDN'T TELL YOU? I COULD TELL THAT THE OFFICE ASSISTANT WASN'T TOO BRIGHT.

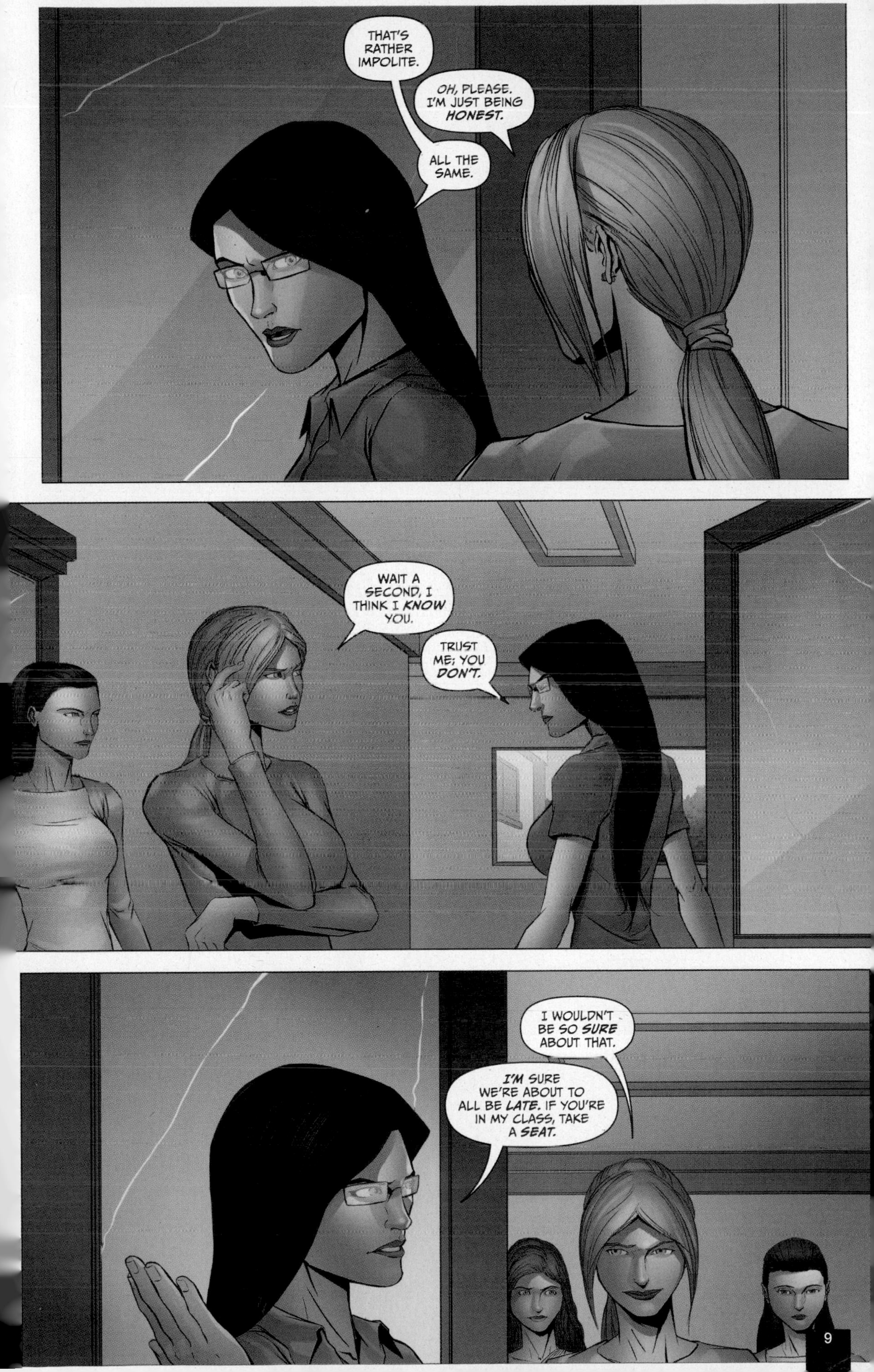
THAT'S RATHER IMPOLITE.
OH, PLEASE. I'M JUST BEING HONEST.
ALL THE SAME.
WAIT A SECOND, I THINK I KNOW YOU.
TRUST ME; YOU DON'T.
I WOULDN'T BE SO SURE ABOUT THAT.
I'M SURE WE'RE ABOUT TO ALL BE LATE. IF YOU'RE IN MY CLASS, TAKE A SEAT.

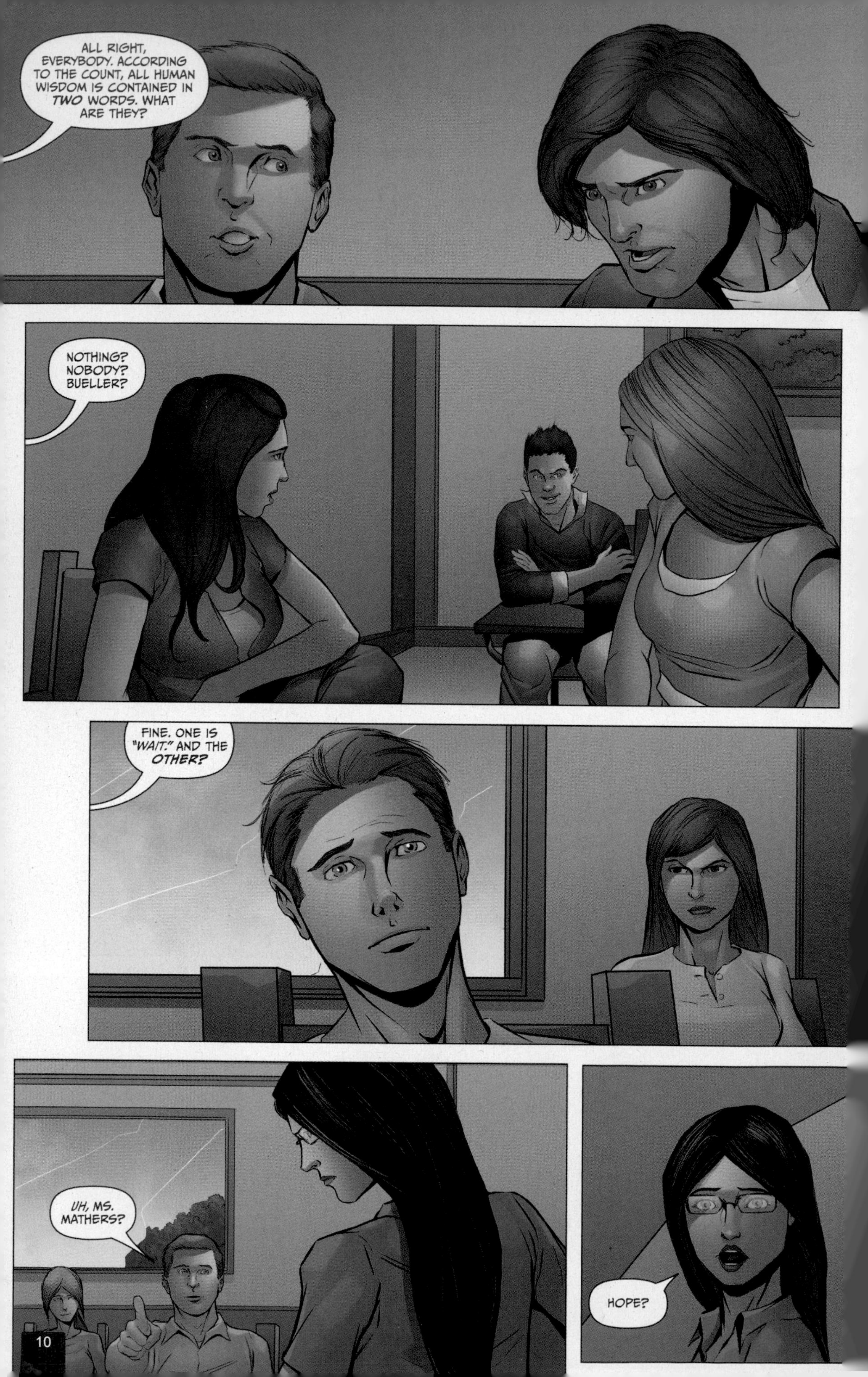
ALL RIGHT, EVERYBODY. ACCORDING TO THE COUNT, ALL HUMAN WISDOM IS CONTAINED IN TWO WORDS. WHAT ARE THEY?
NOTHING? NOBODY? BUELLER?
FINE. ONE IS "WAIT." AND THE OTHER?
UH, MS. MATHERS?
HOPE?

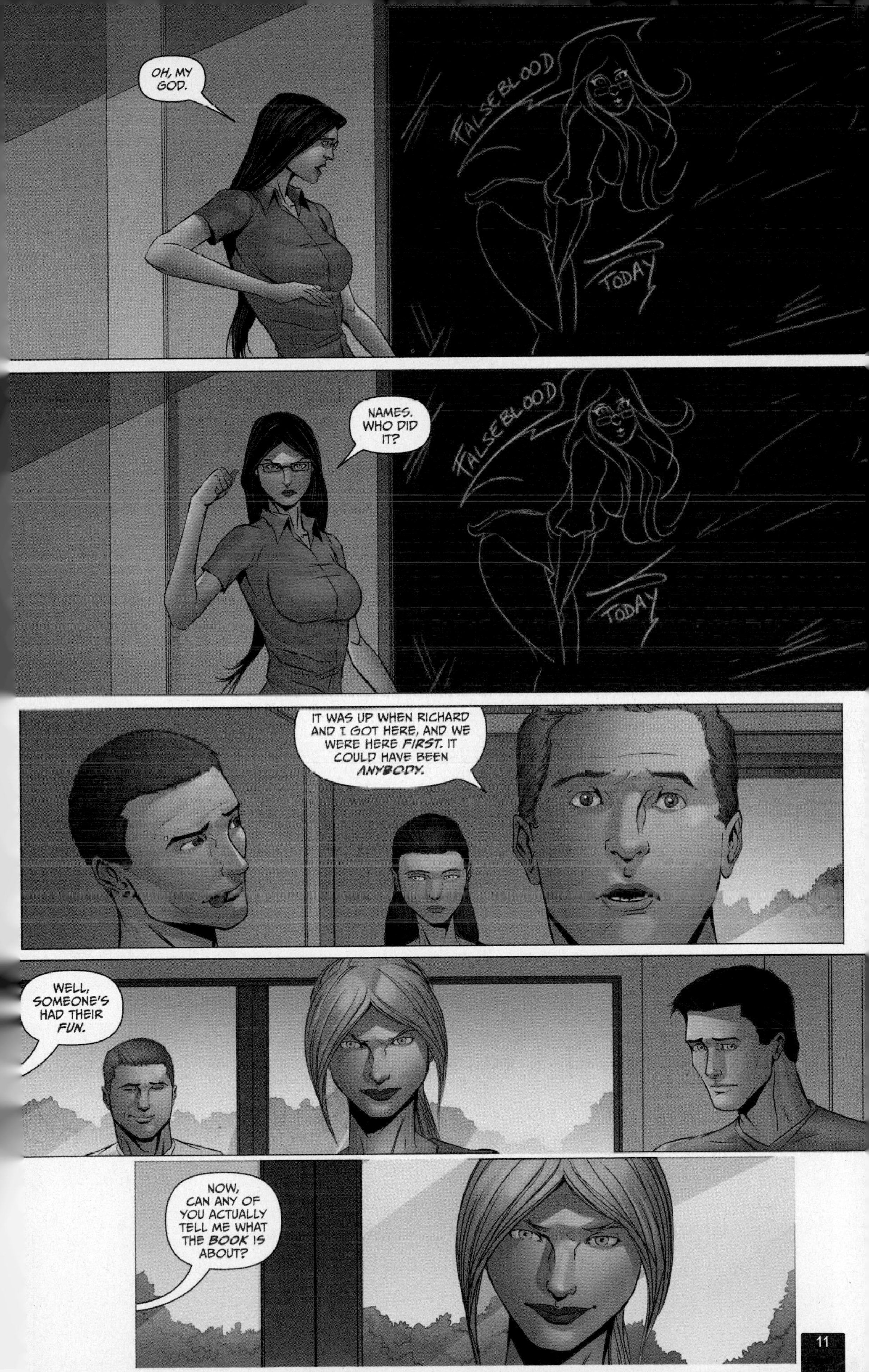

FALSEBLOOD
TODAY
OH, MY GOD.
NAMES. WHO DID IT?
IT WAS UP WHEN RICHARD AND I GOT HERE, AND WE WERE HERE *FIRST.* IT COULD HAVE BEEN *ANYBODY.*
WELL, SOMEONE'S HAD THEIR *FUN.*
NOW, CAN ANY OF YOU ACTUALLY TELL ME WHAT THE *BOOK* IS ABOUT?

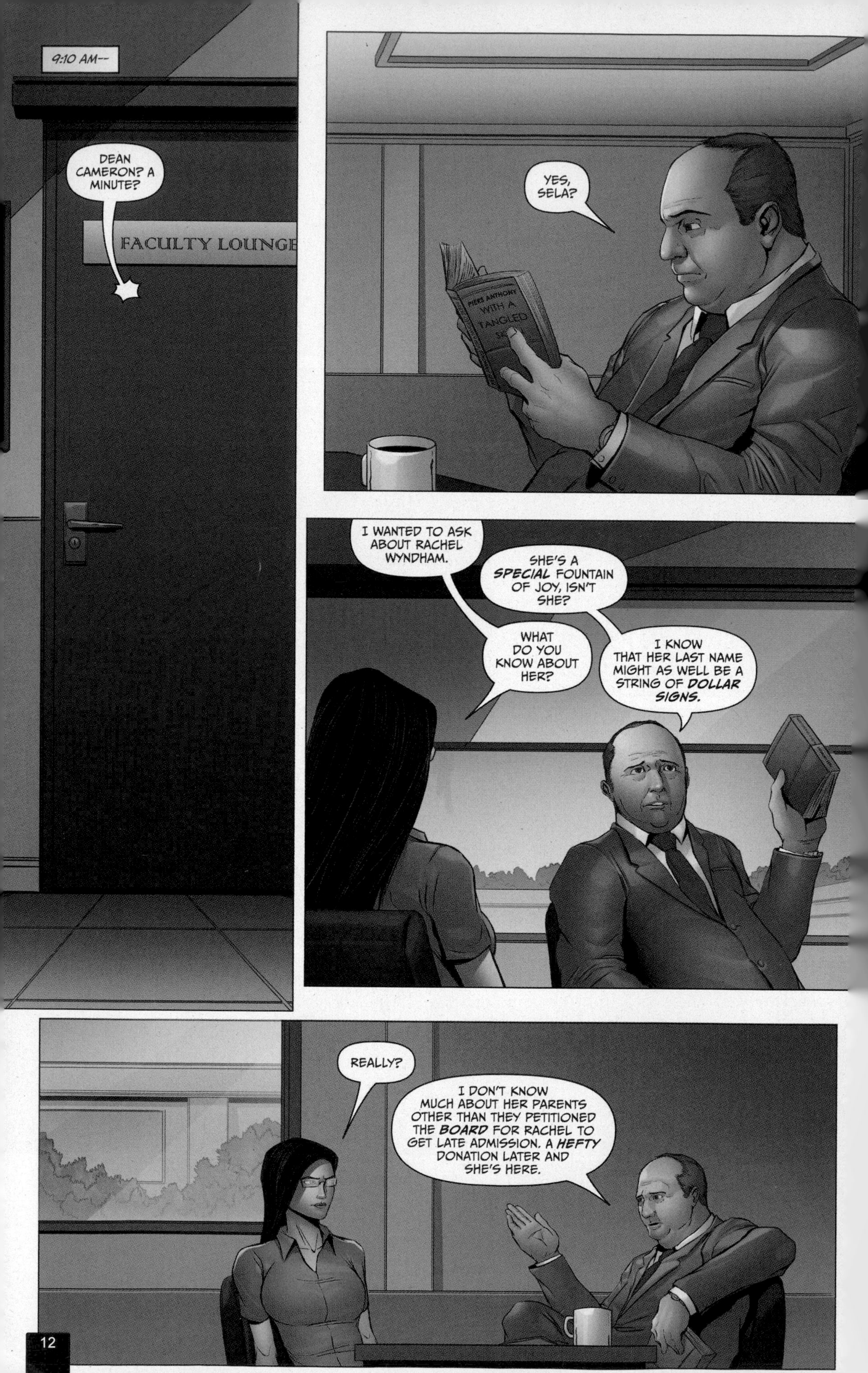

9:10 AM--
DEAN CAMERON? A MINUTE?
FACULTY LOUNGE
YES, SELA?
PIERS ANTHONY WITH A TANGLED
I WANTED TO ASK ABOUT RACHEL WYNDHAM.
SHE'S A SPECIAL FOUNTAIN OF JOY, ISN'T SHE?
WHAT DO YOU KNOW ABOUT HER?
I KNOW THAT HER LAST NAME MIGHT AS WELL BE A STRING OF DOLLAR SIGNS.
REALLY?
I DON'T KNOW MUCH ABOUT HER PARENTS OTHER THAN THEY PETITIONED THE BOARD FOR RACHEL TO GET LATE ADMISSION. A HEFTY DONATION LATER AND SHE'S HERE.

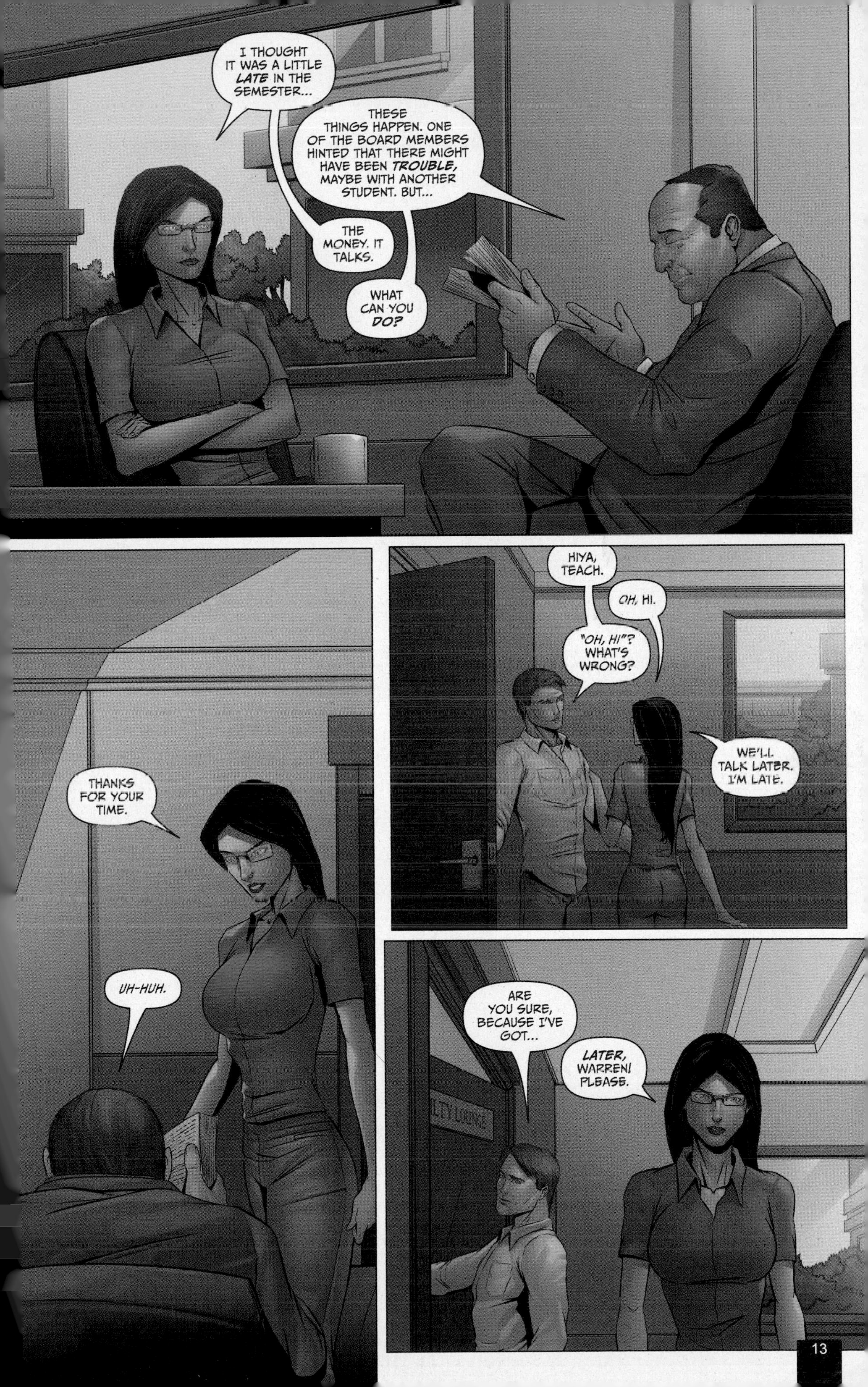
I THOUGHT IT WAS A LITTLE *LATE* IN THE SEMESTER...
THESE THINGS HAPPEN. ONE OF THE BOARD MEMBERS HINTED THAT THERE MIGHT HAVE BEEN *TROUBLE,* MAYBE WITH ANOTHER STUDENT. BUT...
THE MONEY. IT TALKS.
WHAT CAN YOU *DO?*
THANKS FOR YOUR TIME.
UH-HUH.
HIYA, TEACH.
OH, HI.
"OH, HI"? WHAT'S WRONG?
WE'LL TALK LATER. I'M LATE.
ARE YOU SURE, BECAUSE I'VE GOT...
LATER, WARREN! PLEASE.

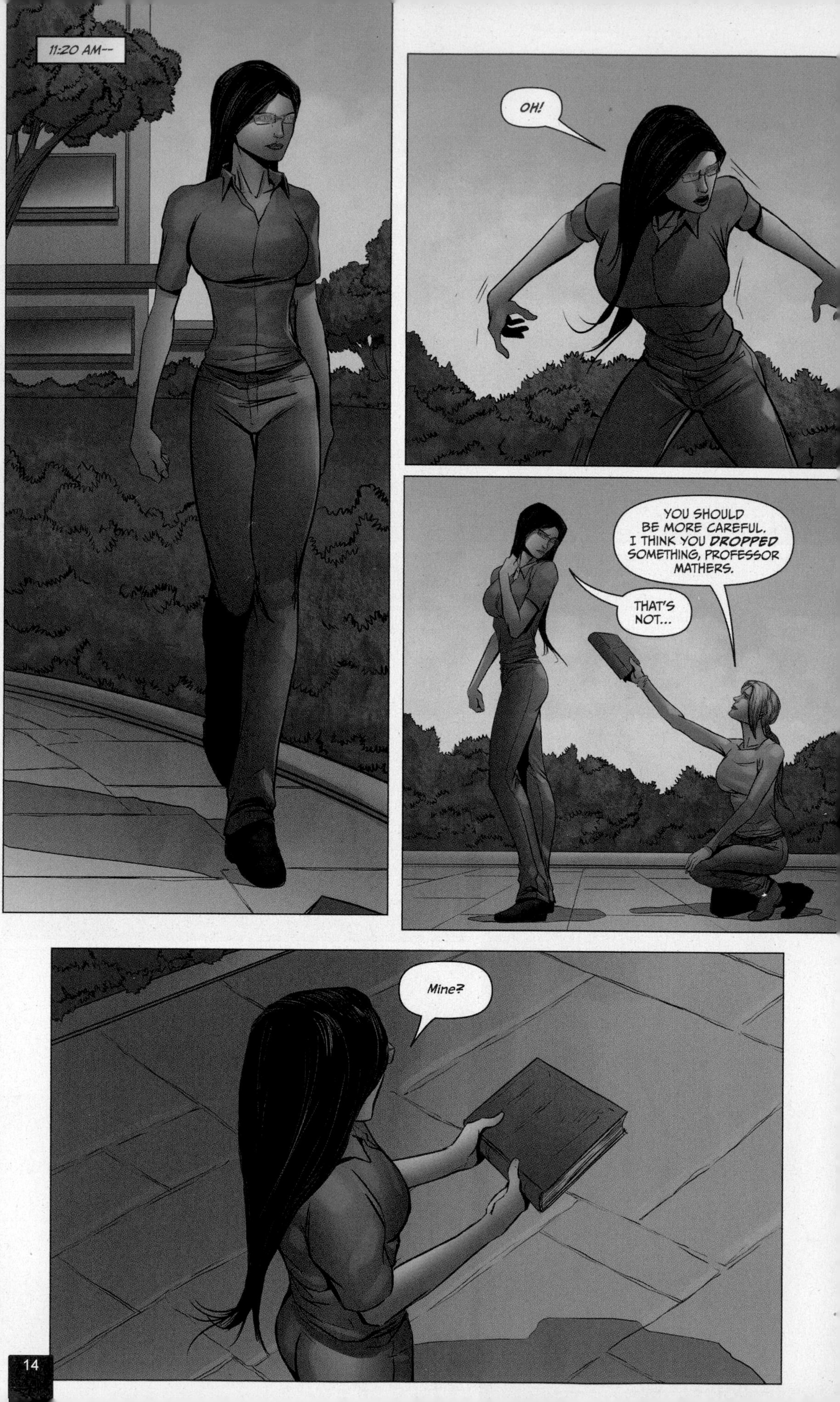
11:20 AM--
OH!
YOU SHOULD BE MORE CAREFUL. I THINK YOU DROPPED SOMETHING, PROFESSOR MATHERS.
THAT'S NOT...
Mine?

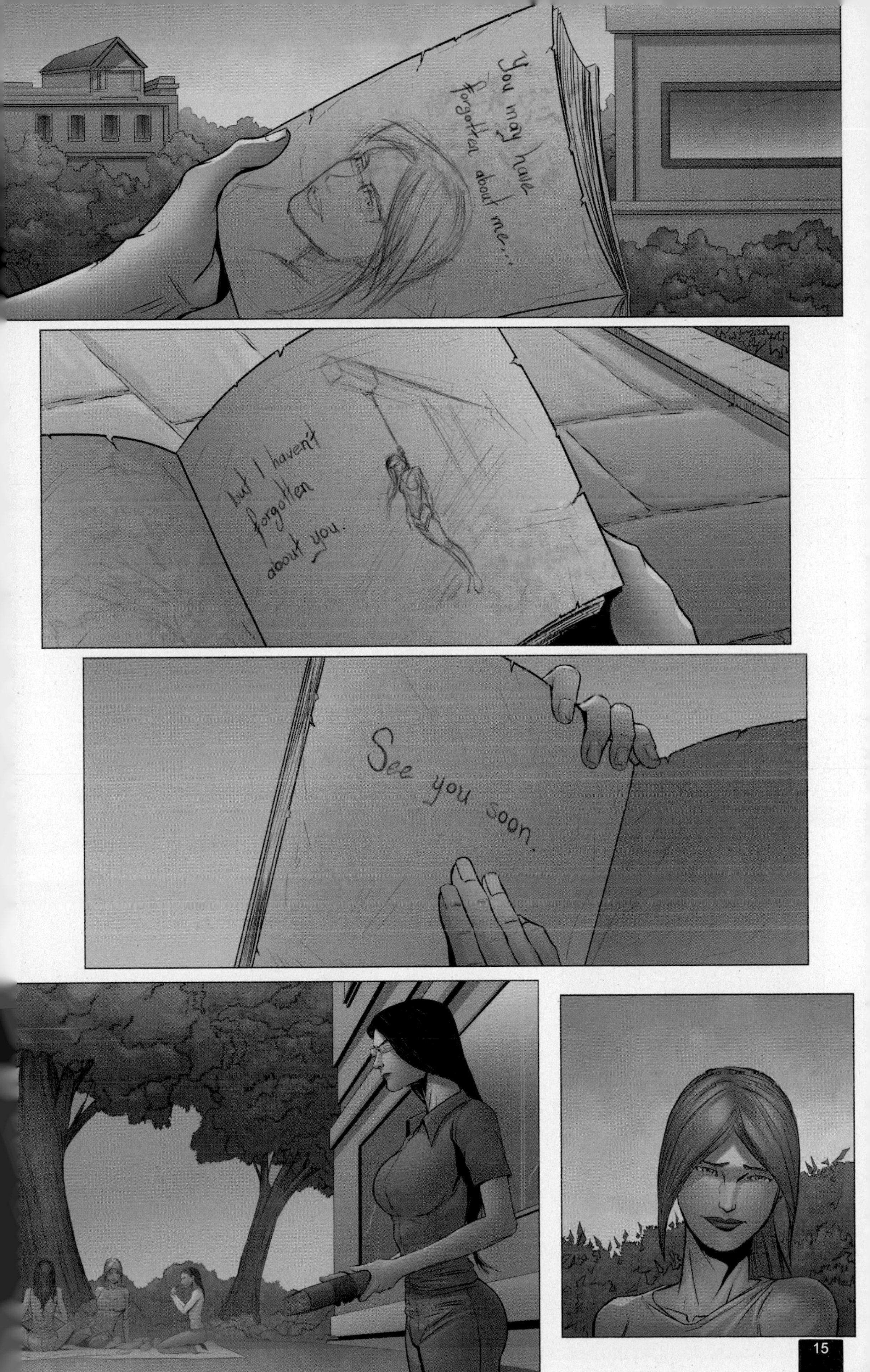
You may have forgotten about me...
but I haven't forgotten about you.
See you soon.

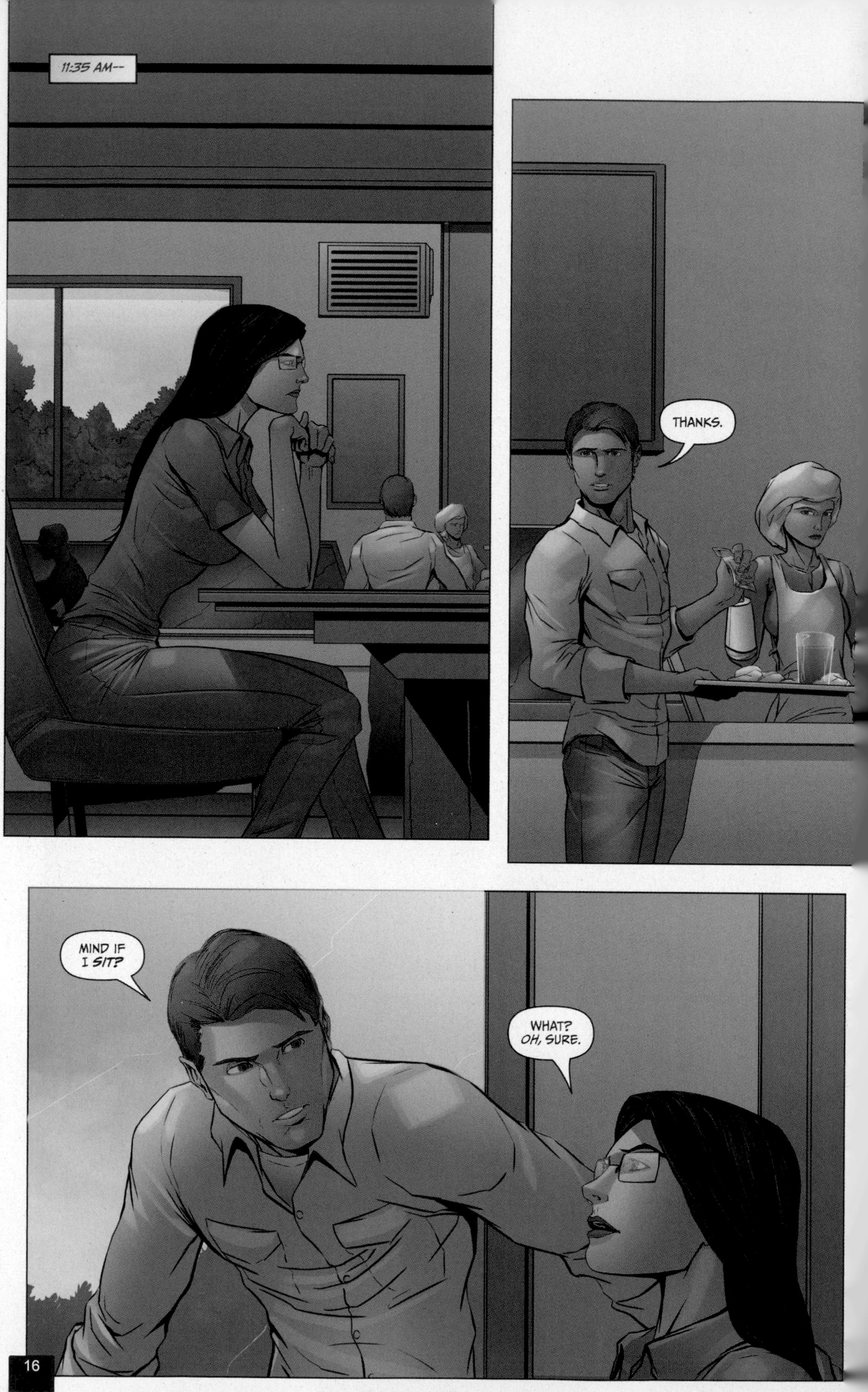
11:35 AM--
THANKS.
MIND IF I *SIT?*
WHAT? *OH,* SURE.

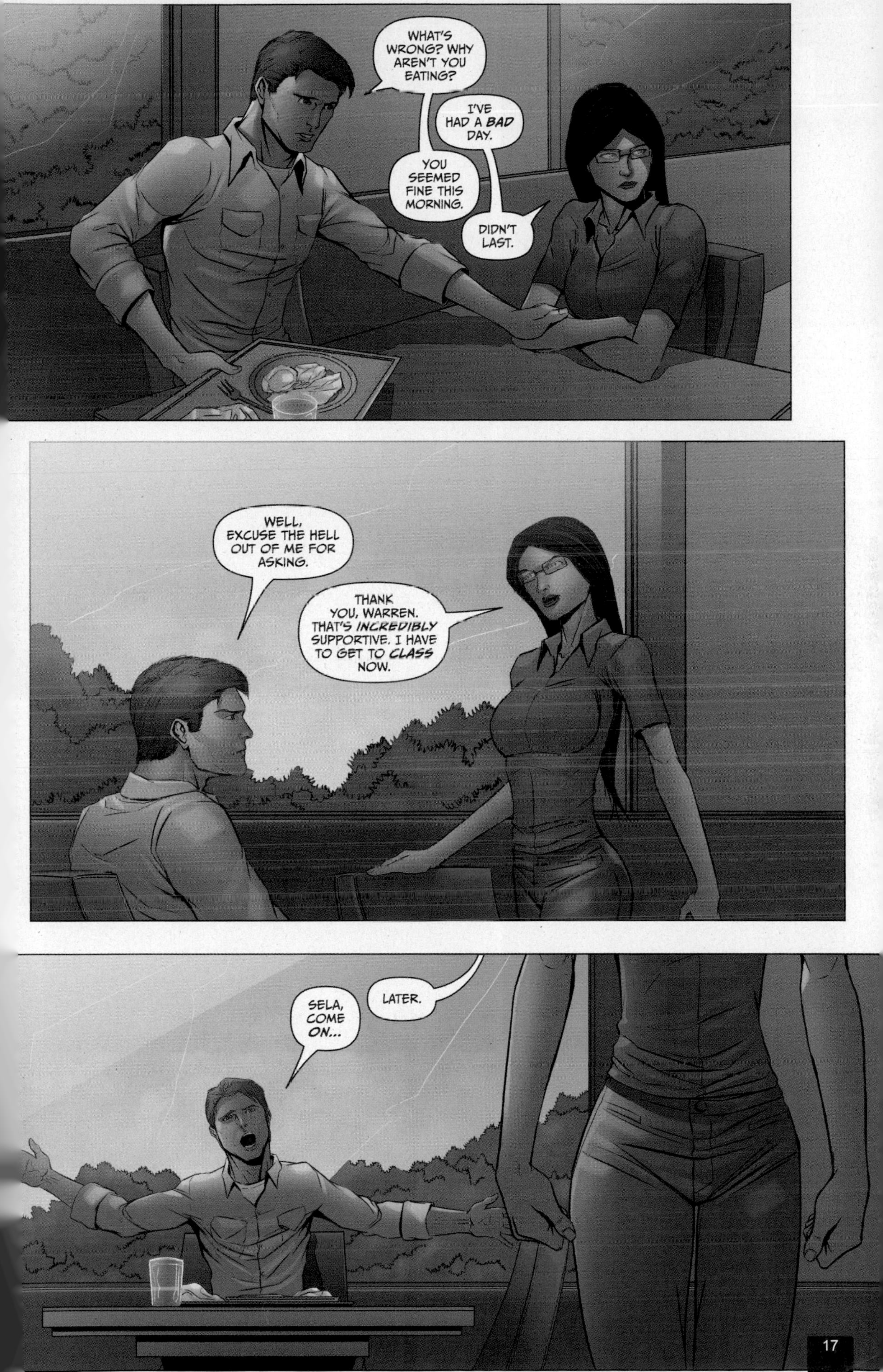
WHAT'S WRONG? WHY AREN'T YOU EATING?
I'VE HAD A BAD DAY.
YOU SEEMED FINE THIS MORNING.
DIDN'T LAST.
WELL, EXCUSE THE HELL OUT OF ME FOR ASKING.
THANK YOU, WARREN. THAT'S INCREDIBLY SUPPORTIVE. I HAVE TO GET TO CLASS NOW.
SELA, COME ON...
LATER.

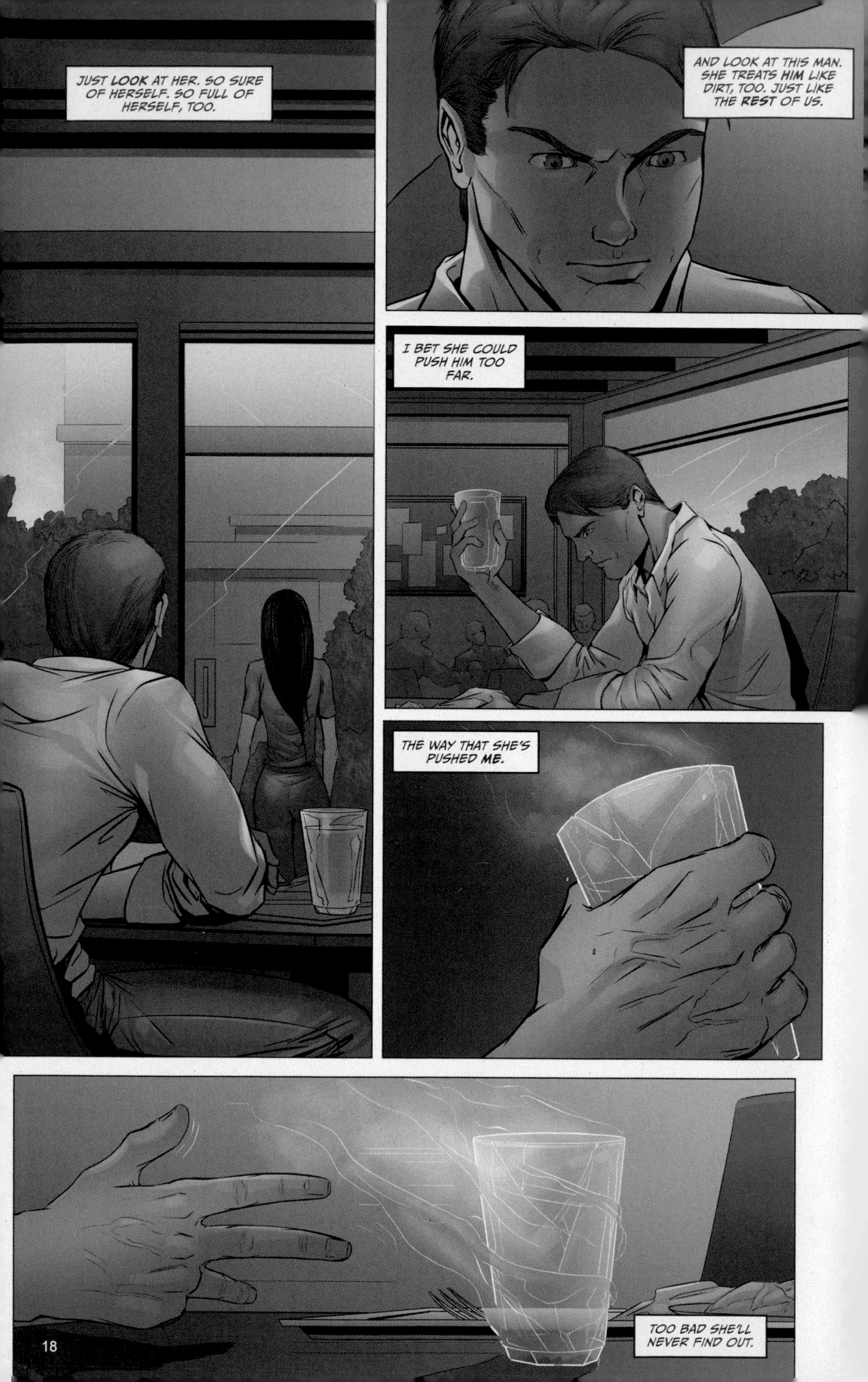
JUST LOOK AT HER. SO SURE OF HERSELF. SO FULL OF HERSELF, TOO.
AND LOOK AT THIS MAN. SHE TREATS HIM LIKE DIRT, TOO. JUST LIKE THE REST OF US.
I BET SHE COULD PUSH HIM TOO FAR.
THE WAY THAT SHE'S PUSHED ME.
TOO BAD SHE'LL NEVER FIND OUT.

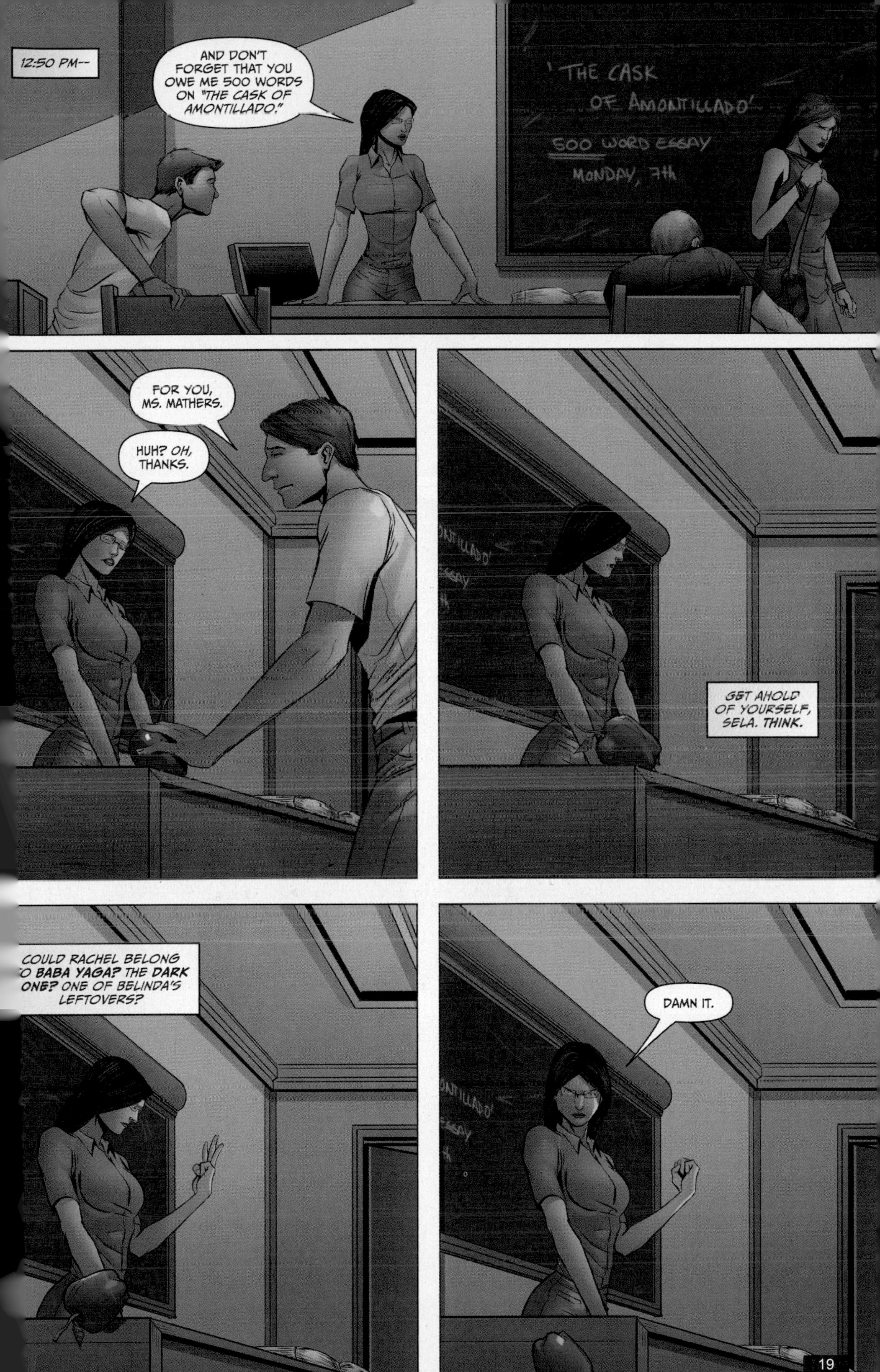
12:50 PM--
AND DON'T FORGET THAT YOU OWE ME 500 WORDS ON "THE CASK OF AMONTILLADO."
'THE CASK OF AMONTILLADO'
500 WORD ESSAY
MONDAY, 7th
FOR YOU, MS. MATHERS.
HUH? OH, THANKS.
GET AHOLD OF YOURSELF, SELA. THINK.
COULD RACHEL BELONG TO BABA YAGA? THE DARK ONE? ONE OF BELINDA'S LEFTOVERS?
DAMN IT.

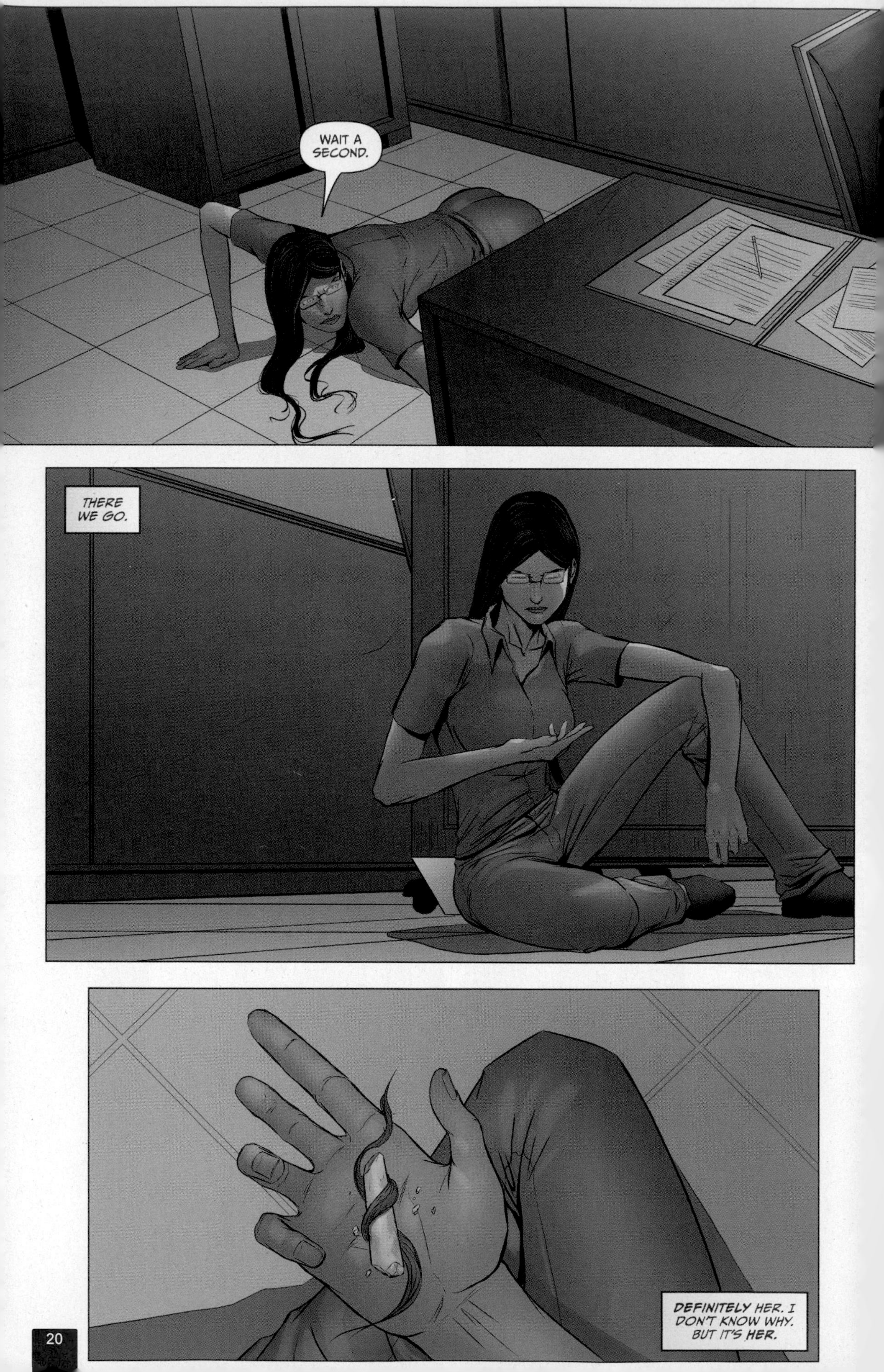
WAIT A SECOND.
THERE WE GO.
DEFINITELY HER. I DON'T KNOW WHY. BUT IT'S HER.

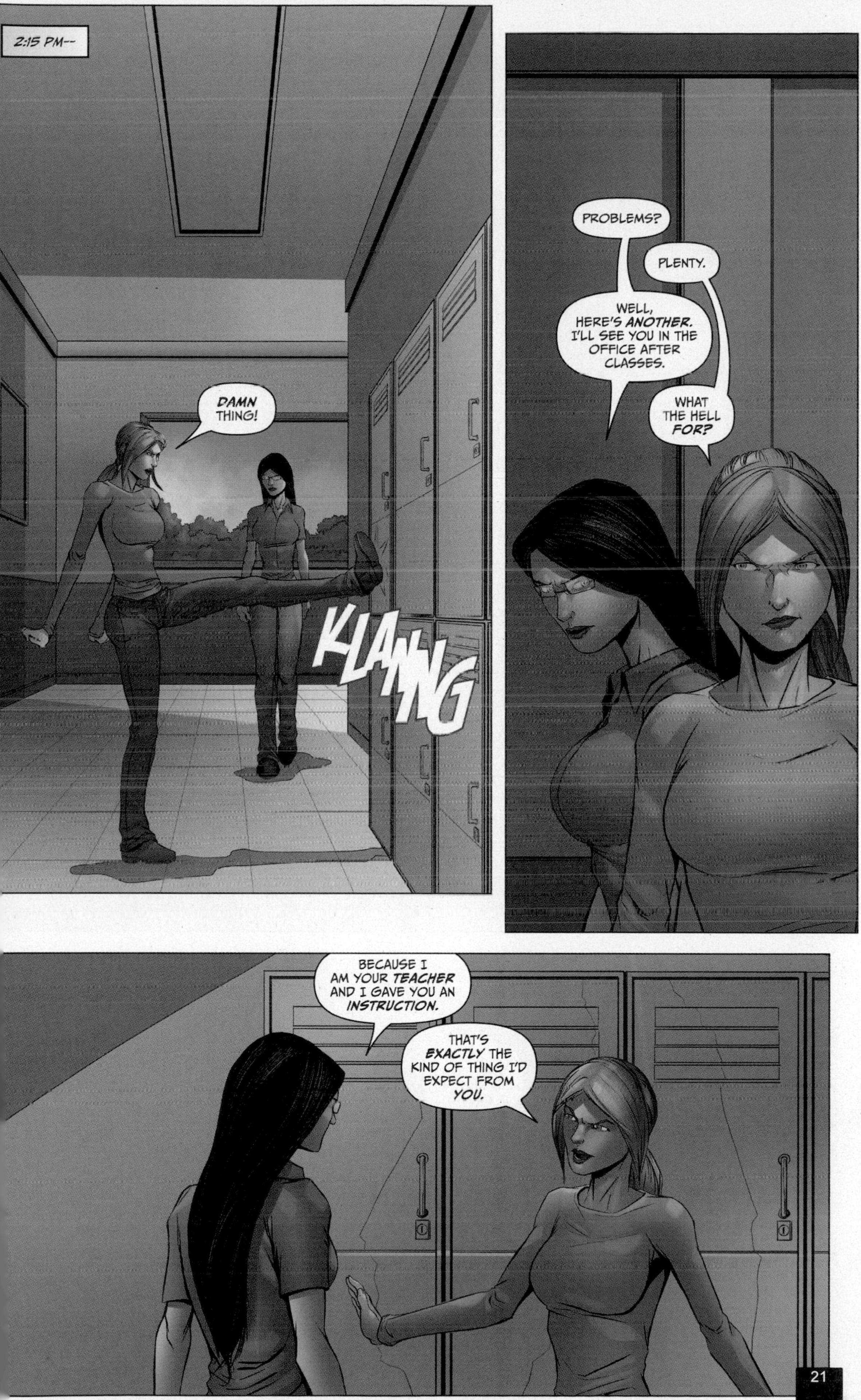
2:15 PM--
DAMN THING!
KLANNG
PROBLEMS?
PLENTY.
WELL, HERE'S ANOTHER. I'LL SEE YOU IN THE OFFICE AFTER CLASSES.
WHAT THE HELL FOR?
BECAUSE I AM YOUR TEACHER AND I GAVE YOU AN INSTRUCTION.
THAT'S EXACTLY THE KIND OF THING I'D EXPECT FROM YOU.

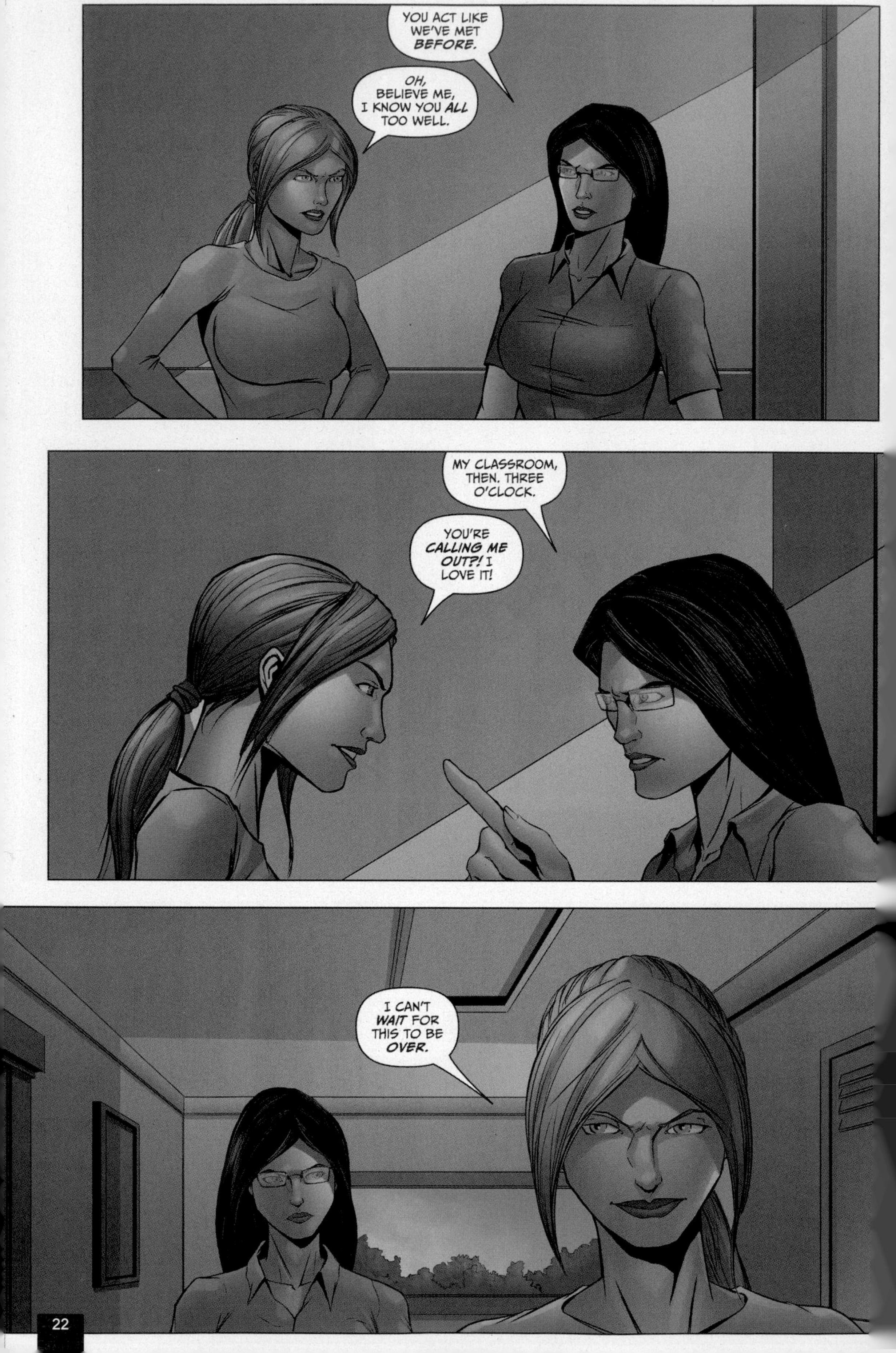
YOU ACT LIKE WE'VE MET BEFORE.
OH, BELIEVE ME, I KNOW YOU ALL TOO WELL.
MY CLASSROOM, THEN. THREE O'CLOCK.
YOU'RE CALLING ME OUT?! I LOVE IT!
I CAN'T WAIT FOR THIS TO BE OVER.

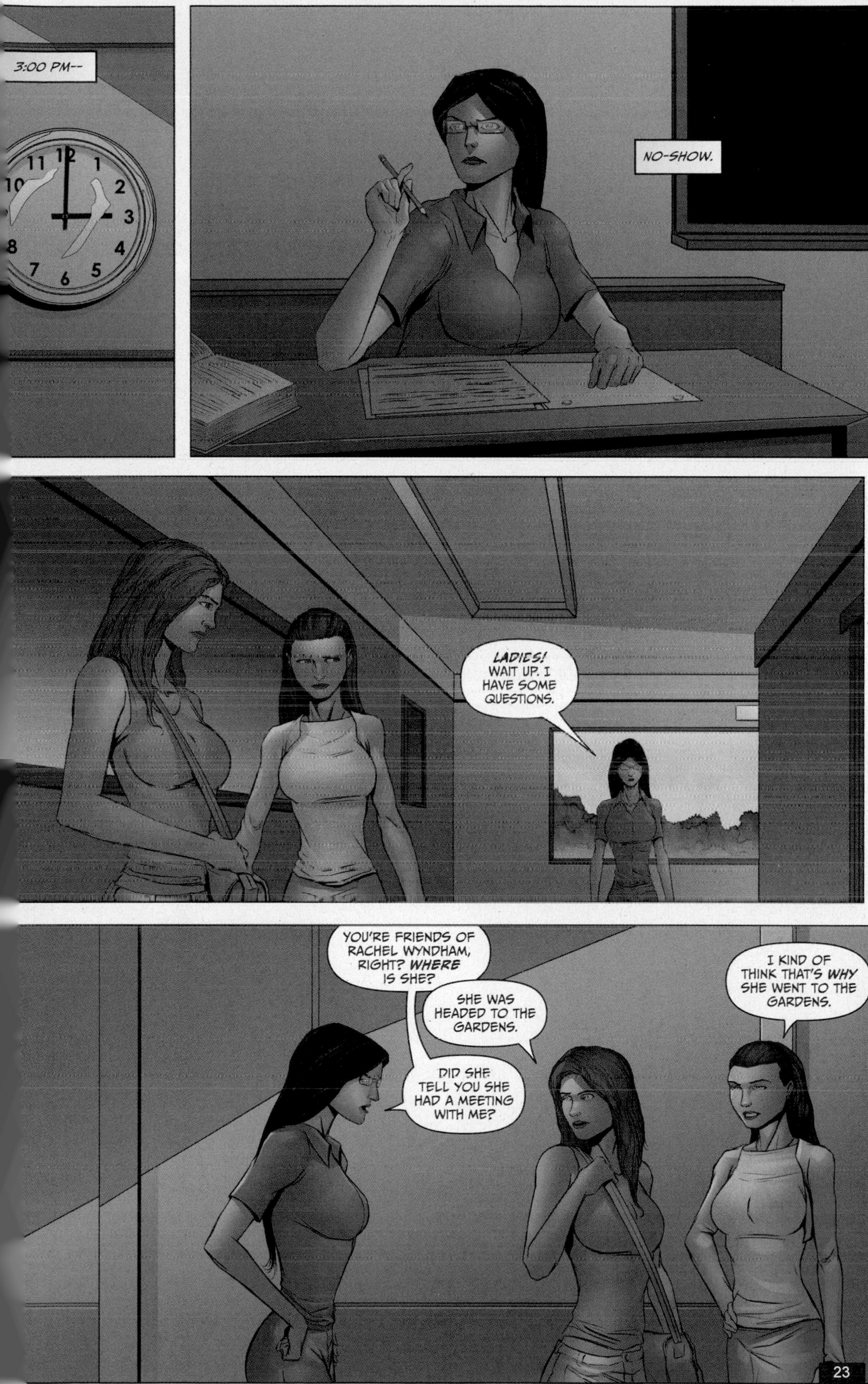
3:00 PM--
NO-SHOW.
LADIES! WAIT UP. I HAVE SOME QUESTIONS.
YOU'RE FRIENDS OF RACHEL WYNDHAM, RIGHT? WHERE IS SHE?
SHE WAS HEADED TO THE GARDENS.
DID SHE TELL YOU SHE HAD A MEETING WITH ME?
I KIND OF THINK THAT'S WHY SHE WENT TO THE GARDENS.

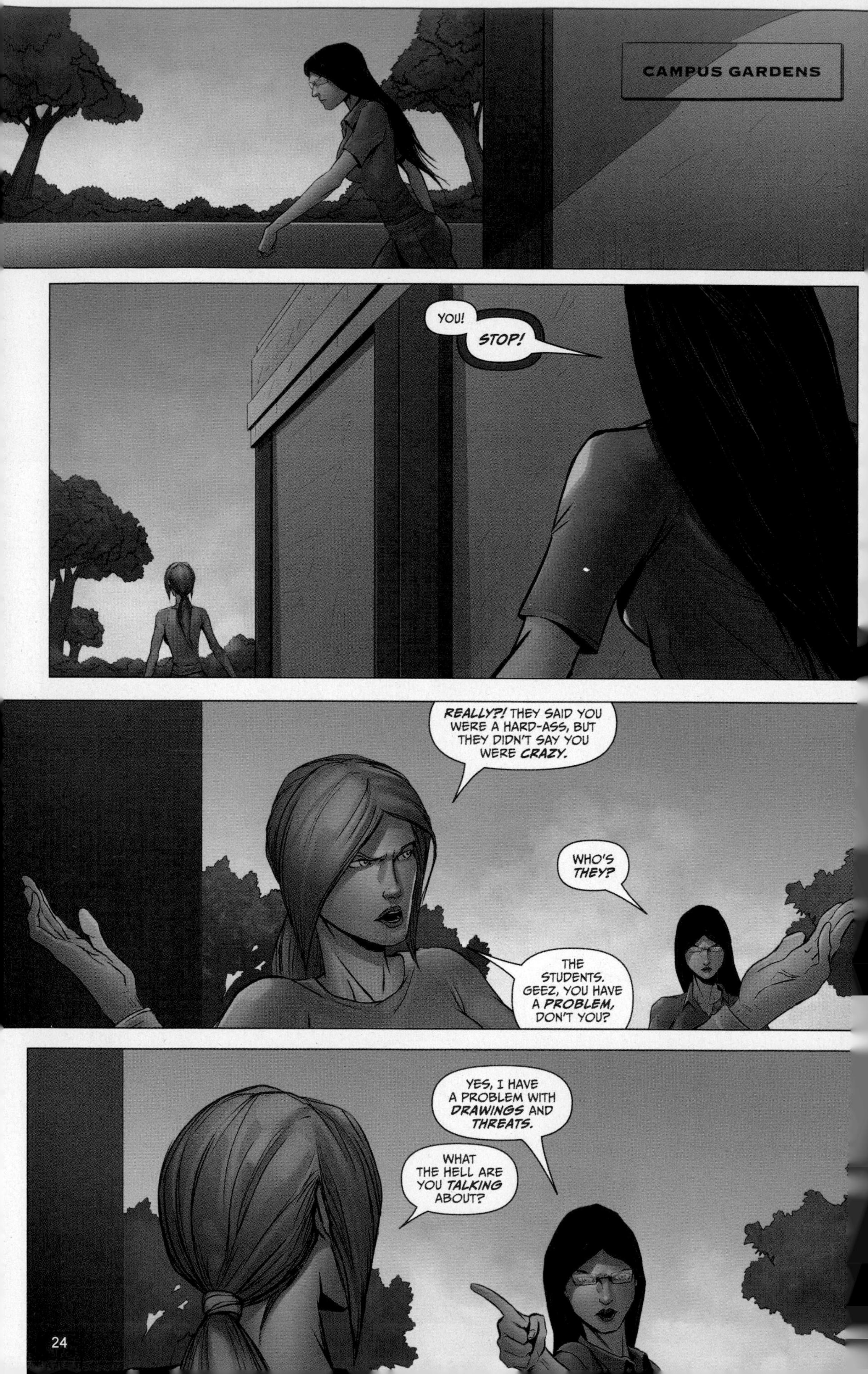
CAMPUS GARDENS
YOU! STOP!
REALLY?! THEY SAID YOU WERE A HARD-ASS, BUT THEY DIDN'T SAY YOU WERE CRAZY.
WHO'S THEY?
THE STUDENTS. GEEZ, YOU HAVE A PROBLEM, DON'T YOU?
YES, I HAVE A PROBLEM WITH DRAWINGS AND THREATS.
WHAT THE HELL ARE YOU TALKING ABOUT?

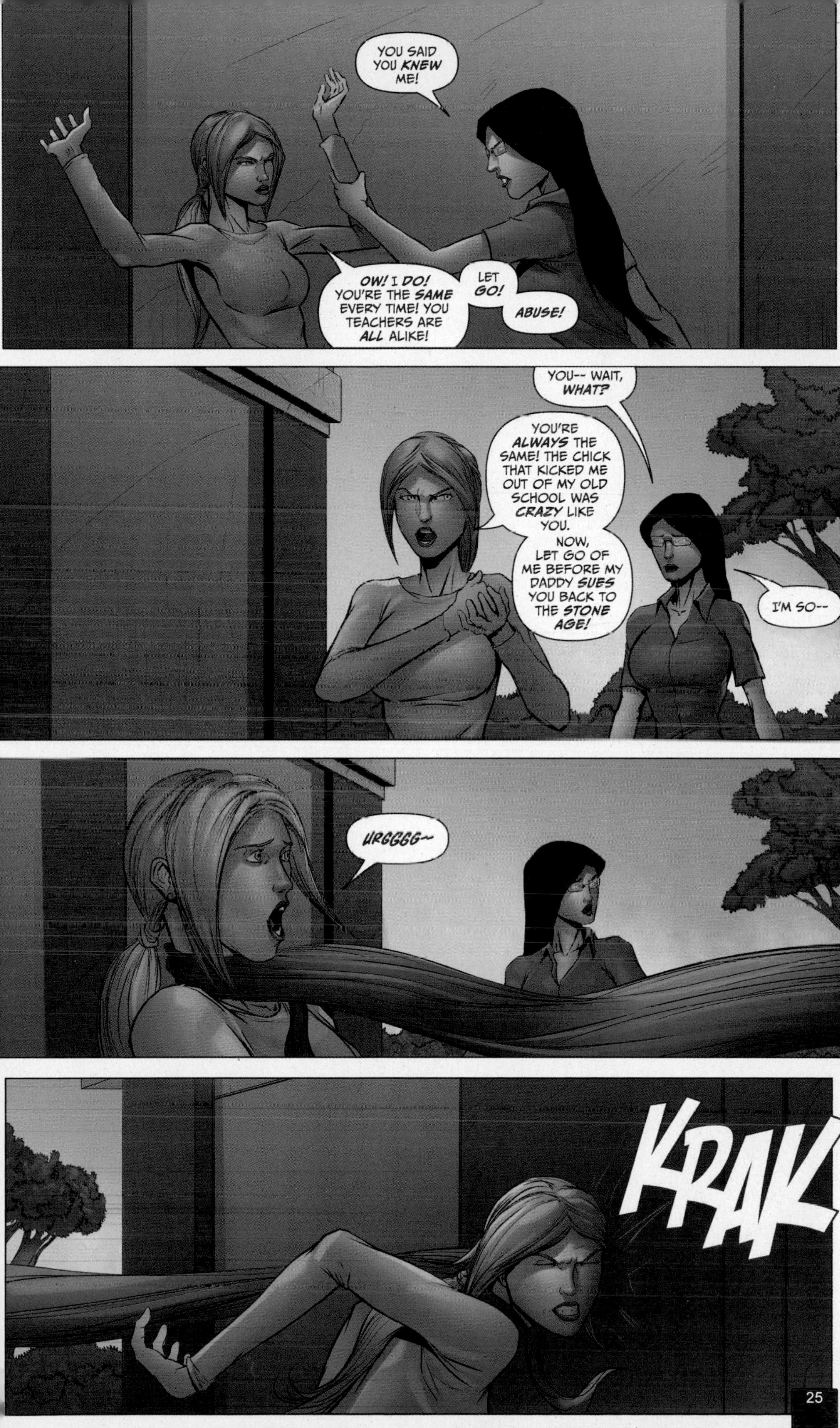

YOU SAID YOU *KNEW* ME!
OW! I *DO!* YOU'RE THE *SAME* EVERY TIME! YOU TEACHERS ARE *ALL* ALIKE!
LET *GO!*
ABUSE!
YOU-- WAIT, *WHAT?*
YOU'RE *ALWAYS* THE SAME! THE CHICK THAT KICKED ME OUT OF MY OLD SCHOOL WAS *CRAZY* LIKE YOU.
NOW, LET GO OF ME BEFORE MY DADDY *SUES* YOU BACK TO THE *STONE AGE!*
I'M SO--
URGGGG--
KRAK

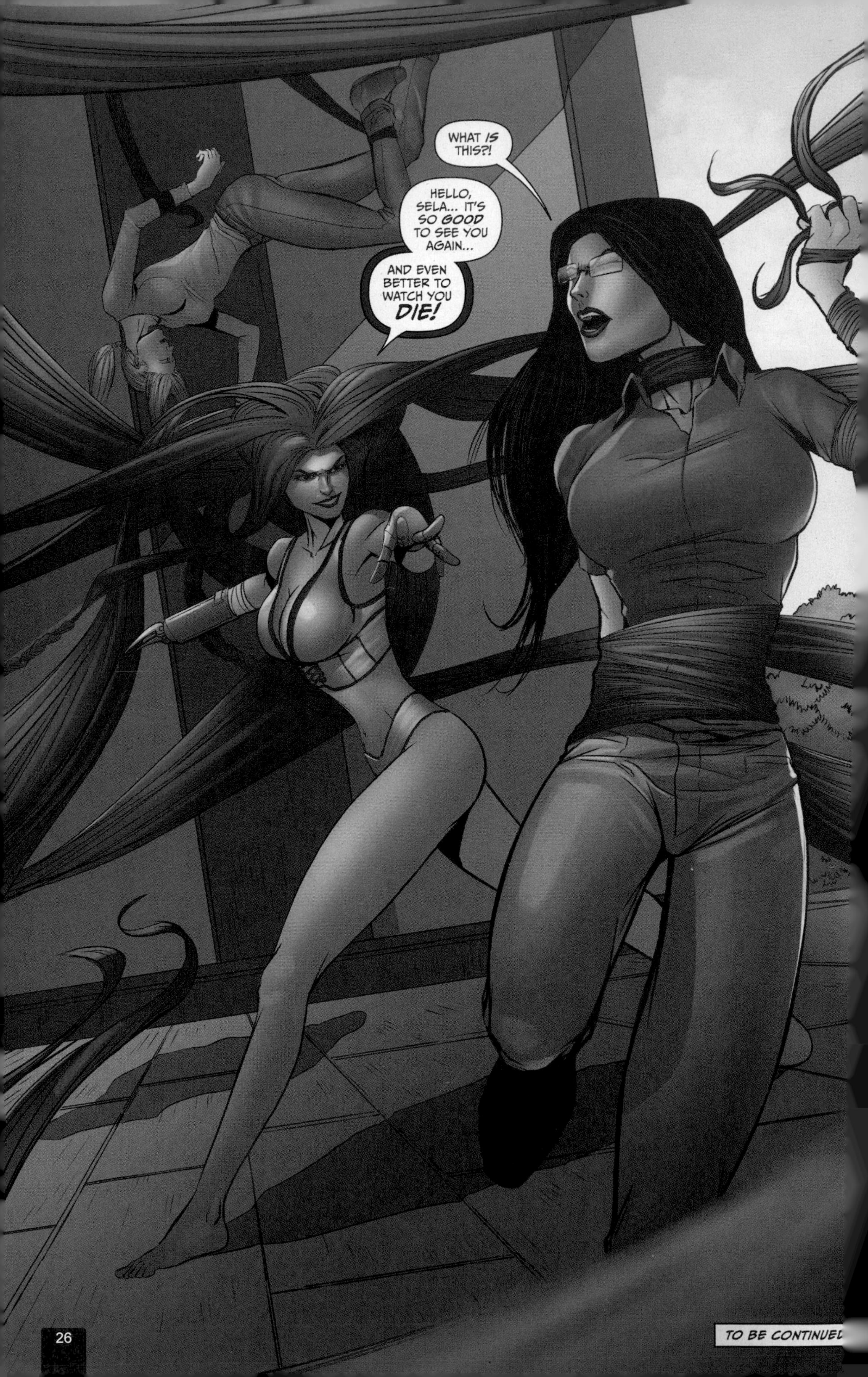
WHAT IS THIS?!
HELLO, SELA... IT'S SO GOOD TO SEE YOU AGAIN...
AND EVEN BETTER TO WATCH YOU DIE!
TO BE CONTINUED

Grimm Fairy Tales

Volume 15

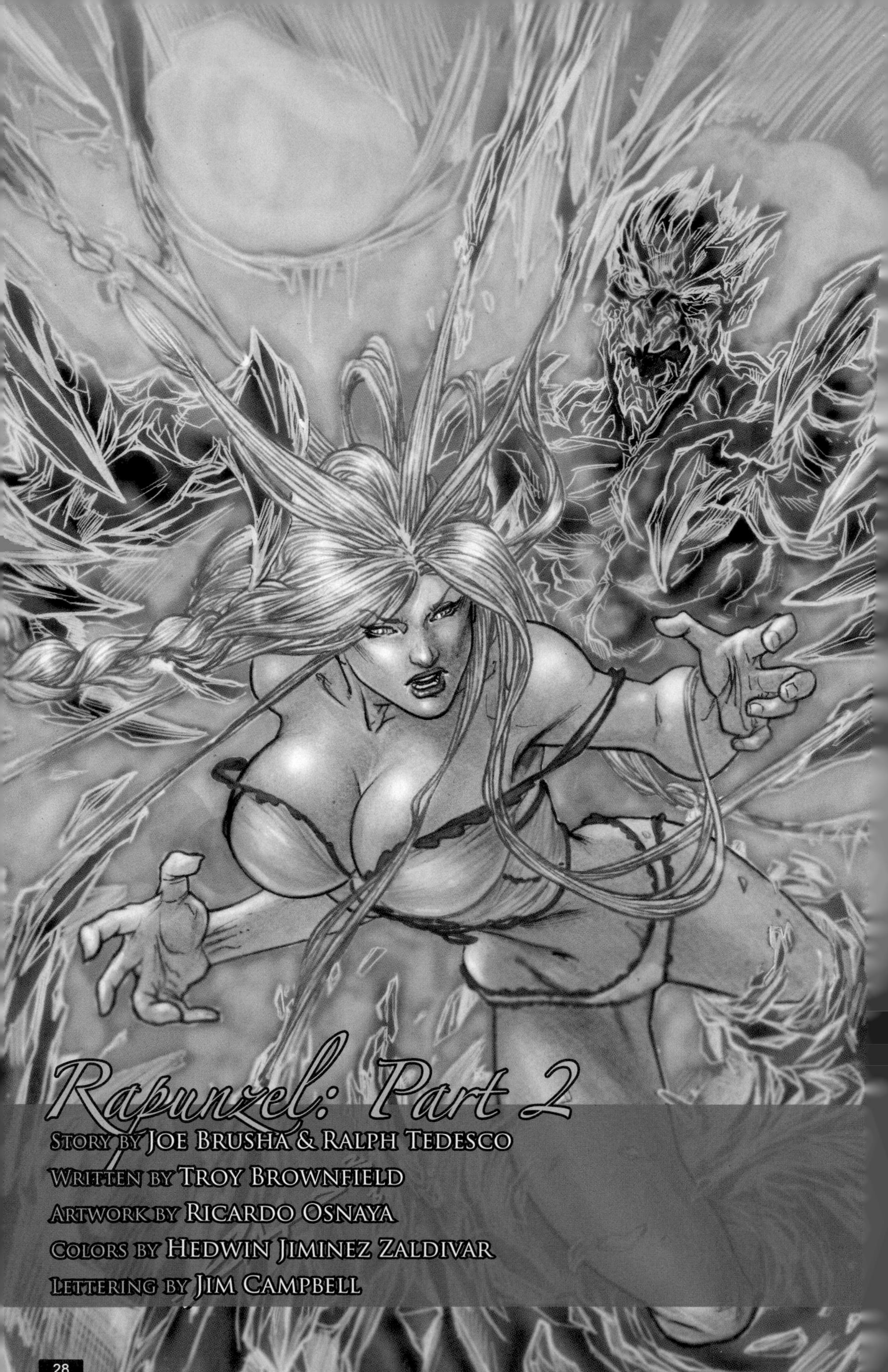

Rapunzel: Part 2
Story by Joe Brusha & Ralph Tedesco
Written by Troy Brownfield
Artwork by Ricardo Osnaya
Colors by Hedwin Jiminez Zaldivar
Lettering by Jim Campbell

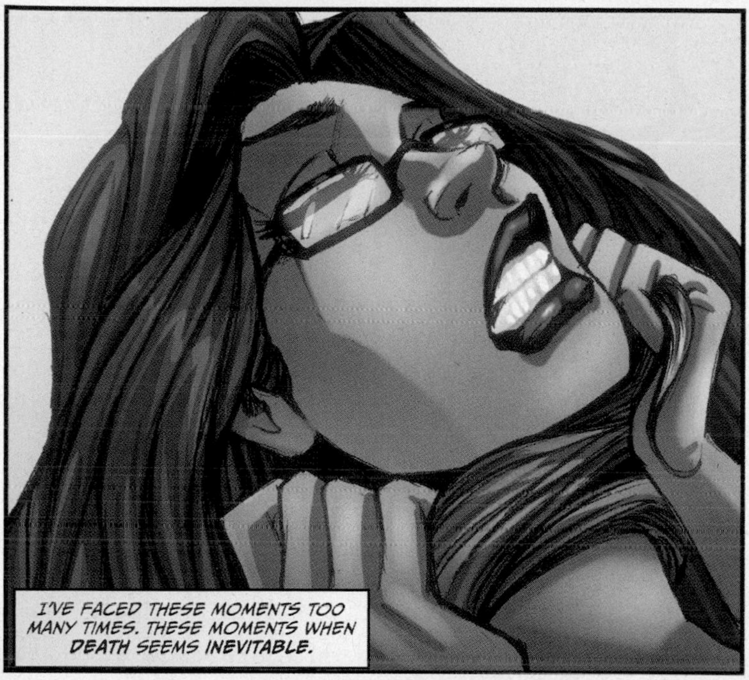
I'VE FACED THESE MOMENTS TOO MANY TIMES. THESE MOMENTS WHEN **DEATH** SEEMS **INEVITABLE.**

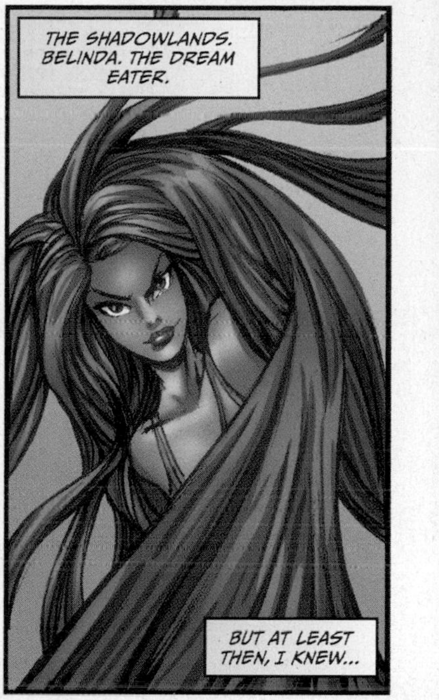
THE SHADOWLANDS. BELINDA. THE DREAM EATER.
BUT AT LEAST THEN, I KNEW...

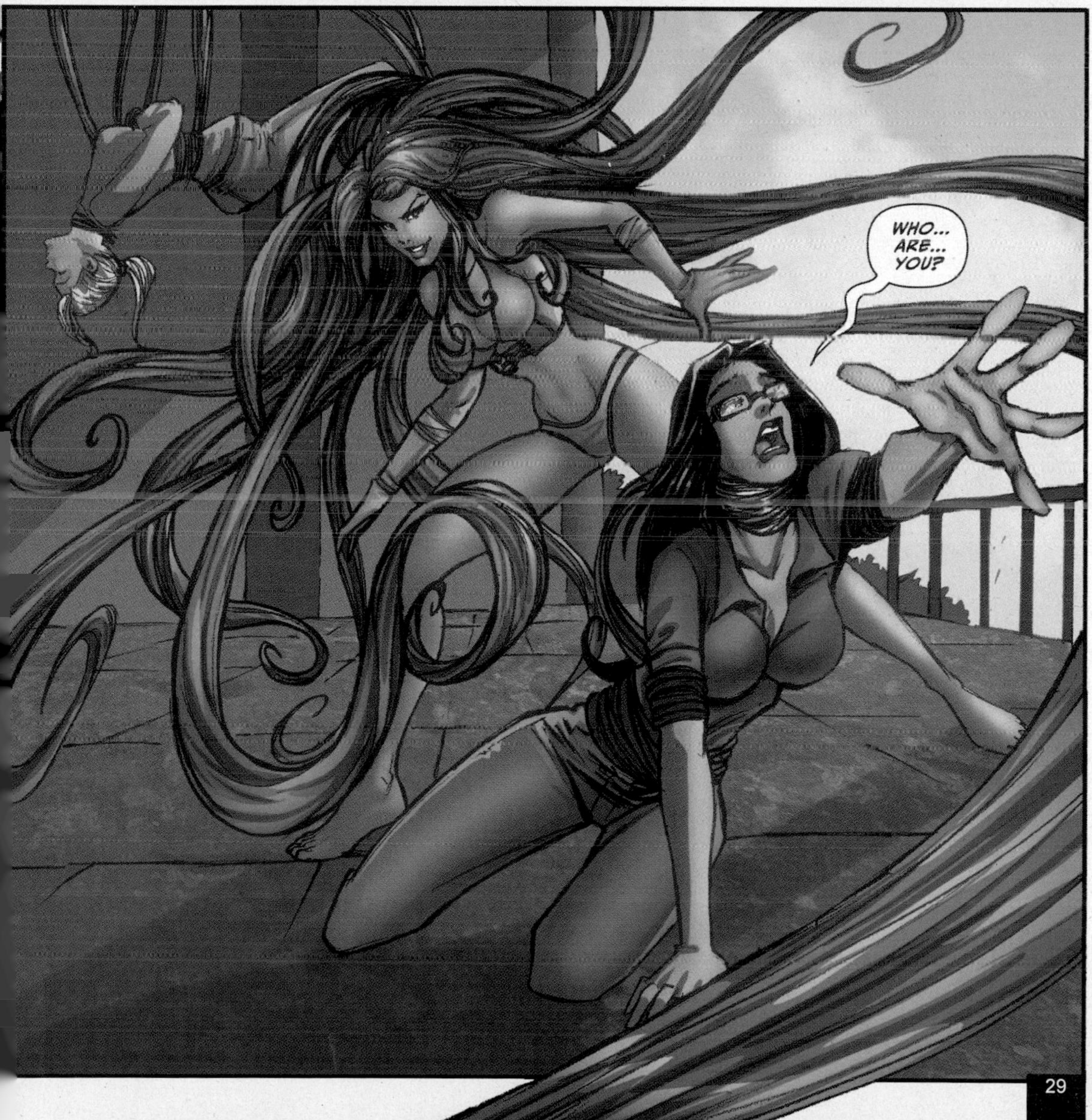
WHO... ARE... YOU?

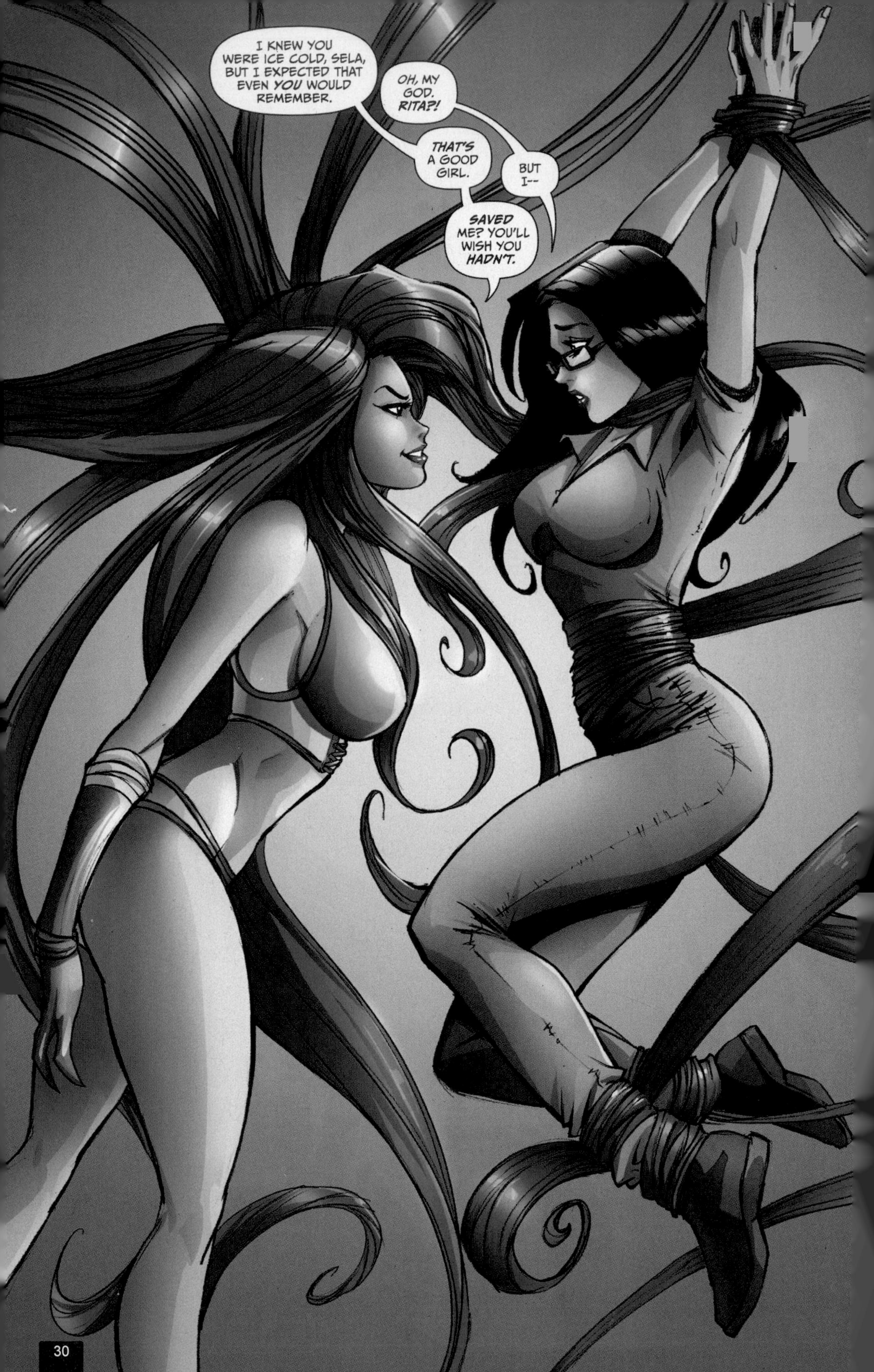
I KNEW YOU WERE ICE COLD, SELA, BUT I EXPECTED THAT EVEN *YOU* WOULD REMEMBER.
OH, MY GOD. *RITA?!*
THAT'S A GOOD GIRL.
BUT I--
SAVED ME? YOU'LL WISH YOU *HADN'T.*

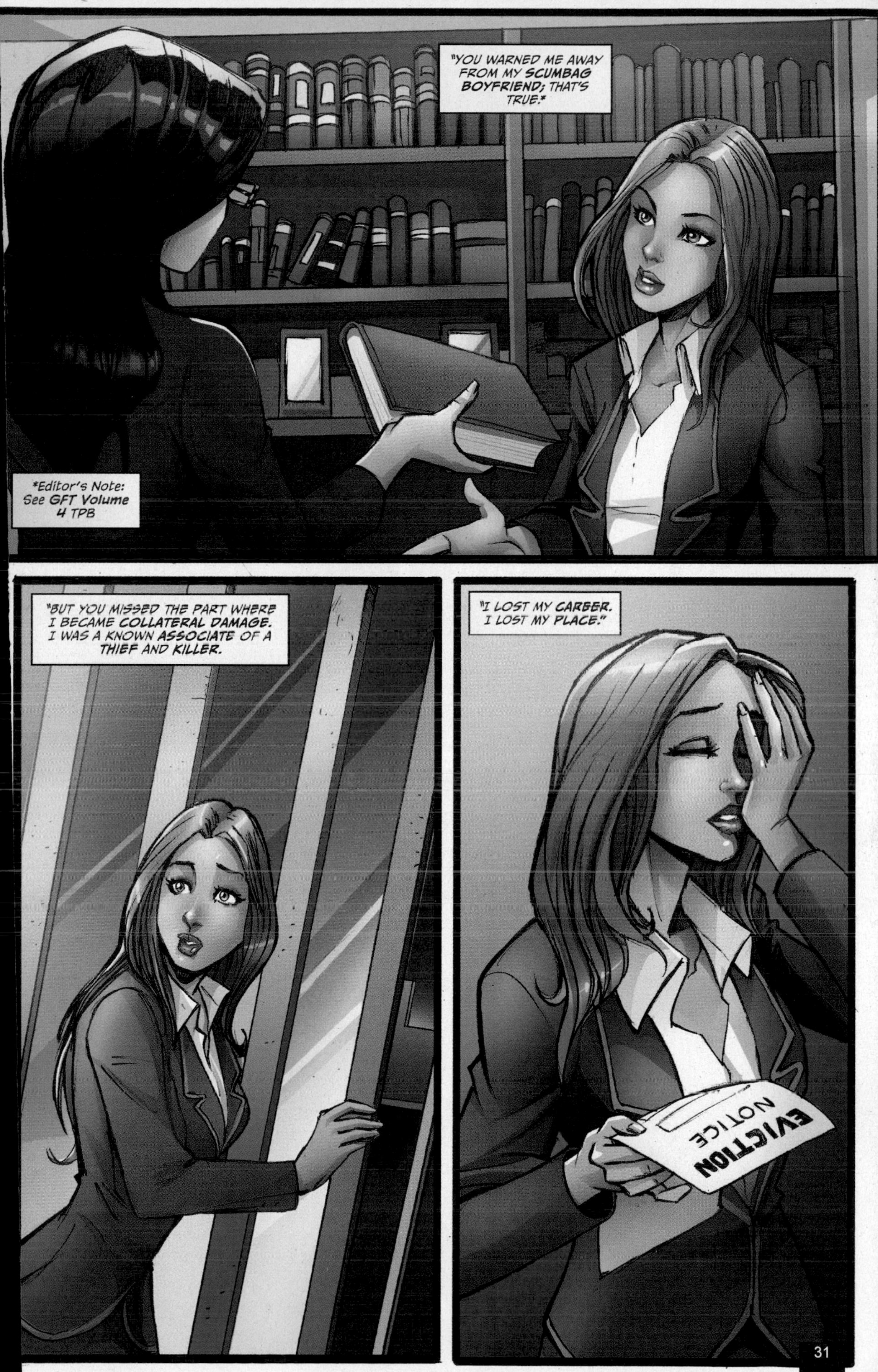
"YOU WARNED ME AWAY FROM MY SCUMBAG BOYFRIEND; THAT'S TRUE.*
*Editor's Note: See GFT Volume 4 TPB
"BUT YOU MISSED THE PART WHERE I BECAME COLLATERAL DAMAGE. I WAS A KNOWN ASSOCIATE OF A THIEF AND KILLER.
"I LOST MY CAREER. I LOST MY PLACE."
EVICTION NOTICE

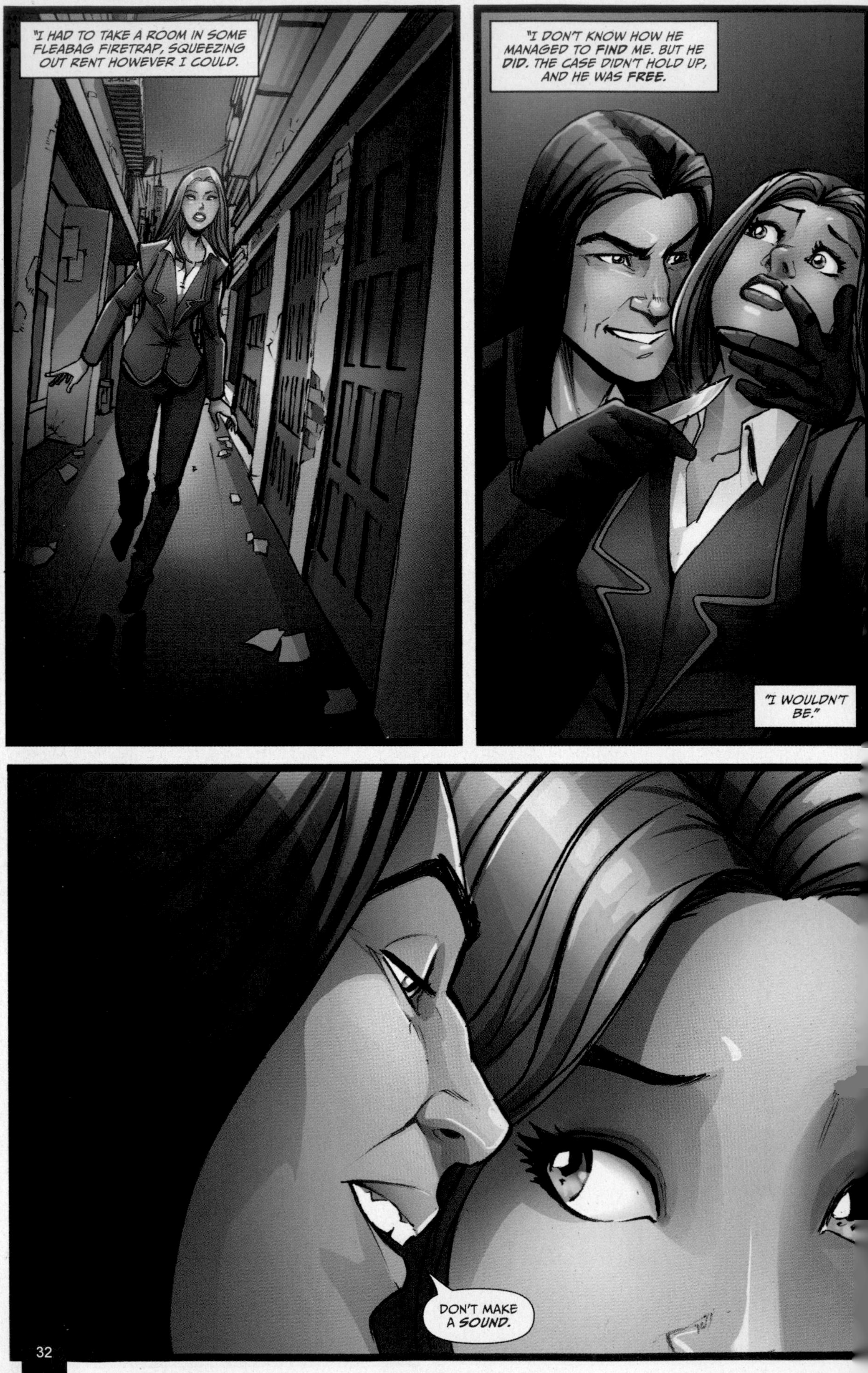
"I HAD TO TAKE A ROOM IN SOME FLEABAG FIRETRAP, SQUEEZING OUT RENT HOWEVER I COULD.
"I DON'T KNOW HOW HE MANAGED TO FIND ME. BUT HE DID. THE CASE DIDN'T HOLD UP, AND HE WAS FREE.
"I WOULDN'T BE."
DON'T MAKE A SOUND.

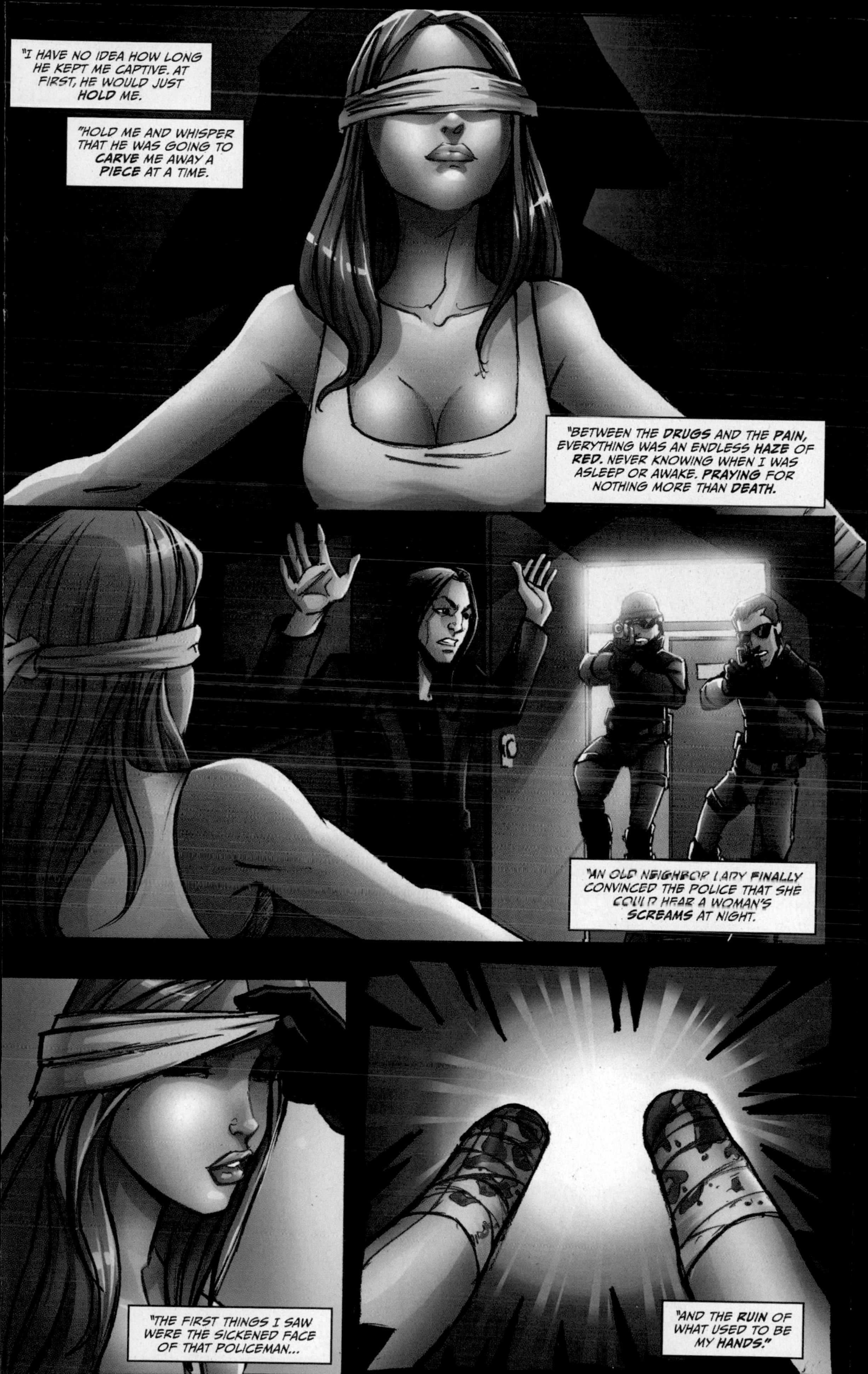
"I HAVE NO IDEA HOW LONG HE KEPT ME CAPTIVE. AT FIRST, HE WOULD JUST HOLD ME.
"HOLD ME AND WHISPER THAT HE WAS GOING TO CARVE ME AWAY A PIECE AT A TIME.
"BETWEEN THE DRUGS AND THE PAIN, EVERYTHING WAS AN ENDLESS HAZE OF RED. NEVER KNOWING WHEN I WAS ASLEEP OR AWAKE. PRAYING FOR NOTHING MORE THAN DEATH.
"AN OLD NEIGHBOR LADY FINALLY CONVINCED THE POLICE THAT SHE COULD HEAR A WOMAN'S SCREAMS AT NIGHT.
"THE FIRST THINGS I SAW WERE THE SICKENED FACE OF THAT POLICEMAN...
"AND THE RUIN OF WHAT USED TO BE MY HANDS."

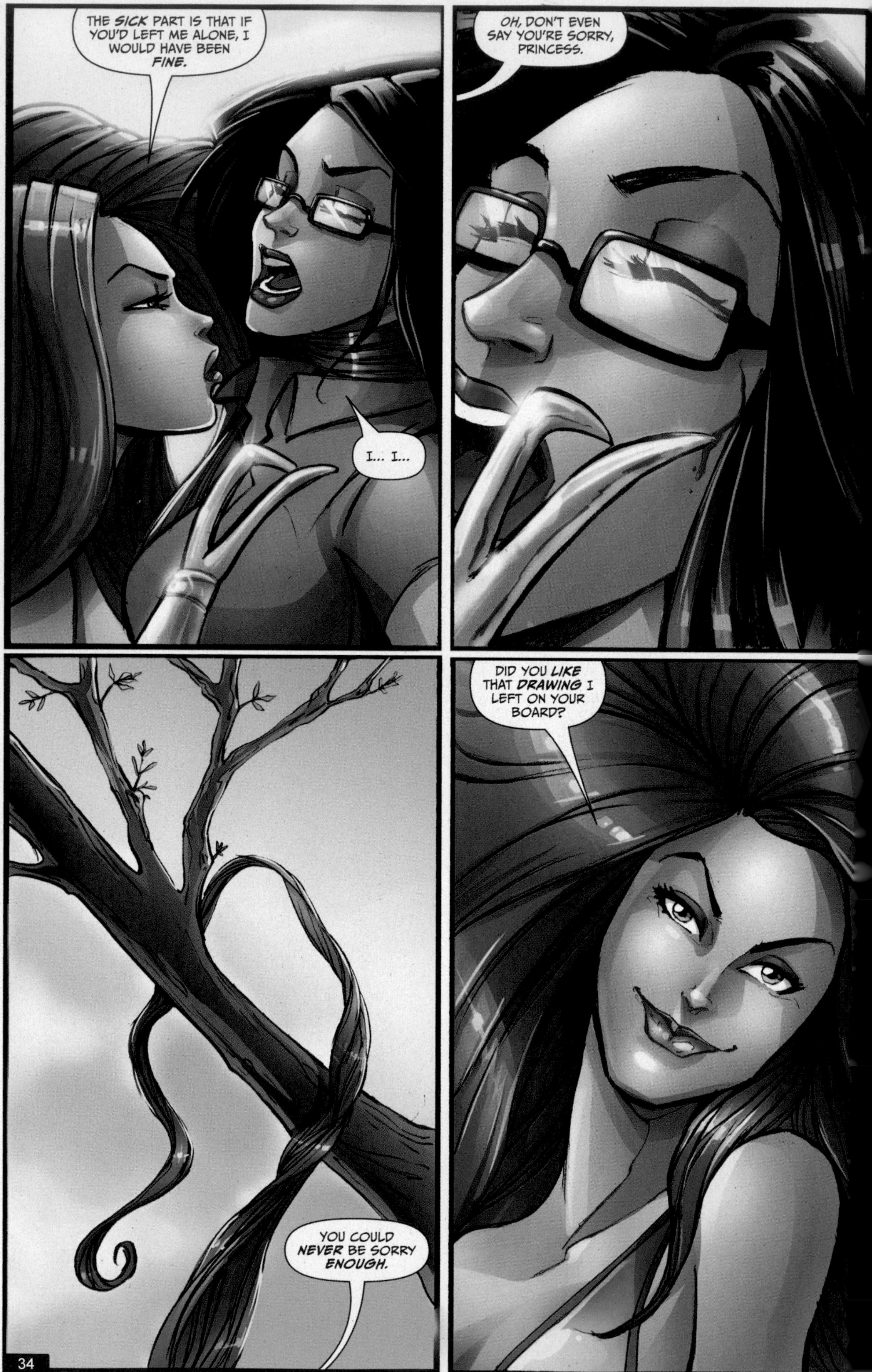
THE SICK PART IS THAT IF YOU'D LEFT ME ALONE, I WOULD HAVE BEEN FINE.
I... I...
OH, DON'T EVEN SAY YOU'RE SORRY, PRINCESS.
YOU COULD NEVER BE SORRY ENOUGH.
DID YOU LIKE THAT DRAWING I LEFT ON YOUR BOARD?

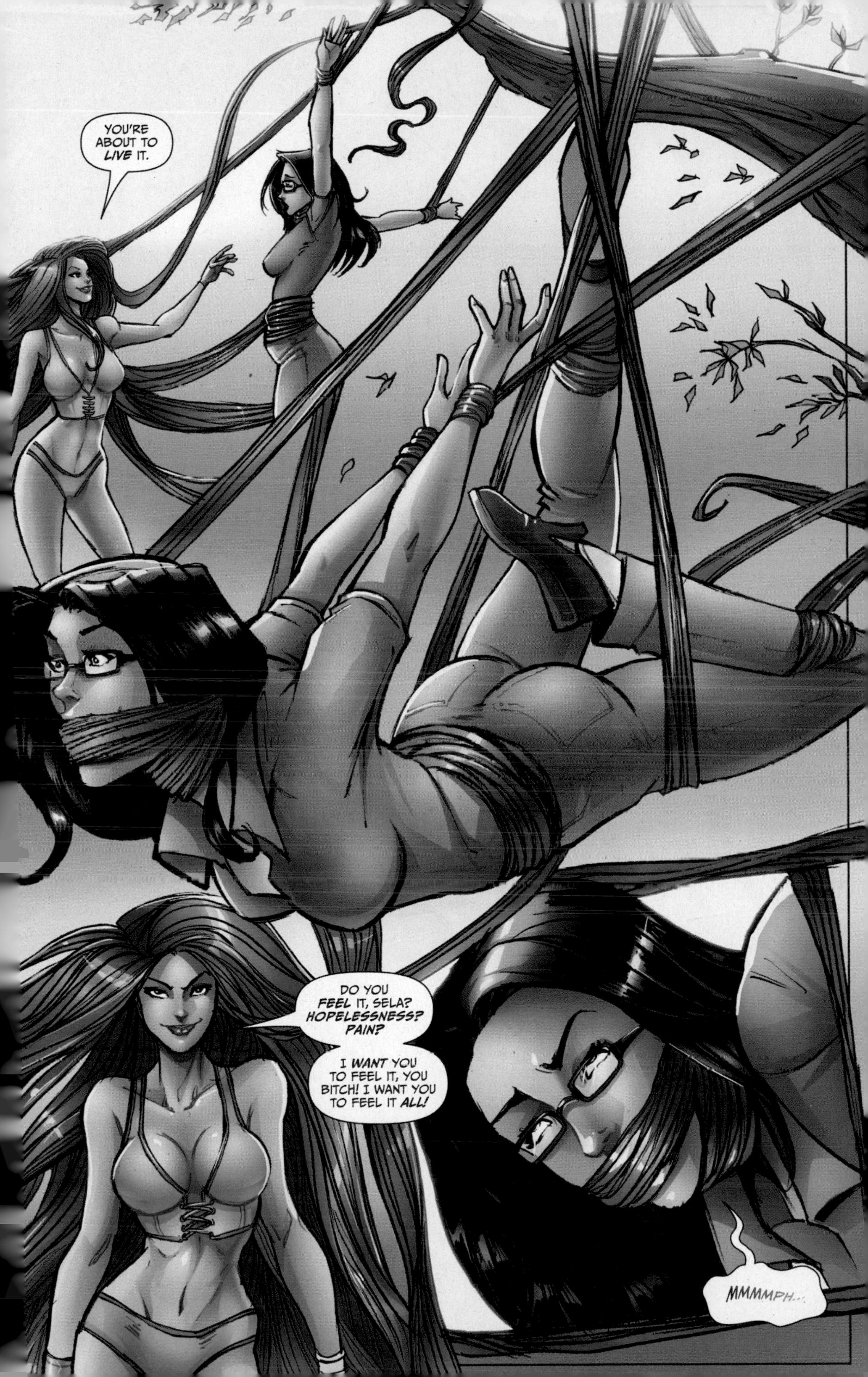
YOU'RE ABOUT TO *LIVE* IT.
DO YOU *FEEL* IT, SELA? *HOPELESSNESS? PAIN?*
I *WANT* YOU TO FEEL IT, YOU BITCH! I WANT YOU TO FEEL IT *ALL!*
MMMMPH...

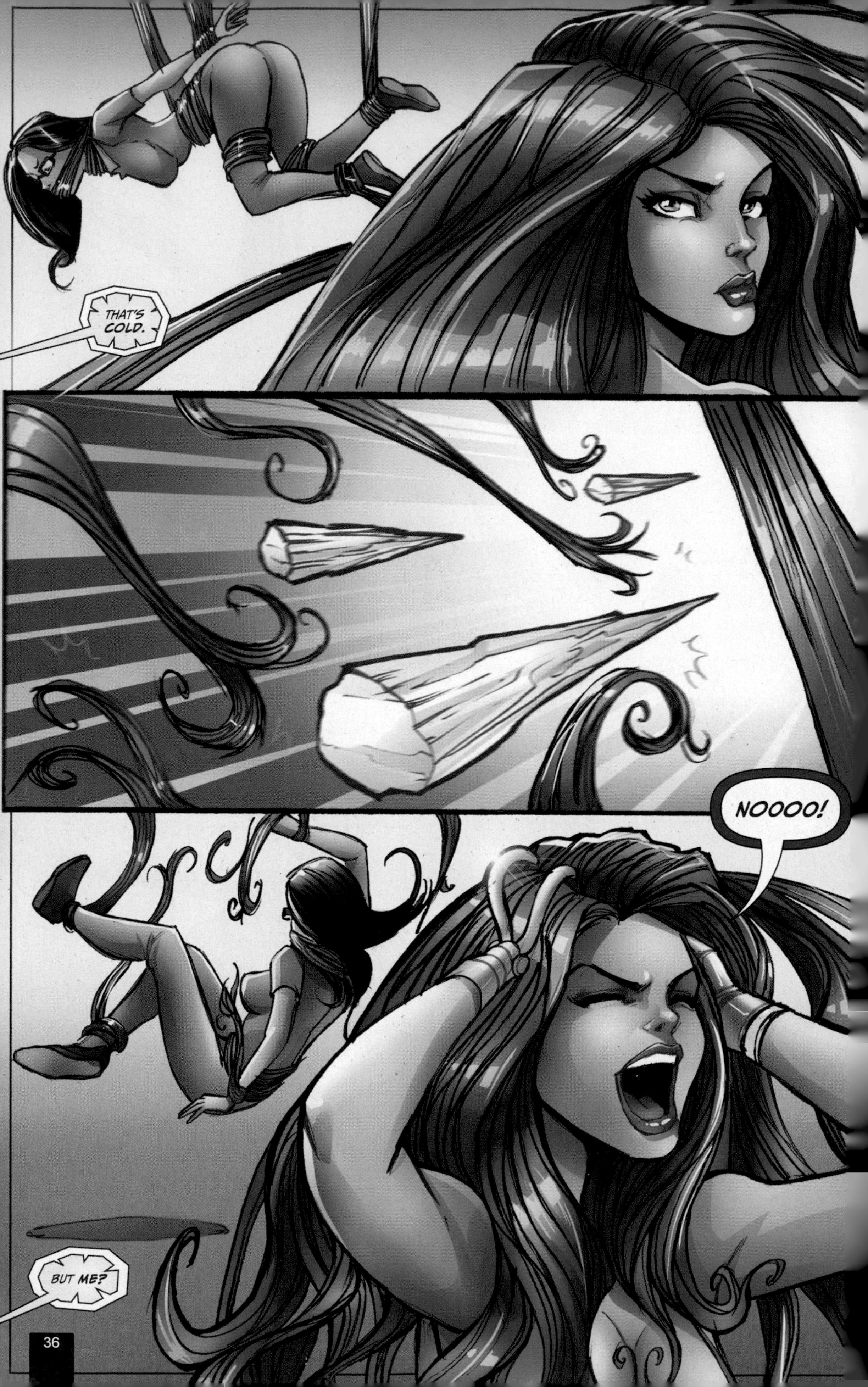
THAT'S COLD.
NOOOO!
BUT ME?

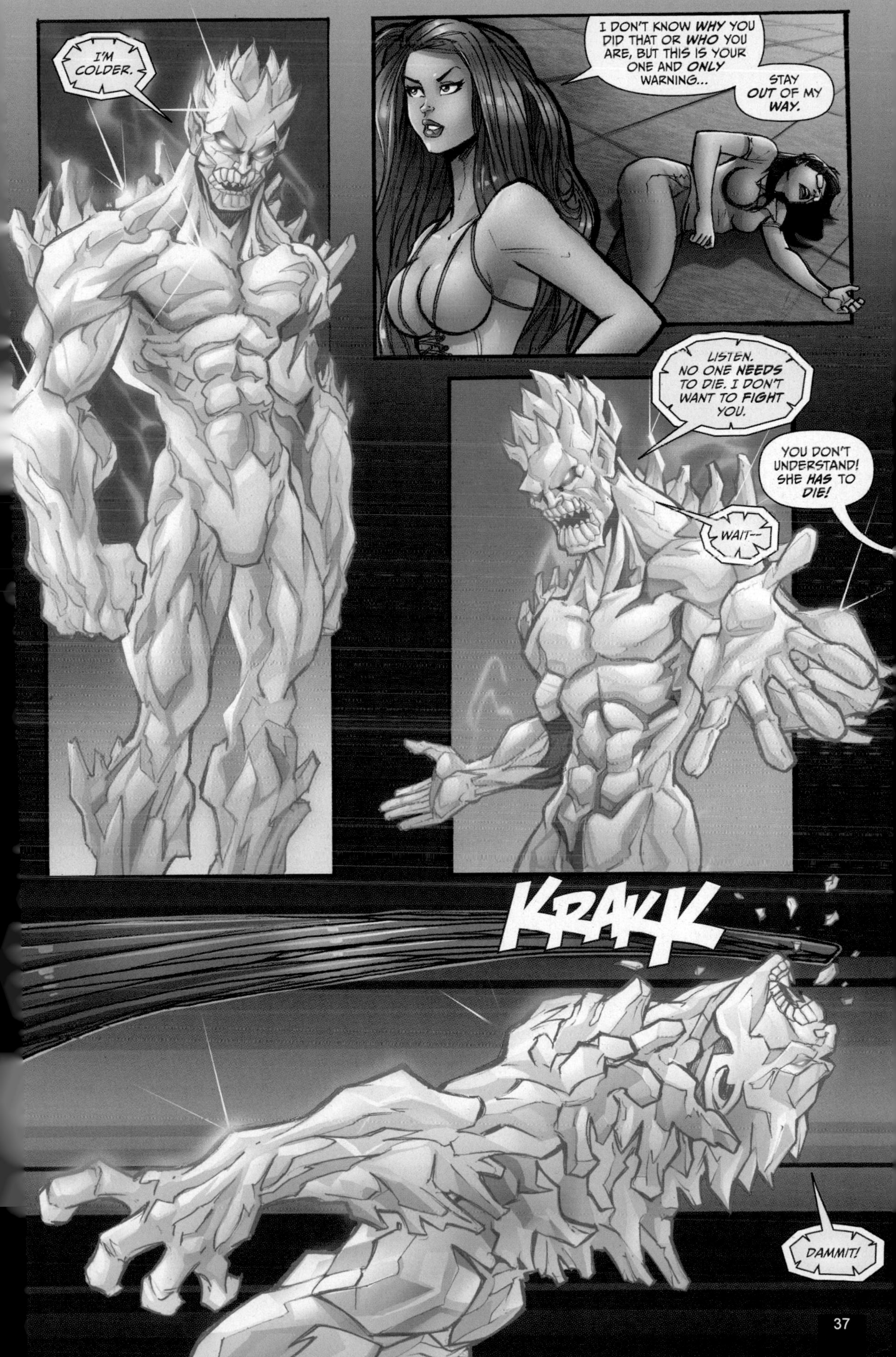
I'M COLDER.
I DON'T KNOW WHY YOU DID THAT OR WHO YOU ARE, BUT THIS IS YOUR ONE AND ONLY WARNING...
STAY OUT OF MY WAY.
LISTEN. NO ONE NEEDS TO DIE. I DON'T WANT TO FIGHT YOU.
YOU DON'T UNDERSTAND! SHE HAS TO DIE!
WAIT--
KRAKK
DAMMIT!

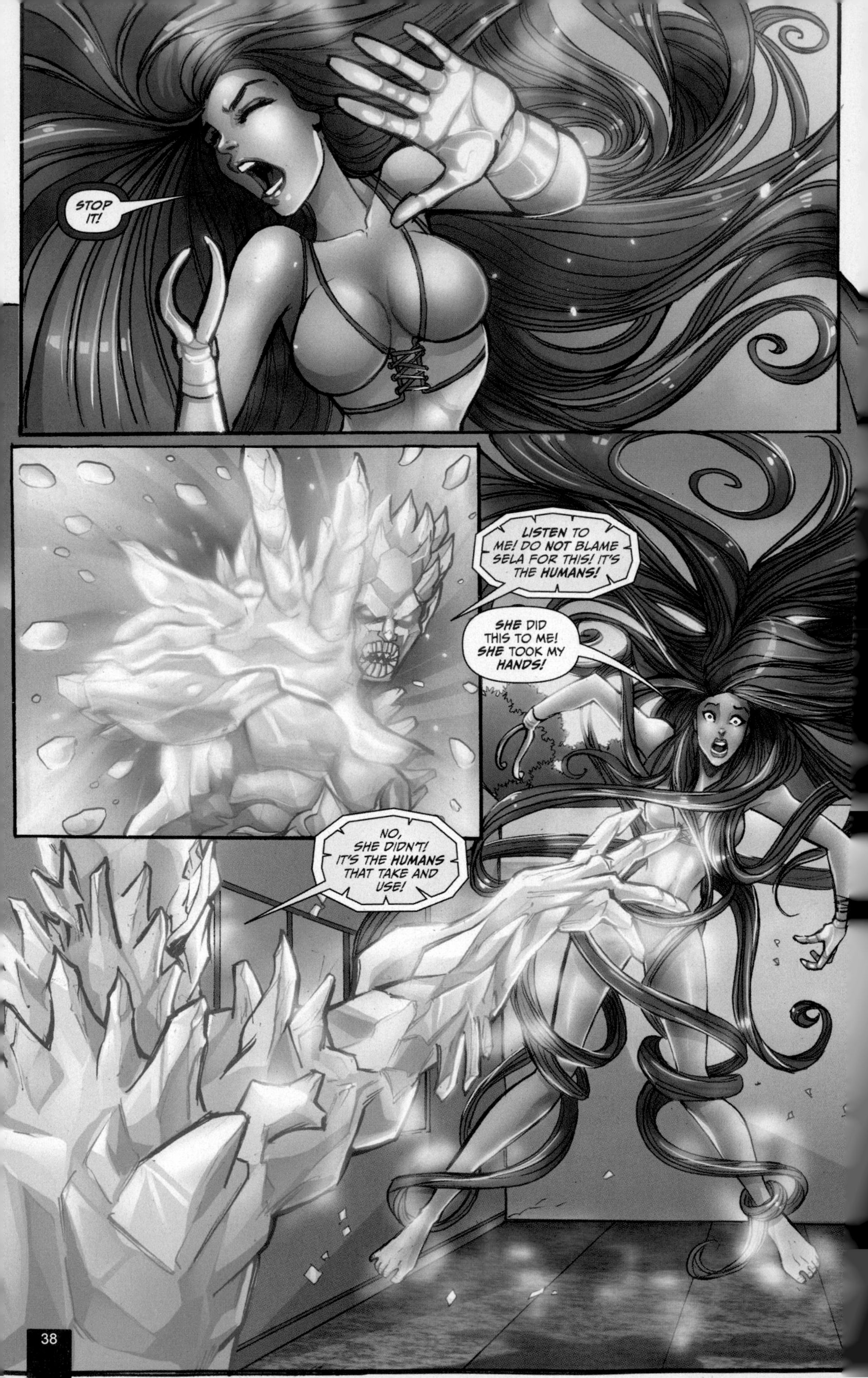
STOP IT!
LISTEN TO ME! DO NOT BLAME SELA FOR THIS! IT'S THE HUMANS!
SHE DID THIS TO ME! SHE TOOK MY HANDS!
NO, SHE DIDN'T! IT'S THE HUMANS THAT TAKE AND USE!

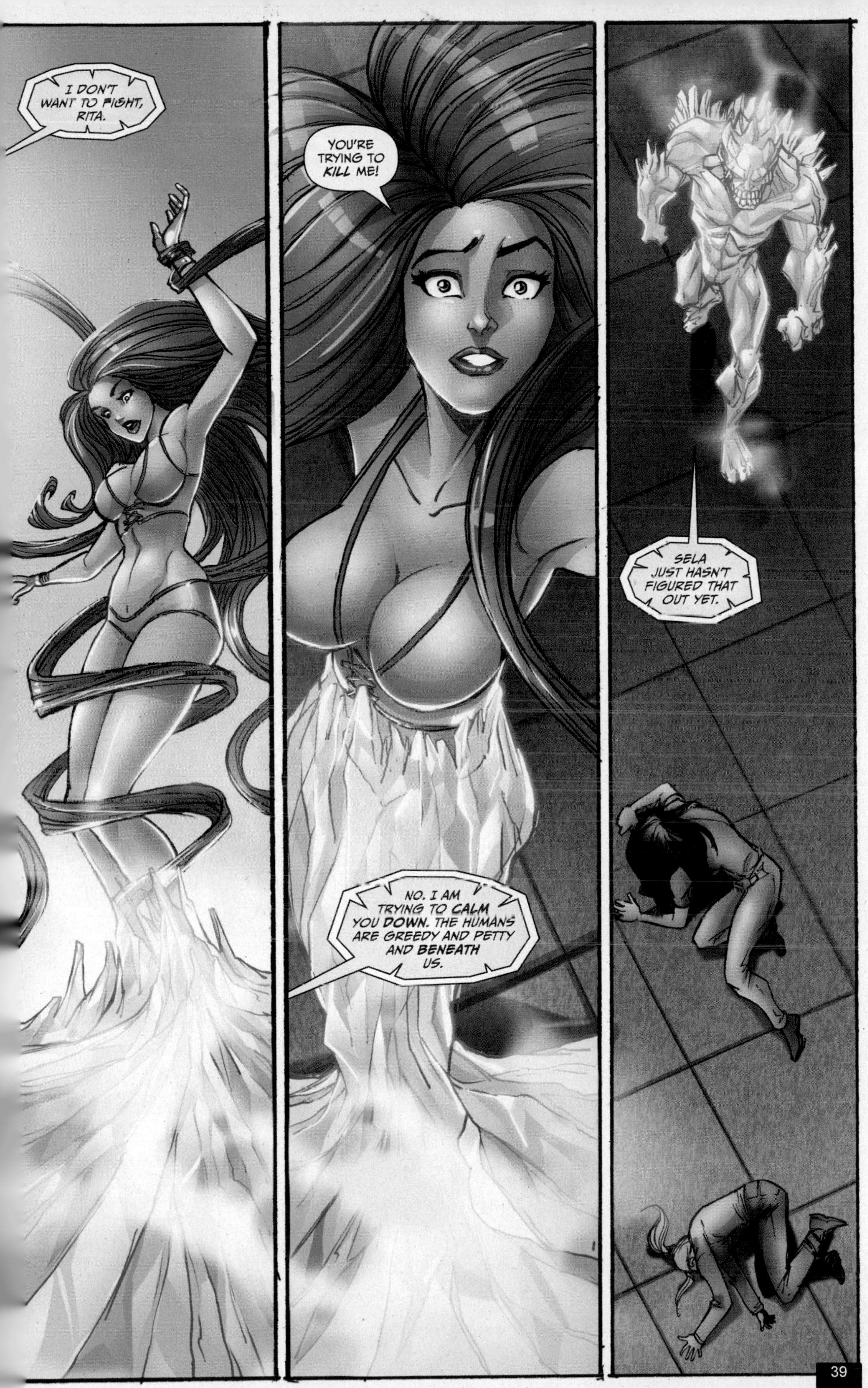
I DON'T WANT TO FIGHT, RITA.
YOU'RE TRYING TO KILL ME!
NO. I AM TRYING TO CALM YOU DOWN. THE HUMANS ARE GREEDY AND PETTY AND BENEATH US.
SELA JUST HASN'T FIGURED THAT OUT YET.

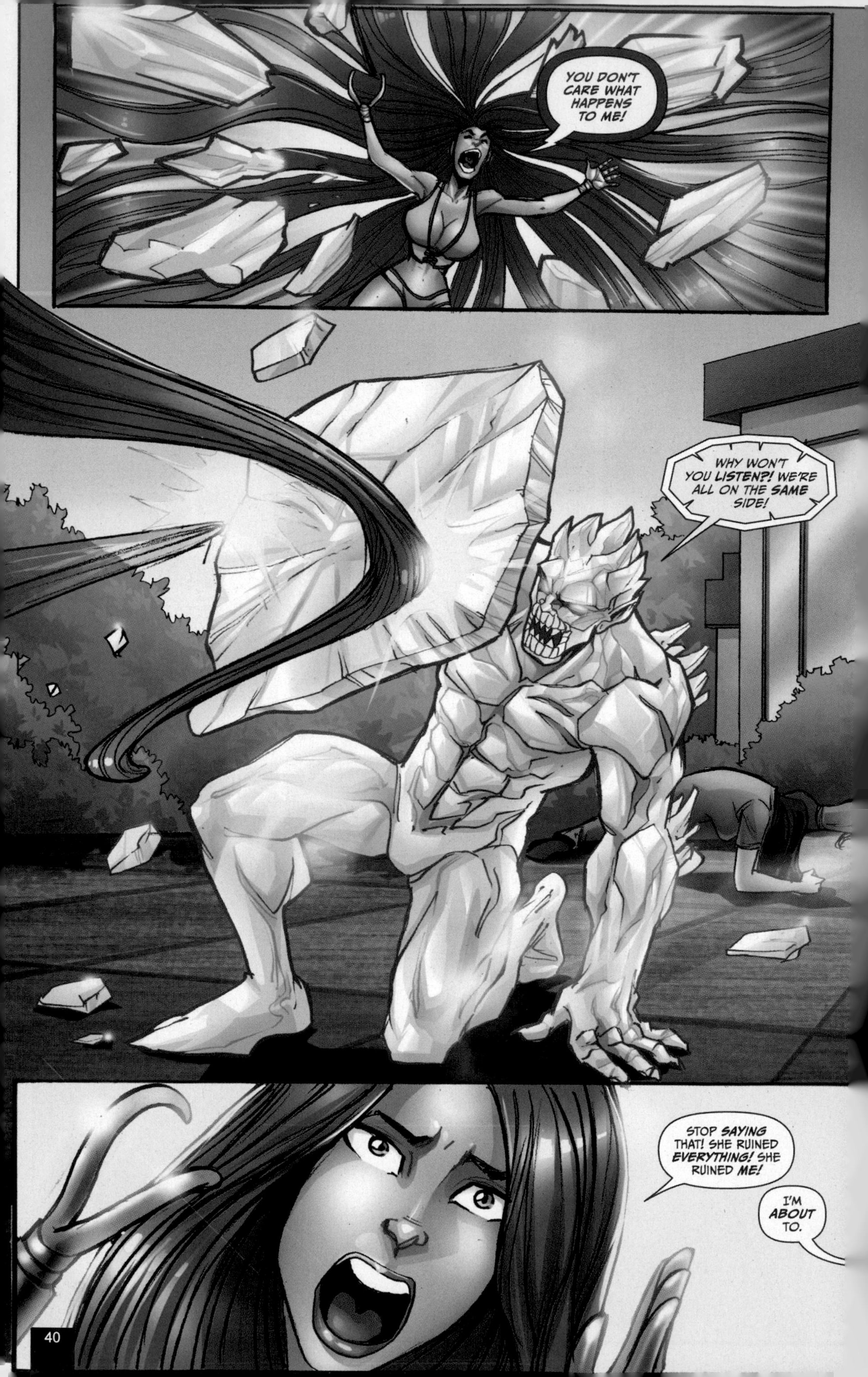

YOU DON'T CARE WHAT HAPPENS TO ME!
WHY WON'T YOU LISTEN?! WE'RE ALL ON THE SAME SIDE!
STOP SAYING THAT! SHE RUINED EVERYTHING! SHE RUINED ME!
I'M ABOUT TO.

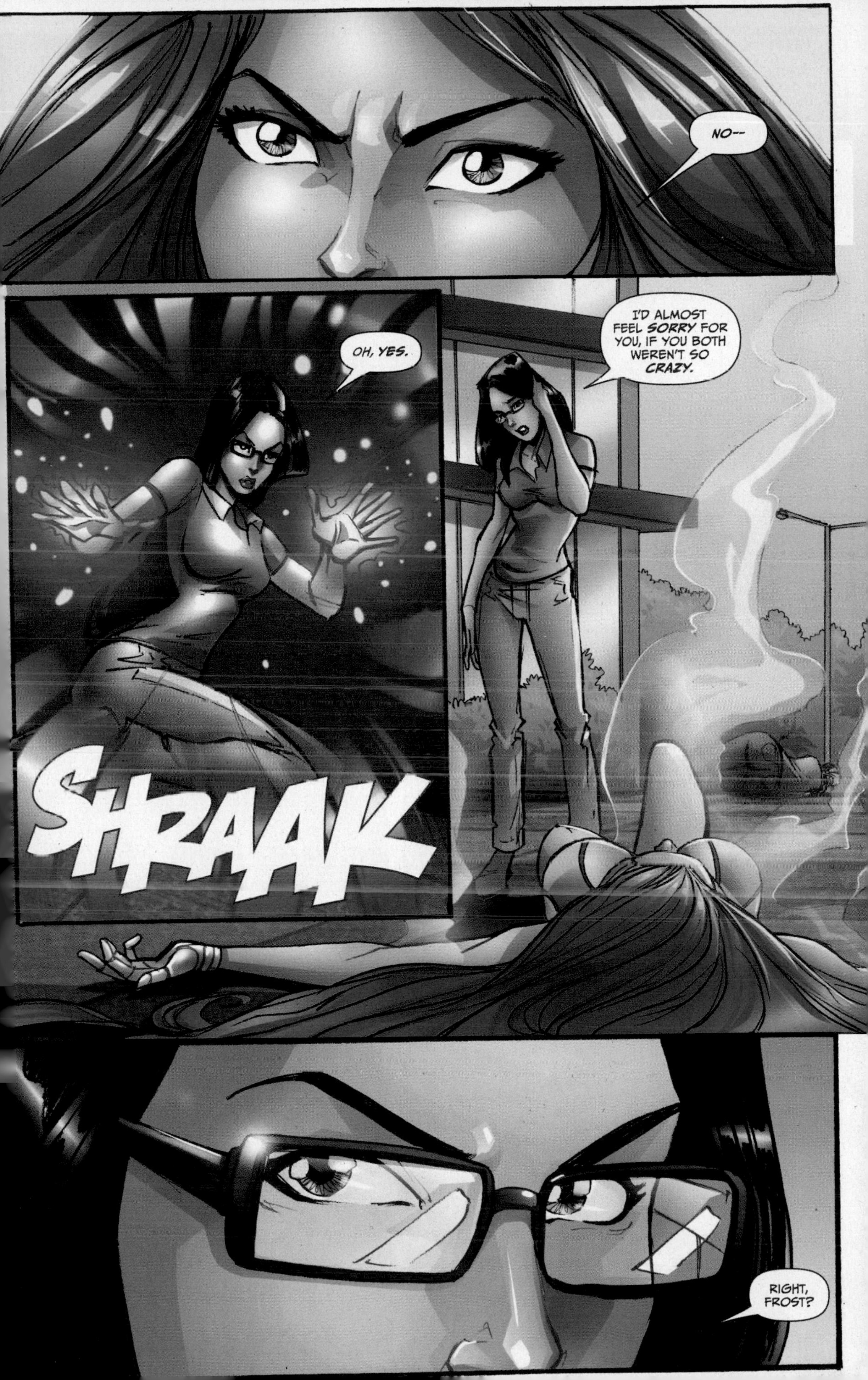
NO--
OH, YES.
I'D ALMOST FEEL SORRY FOR YOU, IF YOU BOTH WEREN'T SO CRAZY.
SHRAAK
RIGHT, FROST?

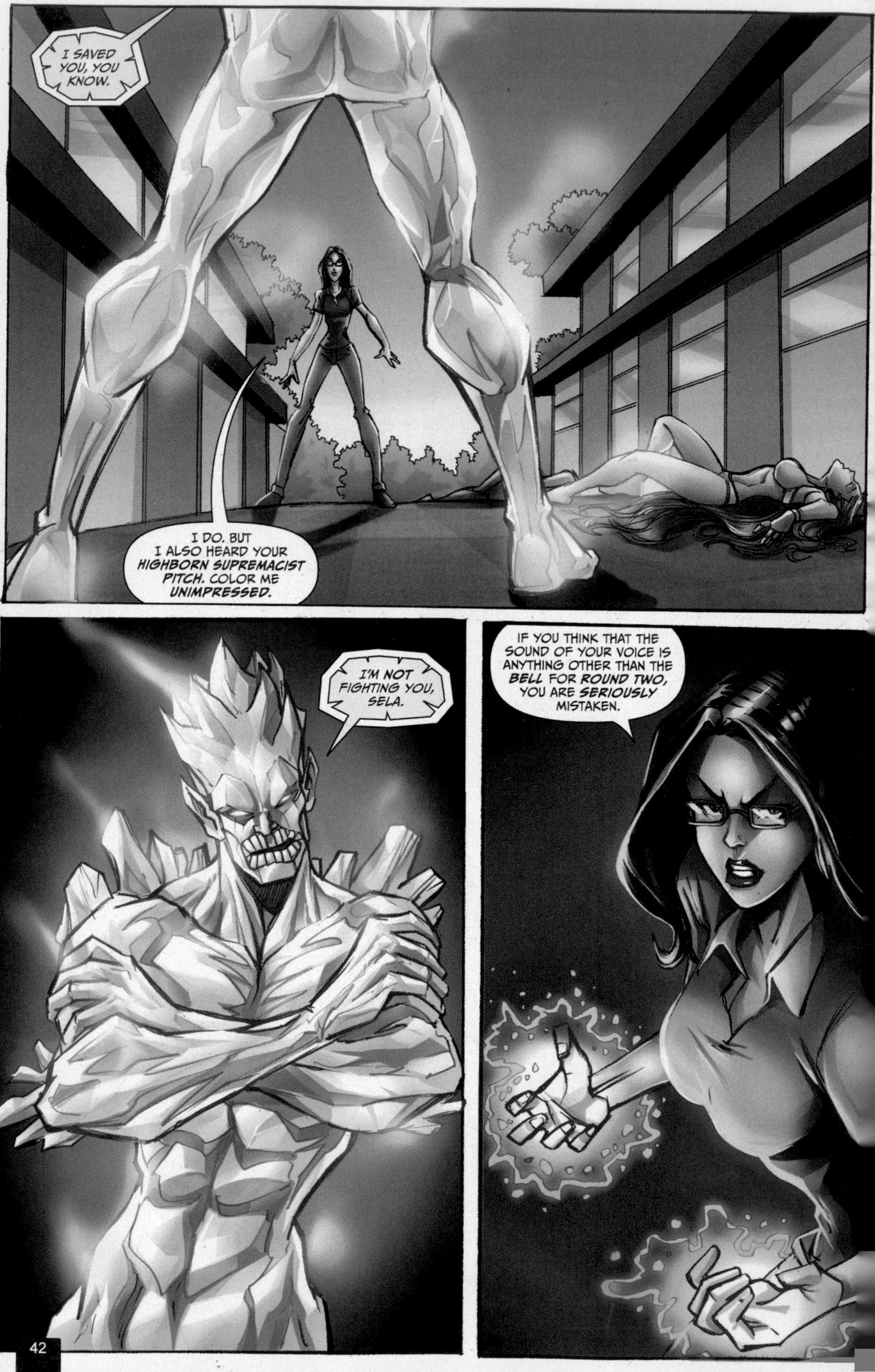
I SAVED YOU, YOU KNOW.
I DO. BUT I ALSO HEARD YOUR HIGHBORN SUPREMACIST PITCH. COLOR ME UNIMPRESSED.
I'M NOT FIGHTING YOU, SELA.
IF YOU THINK THAT THE SOUND OF YOUR VOICE IS ANYTHING OTHER THAN THE BELL FOR ROUND TWO, YOU ARE SERIOUSLY MISTAKEN.

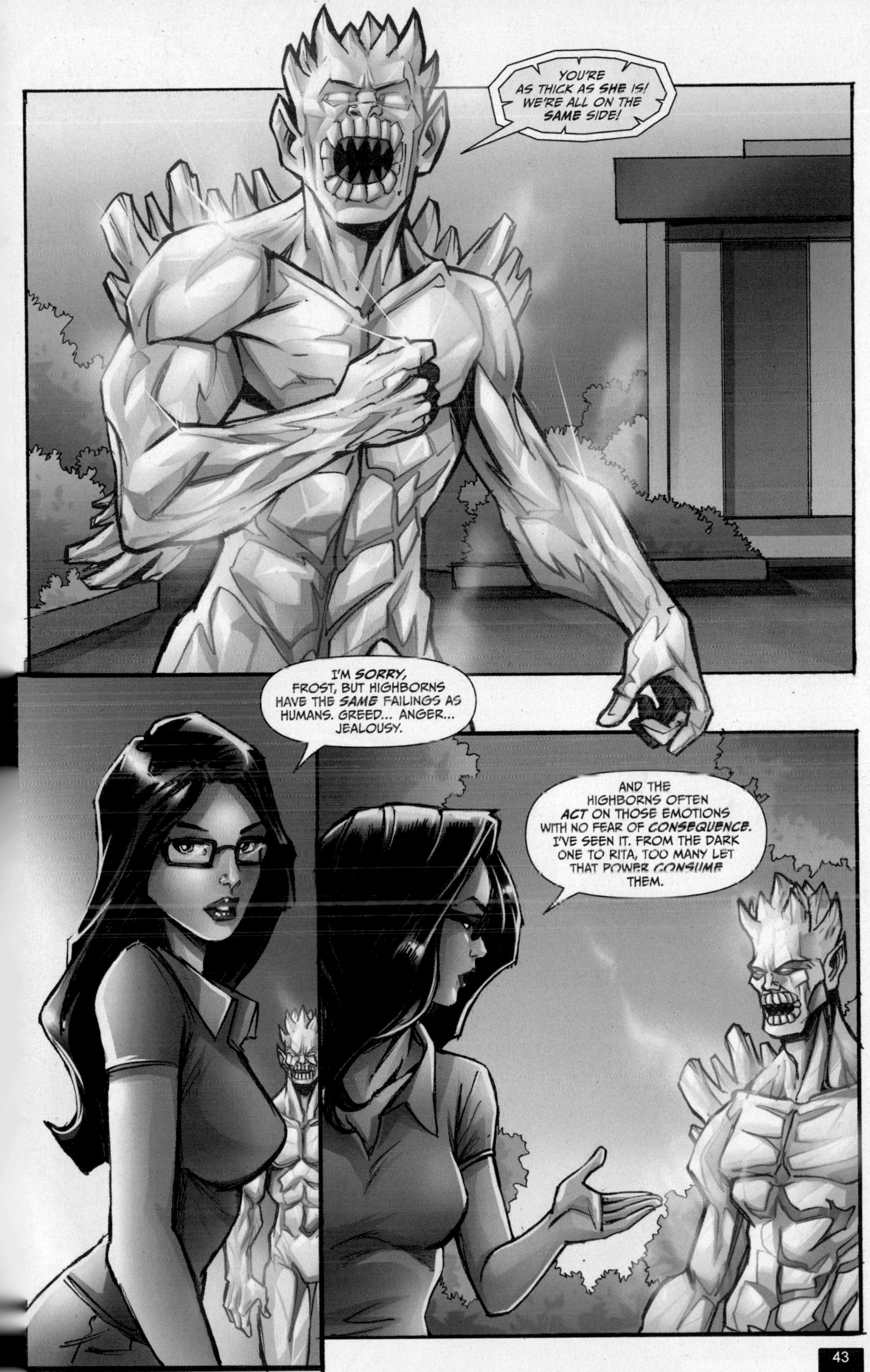
YOU'RE AS THICK AS SHE IS! WE'RE ALL ON THE SAME SIDE!
I'M SORRY, FROST, BUT HIGHBORNS HAVE THE SAME FAILINGS AS HUMANS. GREED... ANGER... JEALOUSY.
AND THE HIGHBORNS OFTEN ACT ON THOSE EMOTIONS WITH NO FEAR OF CONSEQUENCE. I'VE SEEN IT. FROM THE DARK ONE TO RITA, TOO MANY LET THAT POWER CONSUME THEM.

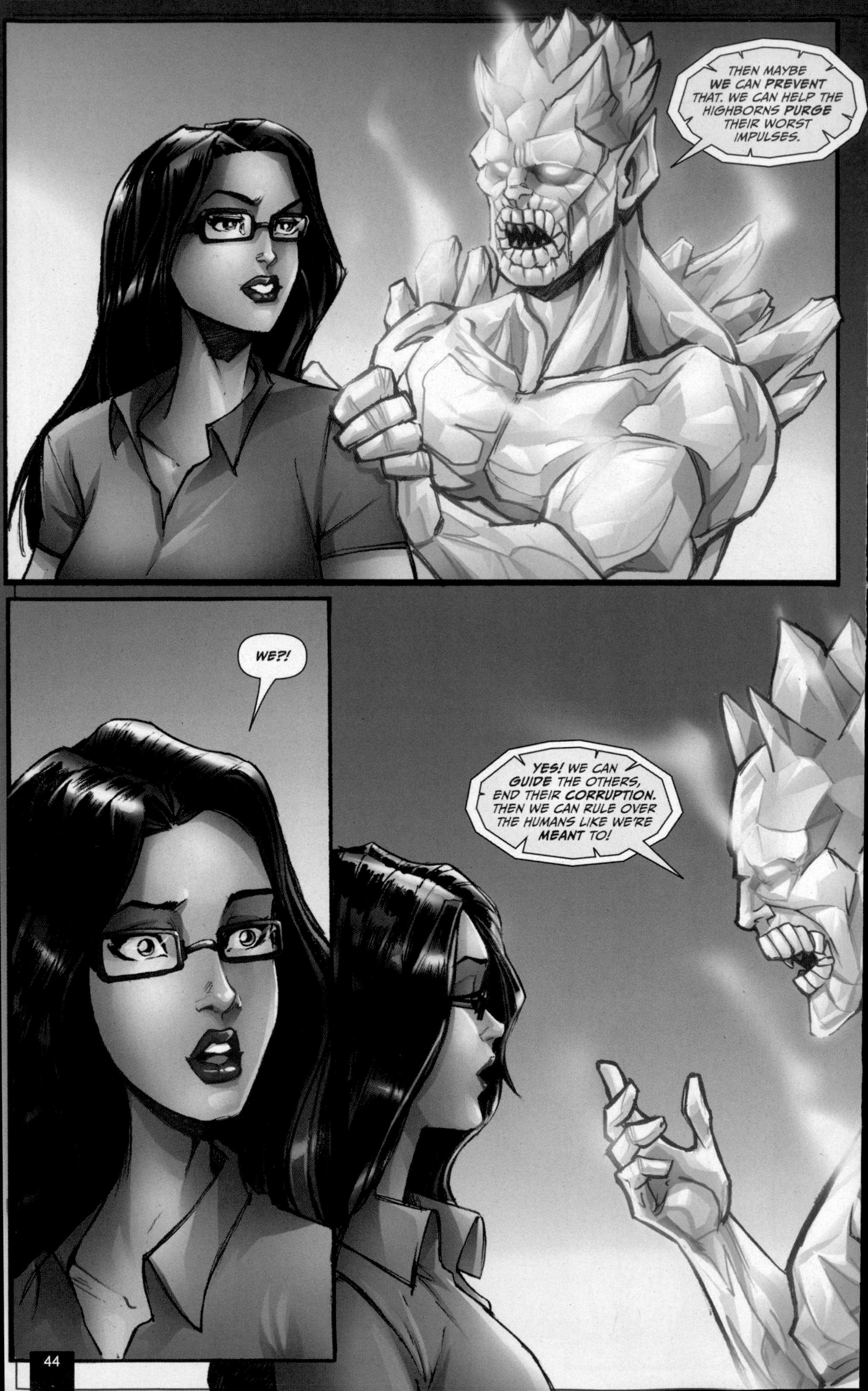
THEN MAYBE WE CAN PREVENT THAT. WE CAN HELP THE HIGHBORNS PURGE THEIR WORST IMPULSES.
WE?!
YES! WE CAN GUIDE THE OTHERS, END THEIR CORRUPTION. THEN WE CAN RULE OVER THE HUMANS LIKE WE'RE MEANT TO!

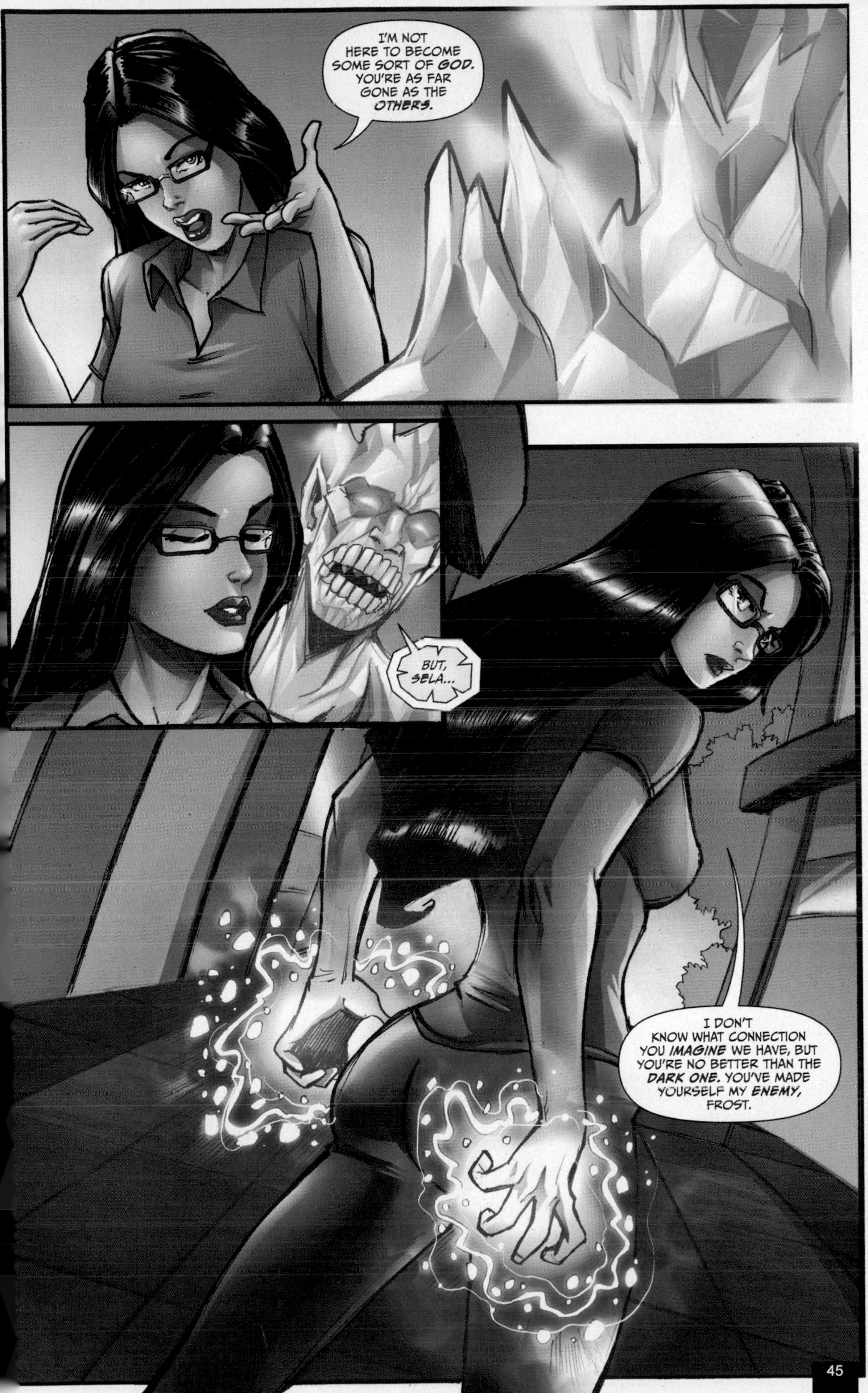
I'M NOT HERE TO BECOME SOME SORT OF GOD. YOU'RE AS FAR GONE AS THE OTHERS.
BUT, SELA...
I DON'T KNOW WHAT CONNECTION YOU IMAGINE WE HAVE, BUT YOU'RE NO BETTER THAN THE DARK ONE. YOU'VE MADE YOURSELF MY ENEMY, FROST.

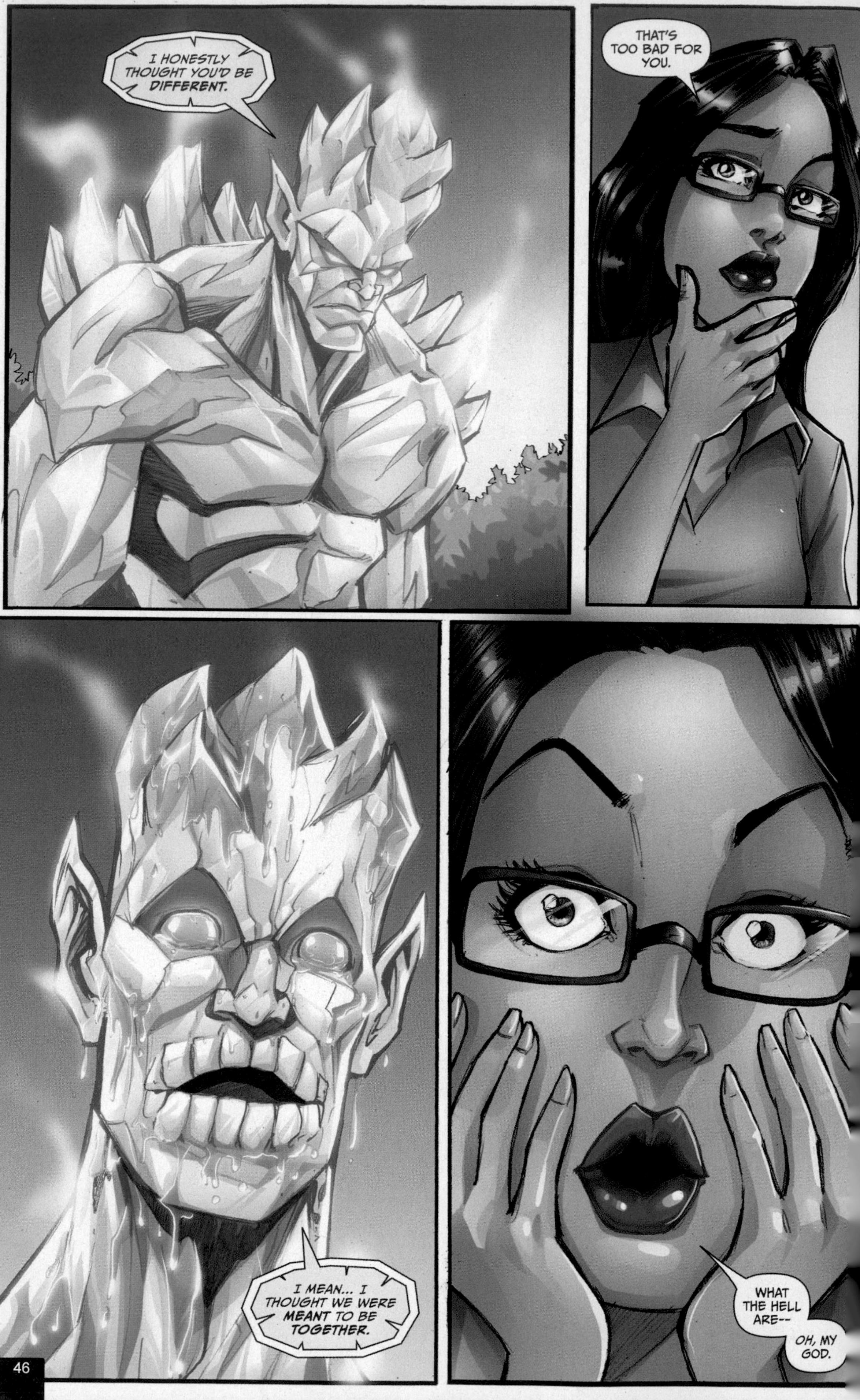
I HONESTLY THOUGHT YOU'D BE DIFFERENT.
THAT'S TOO BAD FOR YOU.
I MEAN... I THOUGHT WE WERE MEANT TO BE TOGETHER.
WHAT THE HELL ARE--
OH, MY GOD.

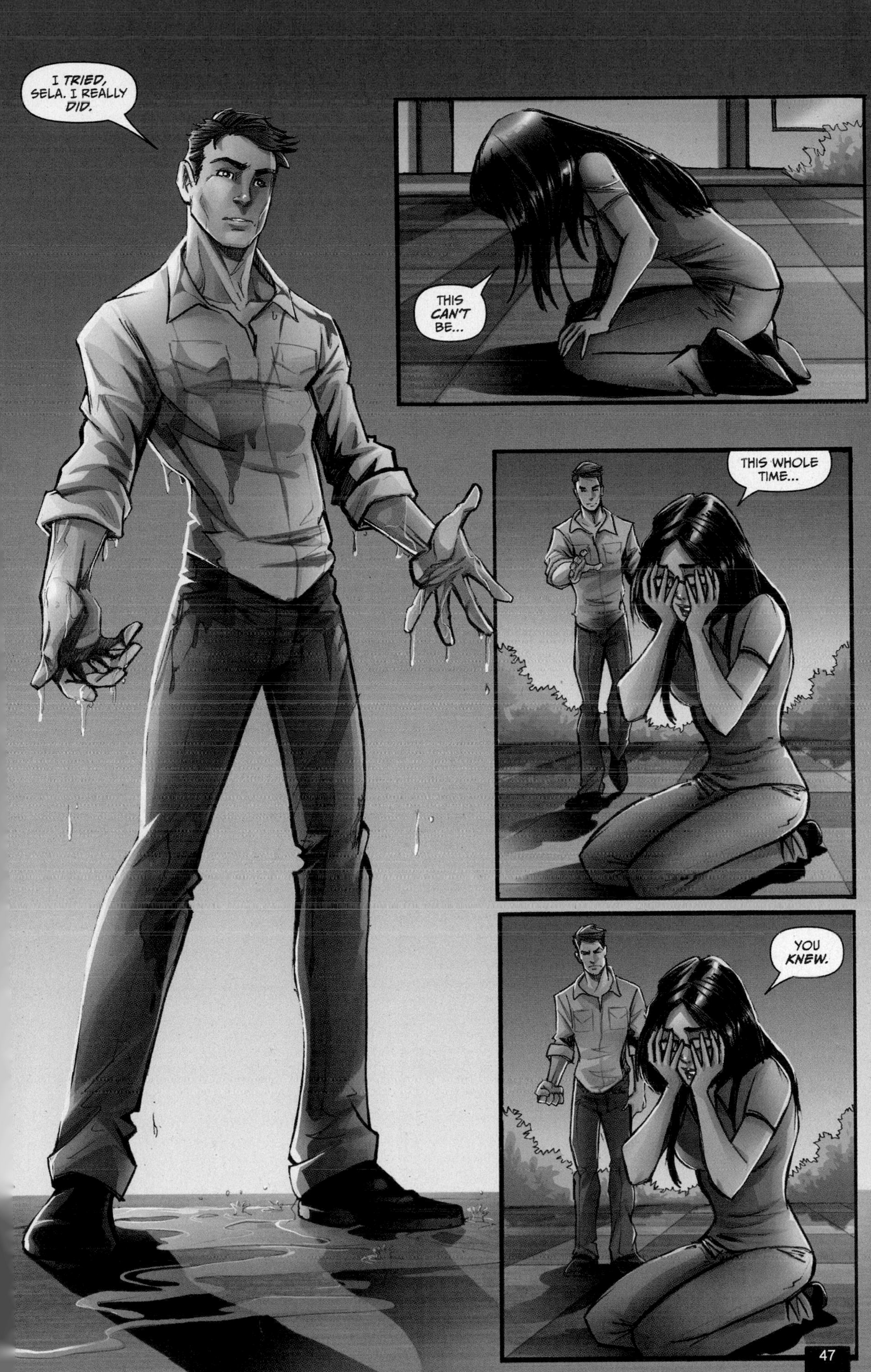
I TRIED, SELA. I REALLY DID.
THIS CAN'T BE...
THIS WHOLE TIME...
YOU KNEW.

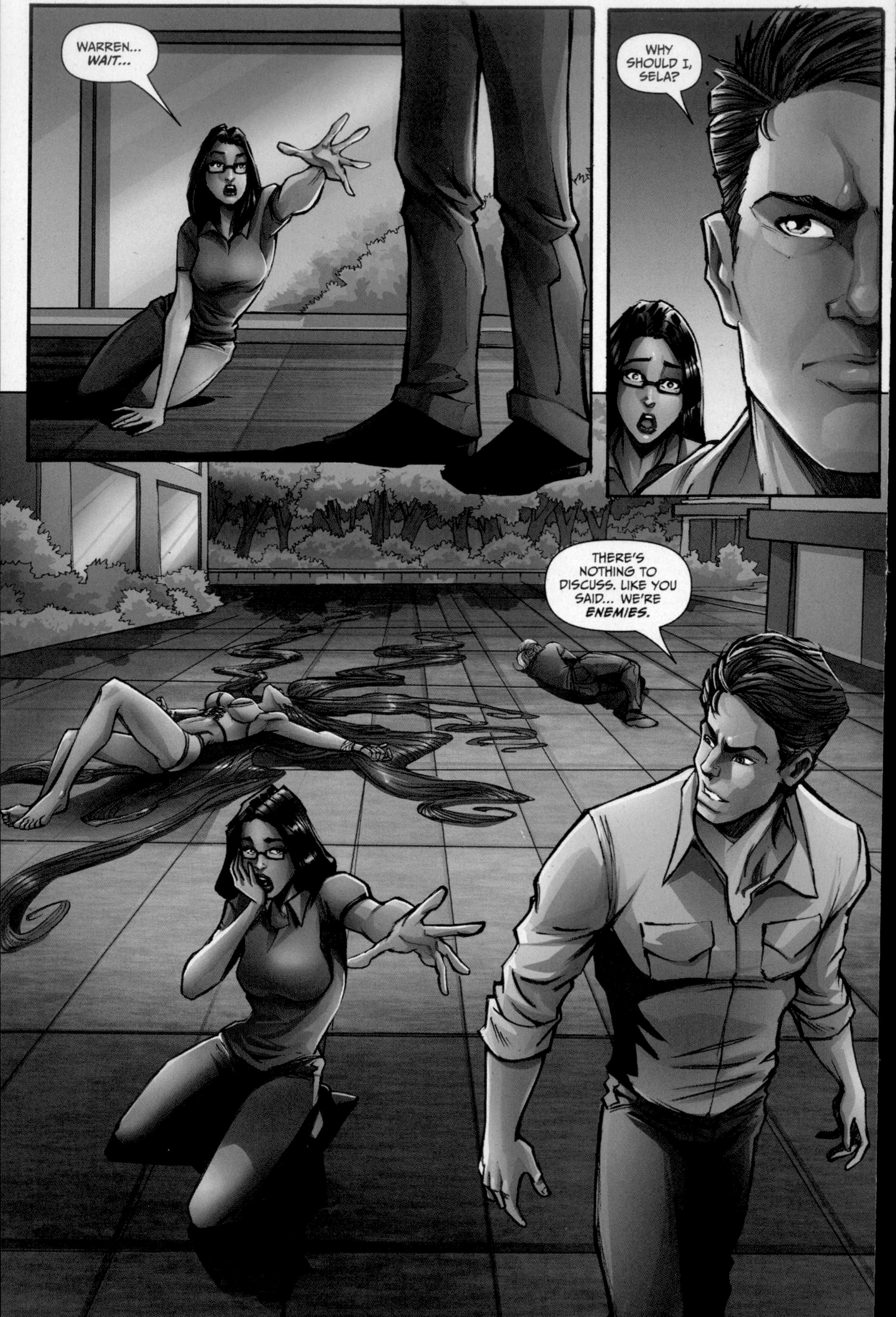
WARREN... WAIT...
WHY SHOULD I, SELA?
THERE'S NOTHING TO DISCUSS. LIKE YOU SAID... WE'RE ENEMIES.

Grimm Fairy Tales

Volume 15

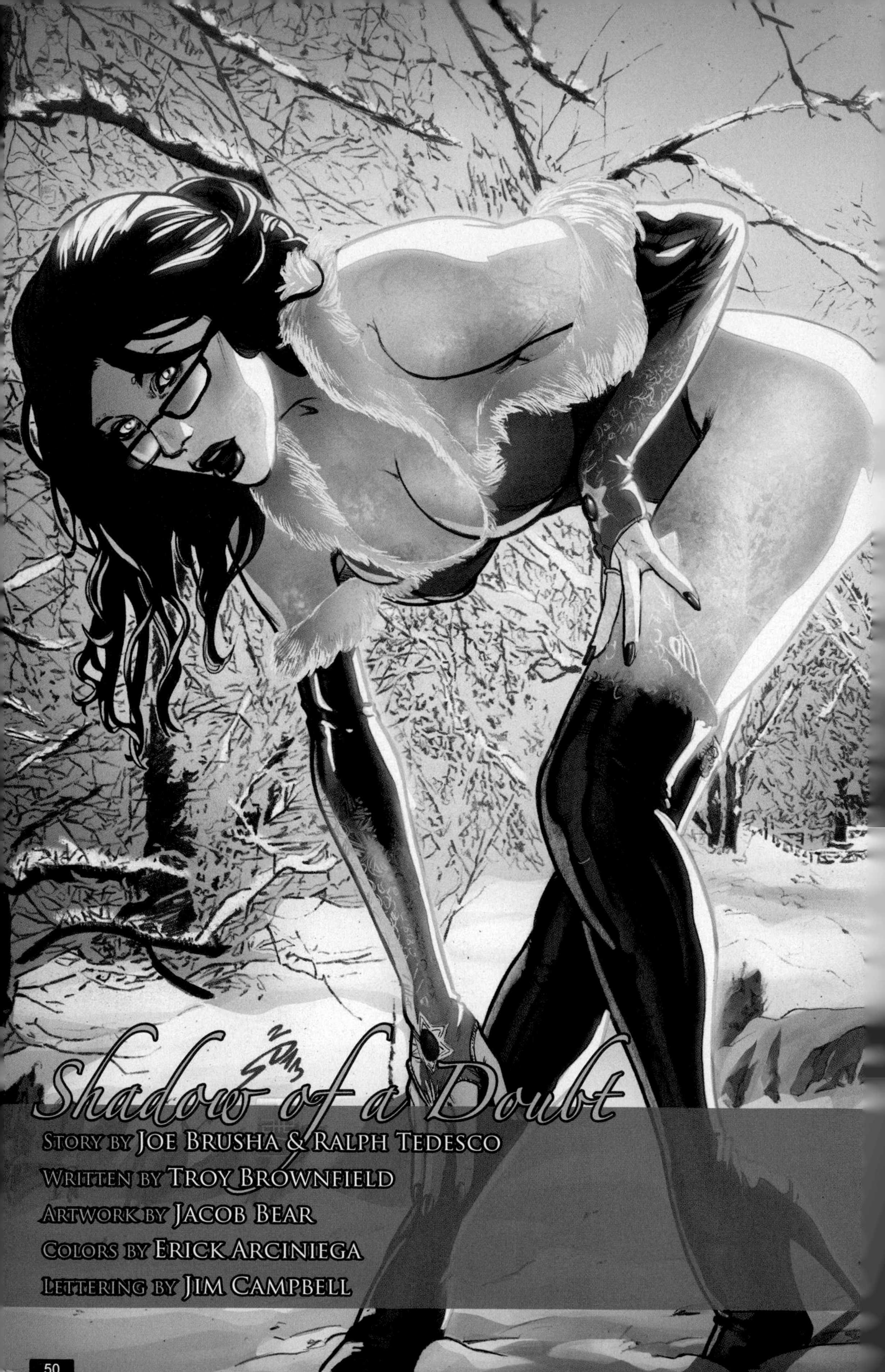
Shadow of a Doubt
Story by Joe Brusha & Ralph Tedesco
Written by Troy Brownfield
Artwork by Jacob Bear
Colors by Erick Arciniega
Lettering by Jim Campbell

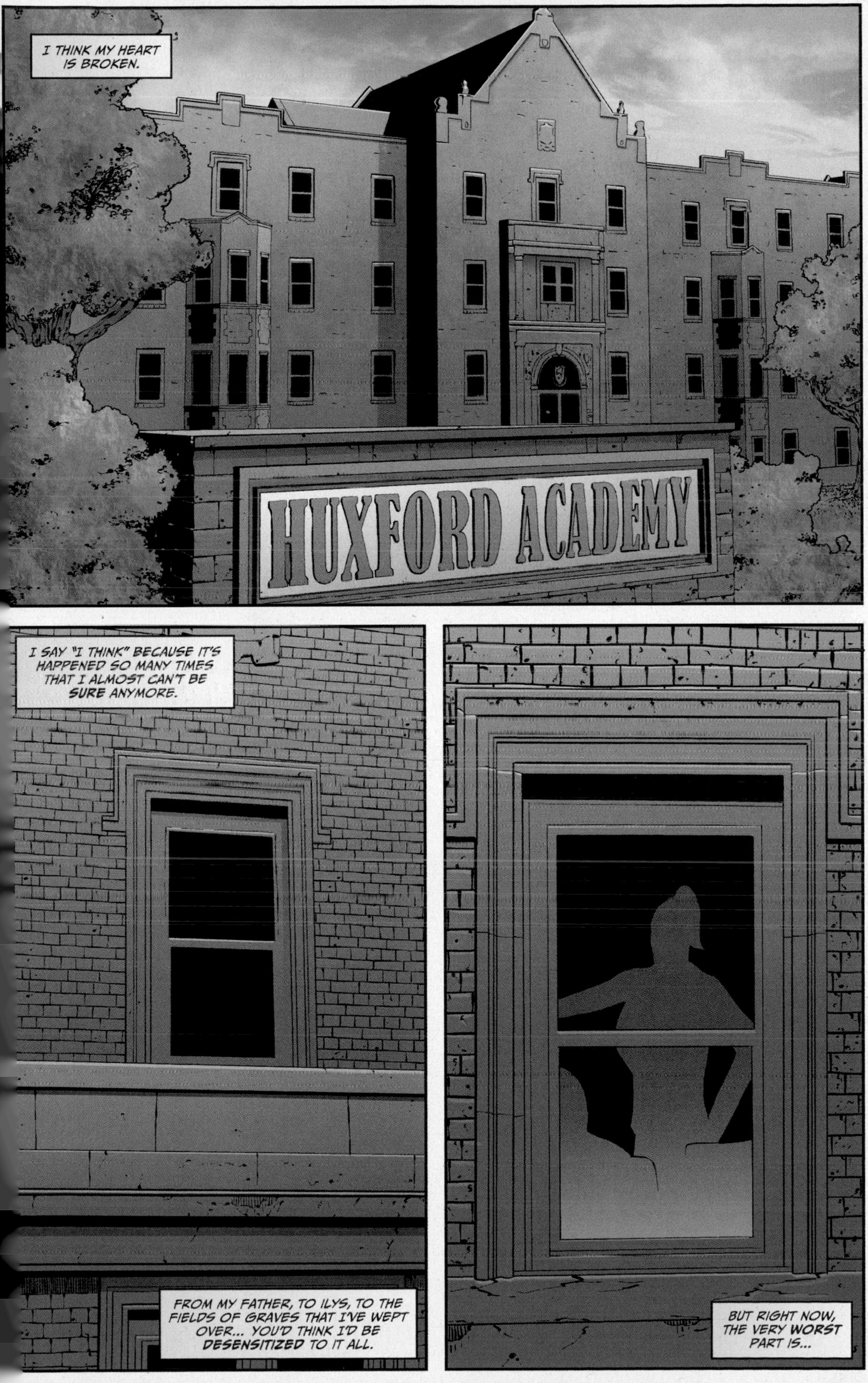
I THINK MY HEART IS BROKEN.
HUXFORD ACADEMY
I SAY "I THINK" BECAUSE IT'S HAPPENED SO MANY TIMES THAT I ALMOST CAN'T BE SURE ANYMORE.
FROM MY FATHER, TO ILYS, TO THE FIELDS OF GRAVES THAT I'VE WEPT OVER... YOU'D THINK I'D BE DESENSITIZED TO IT ALL.
BUT RIGHT NOW, THE VERY WORST PART IS...

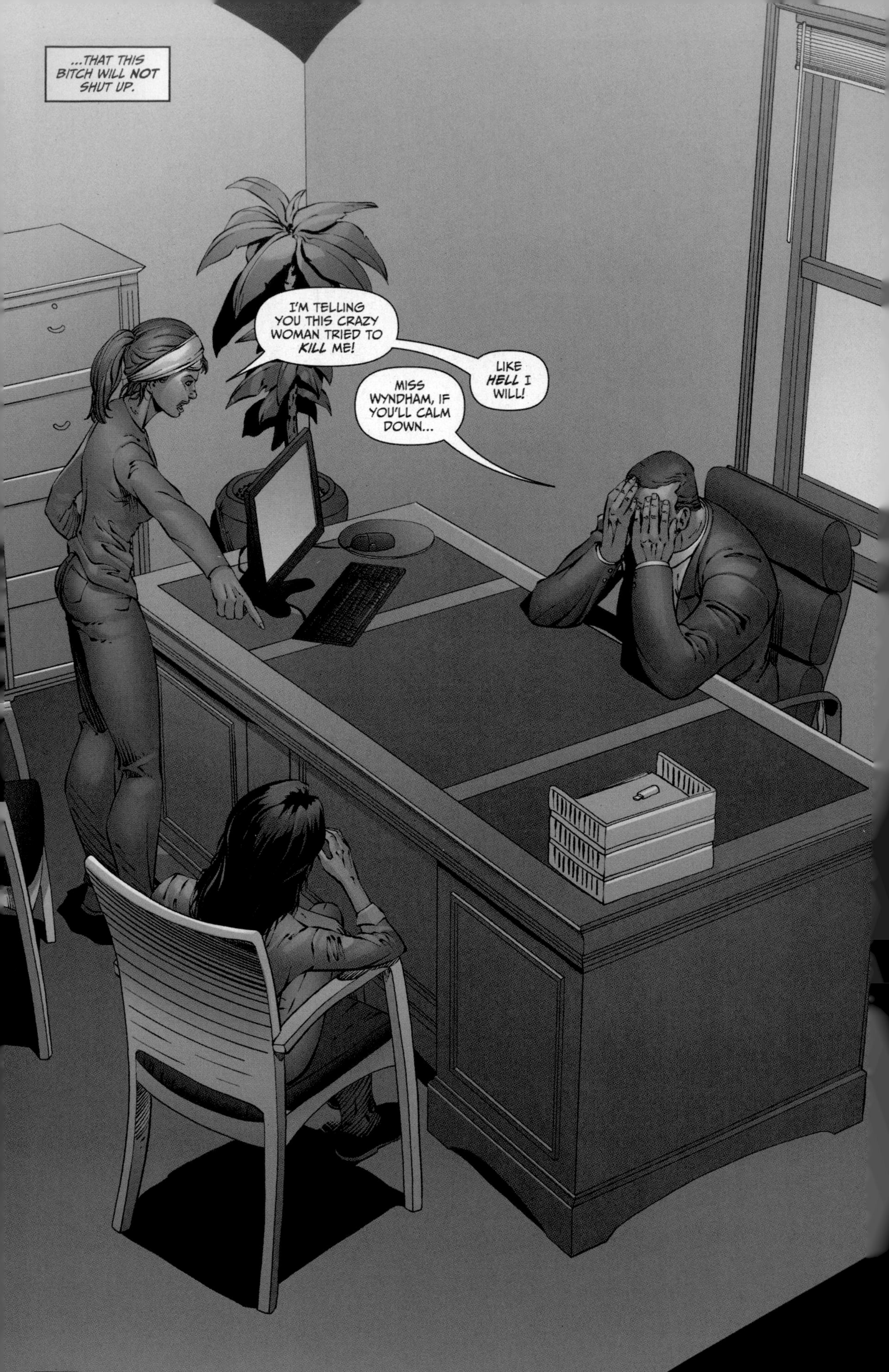
...THAT THIS BITCH WILL NOT SHUT UP.
I'M TELLING YOU THIS CRAZY WOMAN TRIED TO KILL ME!
LIKE HELL I WILL!
MISS WYNDHAM, IF YOU'LL CALM DOWN...

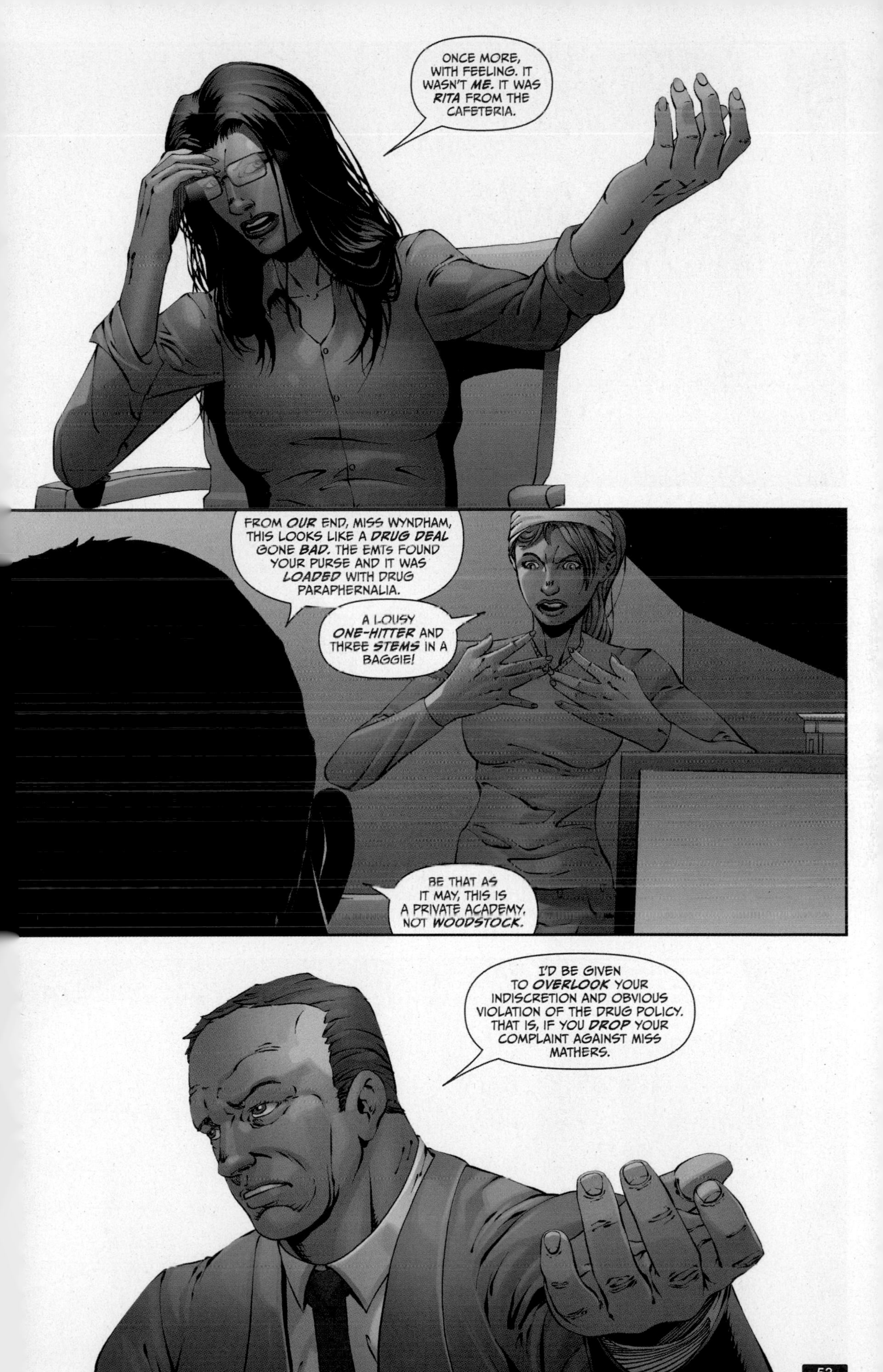
ONCE MORE, WITH FEELING. IT WASN'T ME. IT WAS RITA FROM THE CAFETERIA.
FROM OUR END, MISS WYNDHAM, THIS LOOKS LIKE A DRUG DEAL GONE BAD. THE EMTS FOUND YOUR PURSE AND IT WAS LOADED WITH DRUG PARAPHERNALIA.
A LOUSY ONE-HITTER AND THREE STEMS IN A BAGGIE!
BE THAT AS IT MAY, THIS IS A PRIVATE ACADEMY, NOT WOODSTOCK.
I'D BE GIVEN TO OVERLOOK YOUR INDISCRETION AND OBVIOUS VIOLATION OF THE DRUG POLICY. THAT IS, IF YOU DROP YOUR COMPLAINT AGAINST MISS MATHERS.

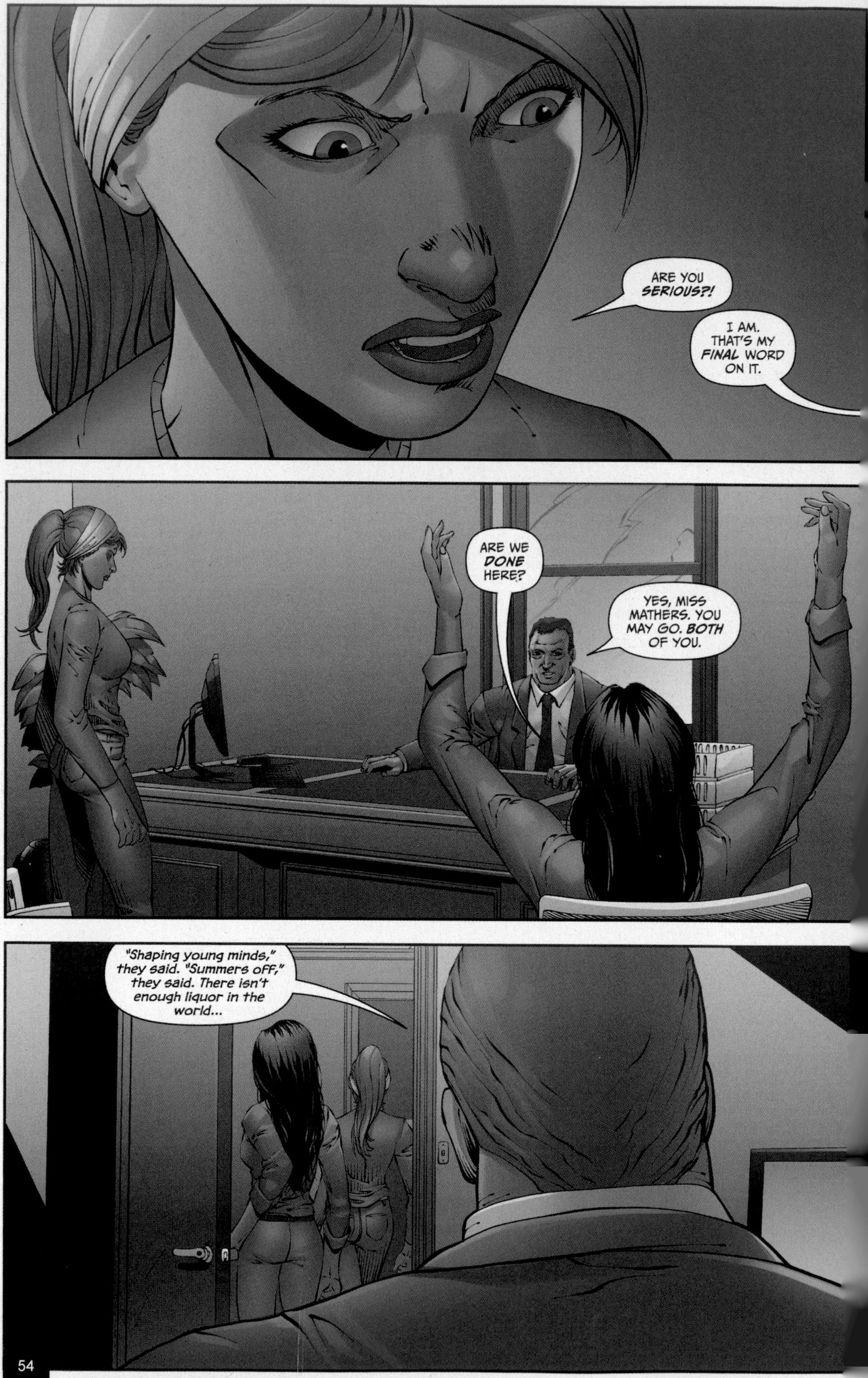
ARE YOU SERIOUS?!
I AM. THAT'S MY FINAL WORD ON IT.
ARE WE DONE HERE?
YES, MISS MATHERS. YOU MAY GO. BOTH OF YOU.
"Shaping young minds," they said. "Summers off," they said. There isn't enough liquor in the world...

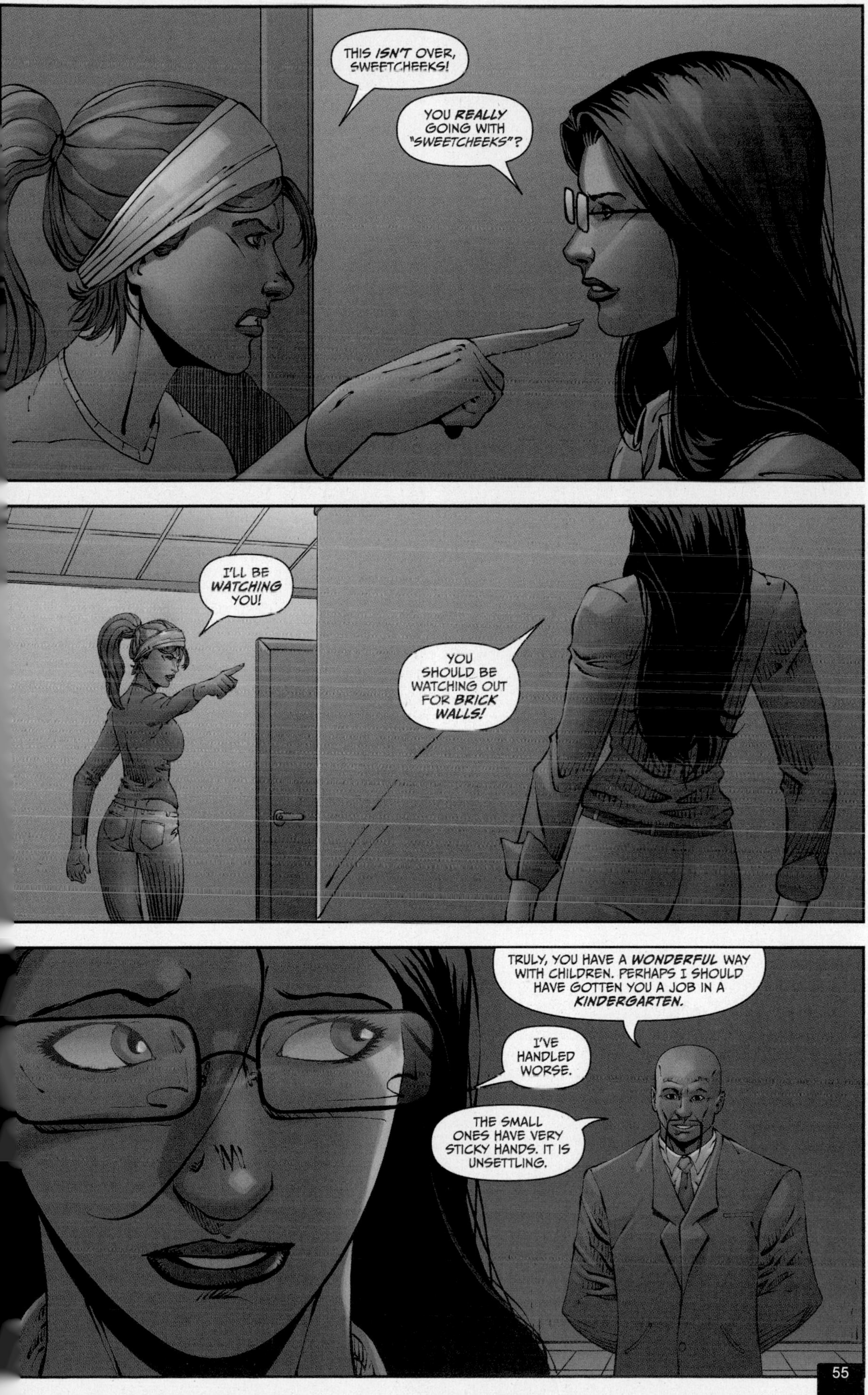

THIS *ISN'T* OVER, SWEETCHEEKS!
YOU *REALLY* GOING WITH "SWEETCHEEKS"?
I'LL BE *WATCHING* YOU!
YOU SHOULD BE WATCHING OUT FOR *BRICK WALLS!*
TRULY, YOU HAVE A *WONDERFUL* WAY WITH CHILDREN. PERHAPS I SHOULD HAVE GOTTEN YOU A JOB IN A *KINDERGARTEN.*
I'VE HANDLED WORSE.
THE SMALL ONES HAVE VERY STICKY HANDS. IT IS UNSETTLING.

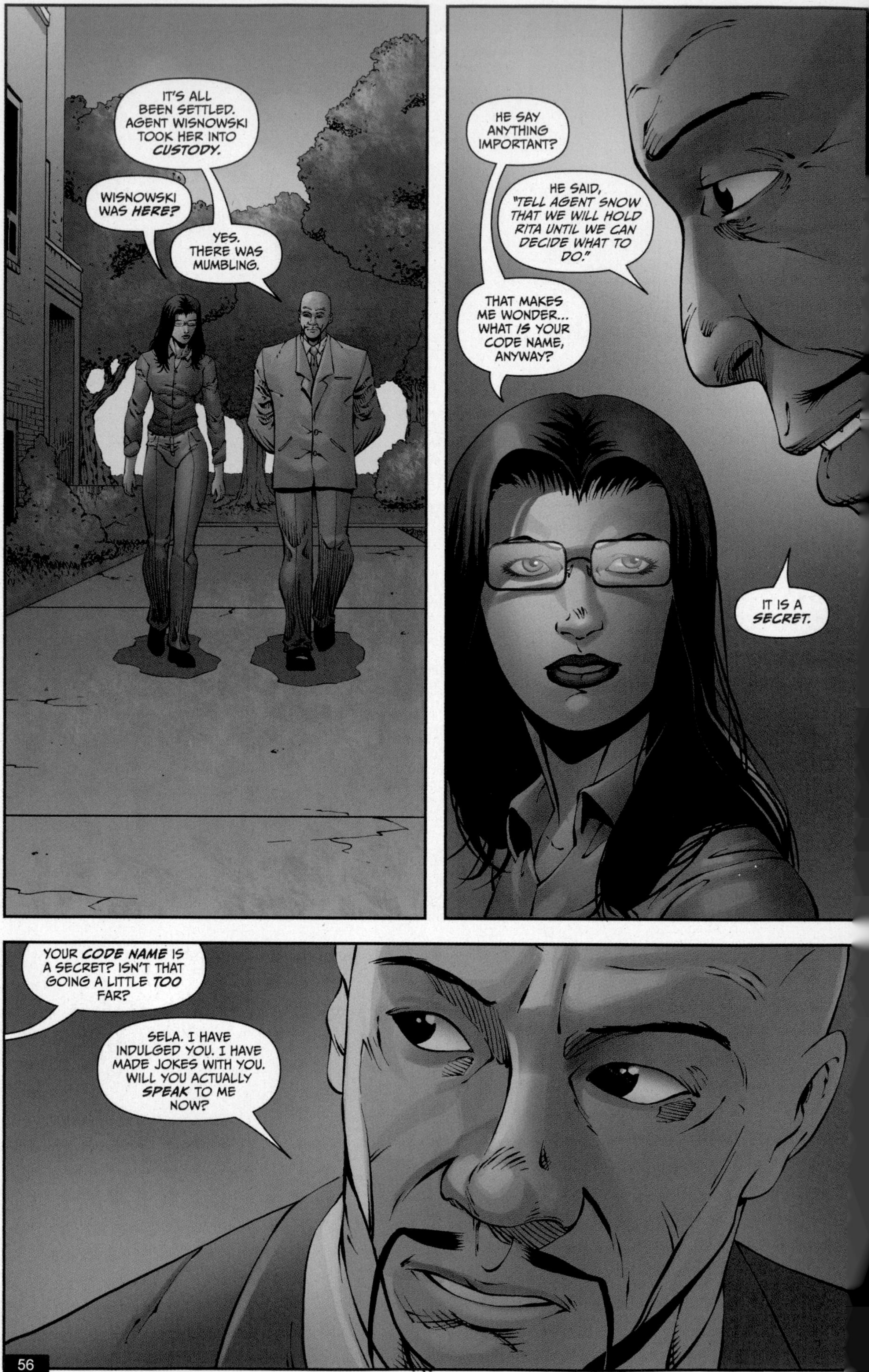
IT'S ALL BEEN SETTLED. AGENT WISNOWSKI TOOK HER INTO CUSTODY.
WISNOWSKI WAS HERE?
YES. THERE WAS MUMBLING.
HE SAY ANYTHING IMPORTANT?
HE SAID, "TELL AGENT SNOW THAT WE WILL HOLD RITA UNTIL WE CAN DECIDE WHAT TO DO."
THAT MAKES ME WONDER... WHAT IS YOUR CODE NAME, ANYWAY?
IT IS A SECRET.
YOUR CODE NAME IS A SECRET? ISN'T THAT GOING A LITTLE TOO FAR?
SELA. I HAVE INDULGED YOU. I HAVE MADE JOKES WITH YOU. WILL YOU ACTUALLY SPEAK TO ME NOW?

SO I TELL SHANG *EVERYTHING.* THEY SAY THAT TALKING ABOUT IT MAKES IT BETTER.

BUT HEARING IT OUT LOUD JUST MAKES IT *WORSE.*

AND I'M *SICK,* SHANG. SICK ABOUT WHAT HAPPENED TO *RITA.* SICK ABOUT *WARREN.*

Sick of it all.

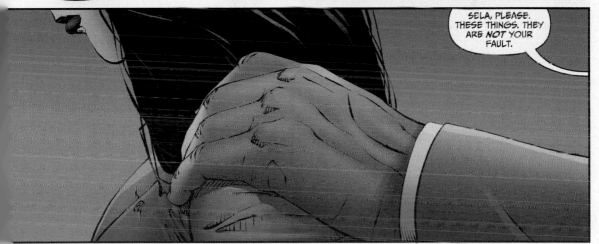

SELA, PLEASE. THESE THINGS. THEY ARE *NOT* YOUR FAULT.

WARREN ... DID YOU *KNOW* THAT HE WAS FROST?

MUST YOU ASK? OF *COURSE* NOT.

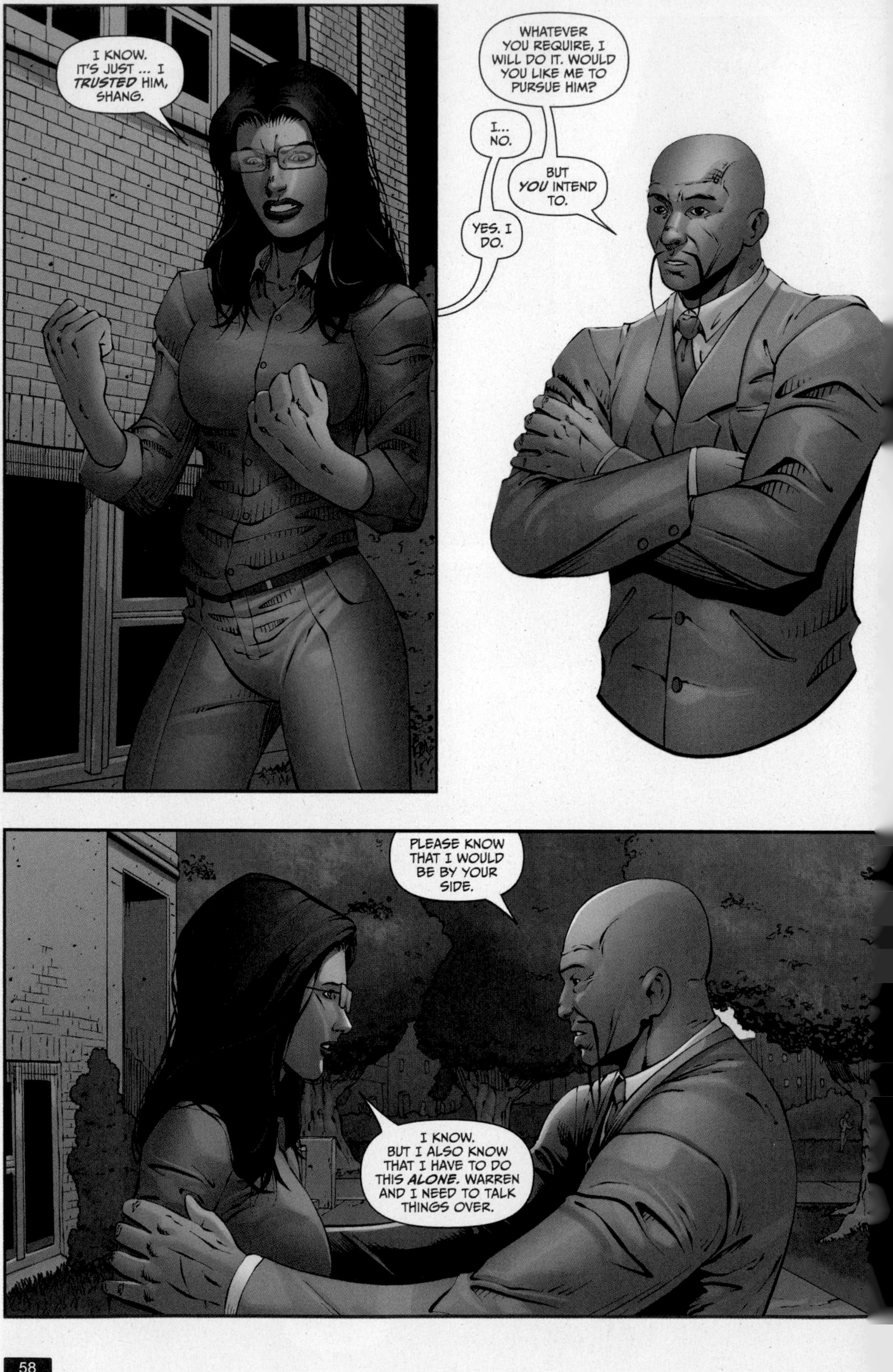
I KNOW. IT'S JUST ... I *TRUSTED* HIM, SHANG.
WHATEVER YOU REQUIRE, I WILL DO IT. WOULD YOU LIKE ME TO PURSUE HIM?
I... NO.
BUT *YOU* INTEND TO.
YES. I DO.
PLEASE KNOW THAT I WOULD BE BY YOUR SIDE.
I KNOW. BUT I ALSO KNOW THAT I HAVE TO DO THIS *ALONE.* WARREN AND I NEED TO TALK THINGS OVER.

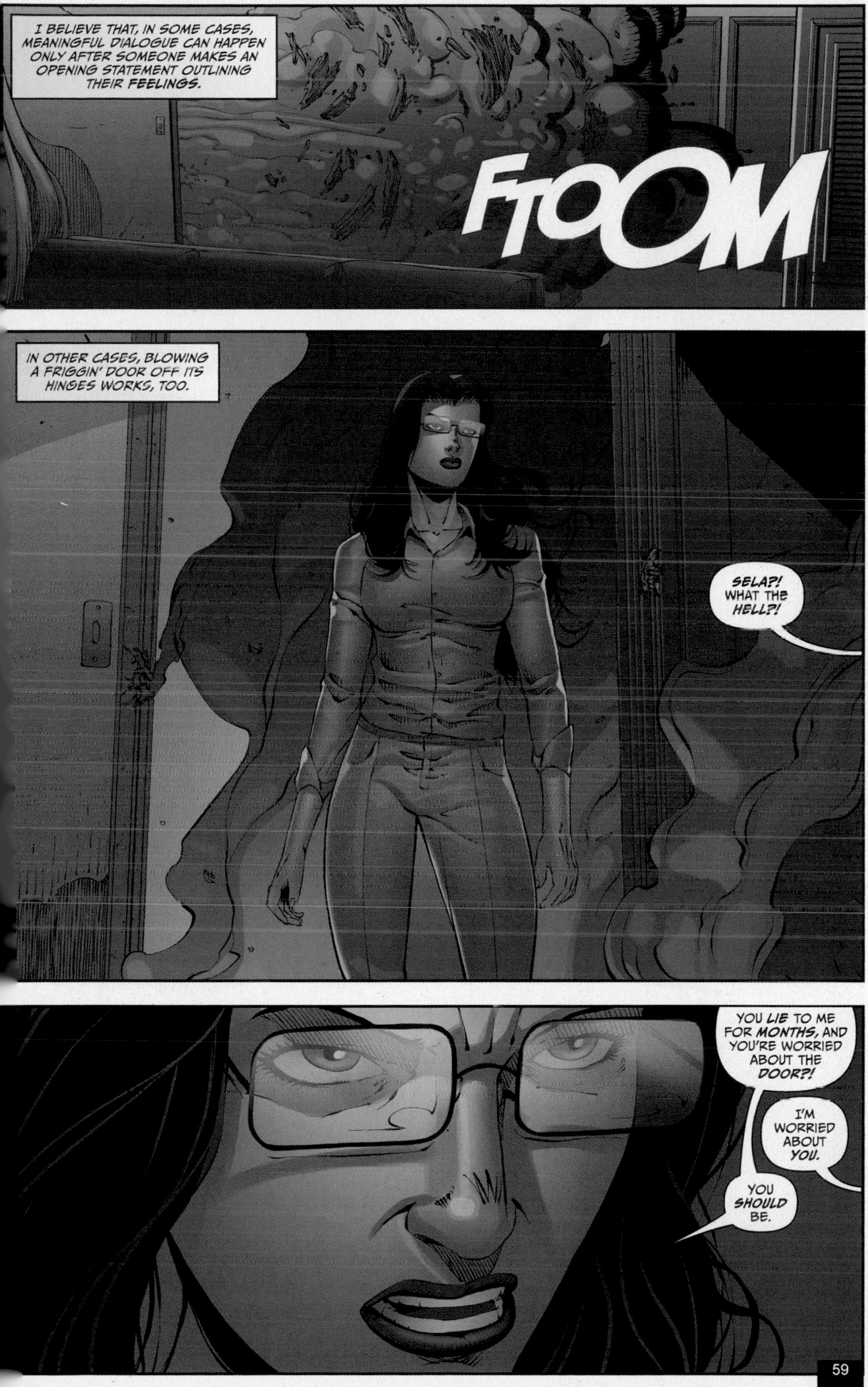
I BELIEVE THAT, IN SOME CASES, MEANINGFUL DIALOGUE CAN HAPPEN ONLY AFTER SOMEONE MAKES AN OPENING STATEMENT OUTLINING THEIR FEELINGS.
FTOOM
IN OTHER CASES, BLOWING A FRIGGIN' DOOR OFF ITS HINGES WORKS, TOO.
SELA?! WHAT THE HELL?!
YOU LIE TO ME FOR MONTHS, AND YOU'RE WORRIED ABOUT THE DOOR?!
I'M WORRIED ABOUT YOU.
YOU SHOULD BE.

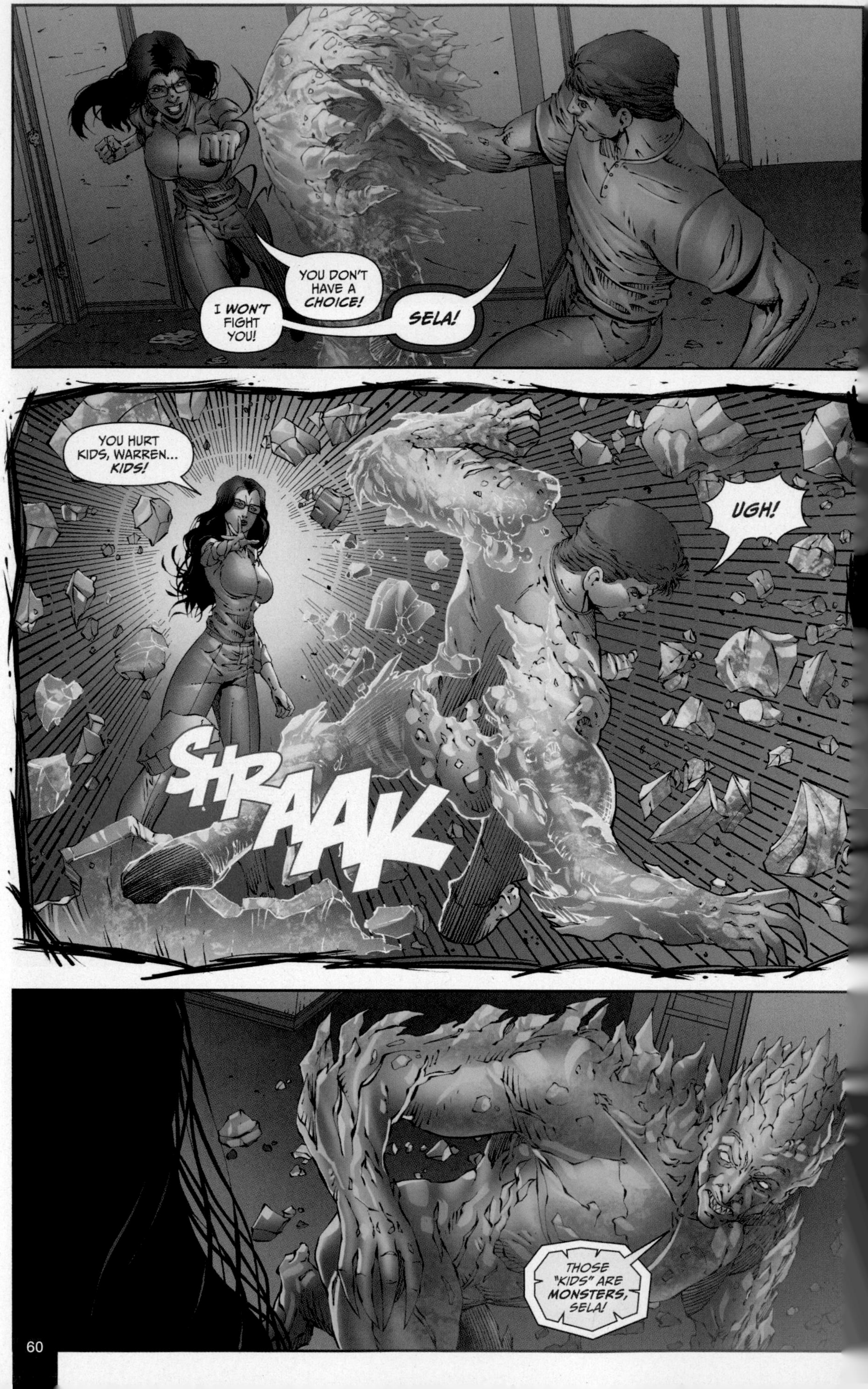
I WON'T FIGHT YOU!
YOU DON'T HAVE A CHOICE!
SELA!
YOU HURT KIDS, WARREN... KIDS!
UGH!
SHRAAK
THOSE "KIDS" ARE MONSTERS, SELA!

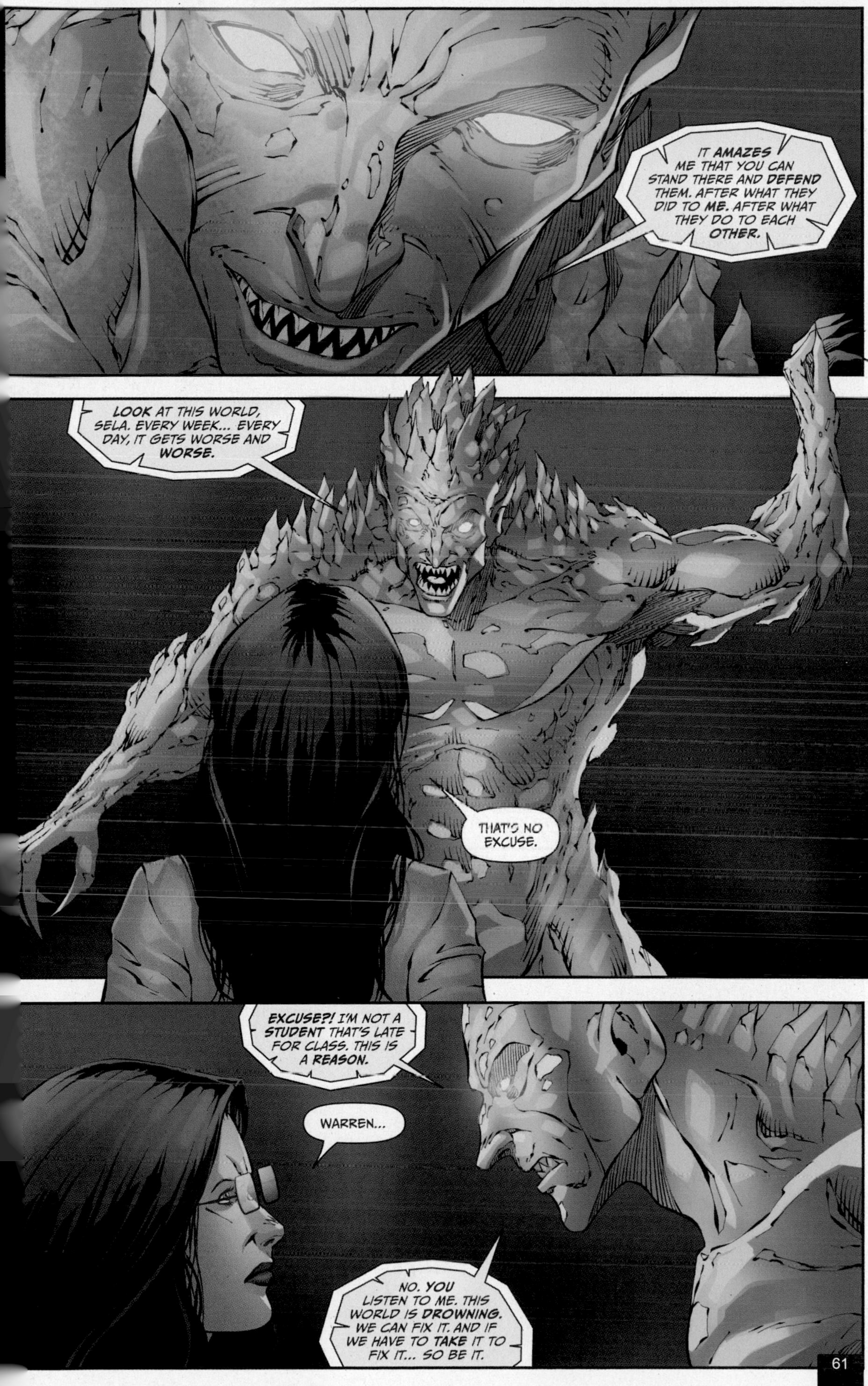
IT AMAZES ME THAT YOU CAN STAND THERE AND DEFEND THEM. AFTER WHAT THEY DID TO ME. AFTER WHAT THEY DO TO EACH OTHER.
LOOK AT THIS WORLD, SELA. EVERY WEEK... EVERY DAY, IT GETS WORSE AND WORSE.
THAT'S NO EXCUSE.
EXCUSE?! I'M NOT A STUDENT THAT'S LATE FOR CLASS. THIS IS A REASON.
WARREN...
NO. YOU LISTEN TO ME. THIS WORLD IS DROWNING. WE CAN FIX IT. AND IF WE HAVE TO TAKE IT TO FIX IT... SO BE IT.

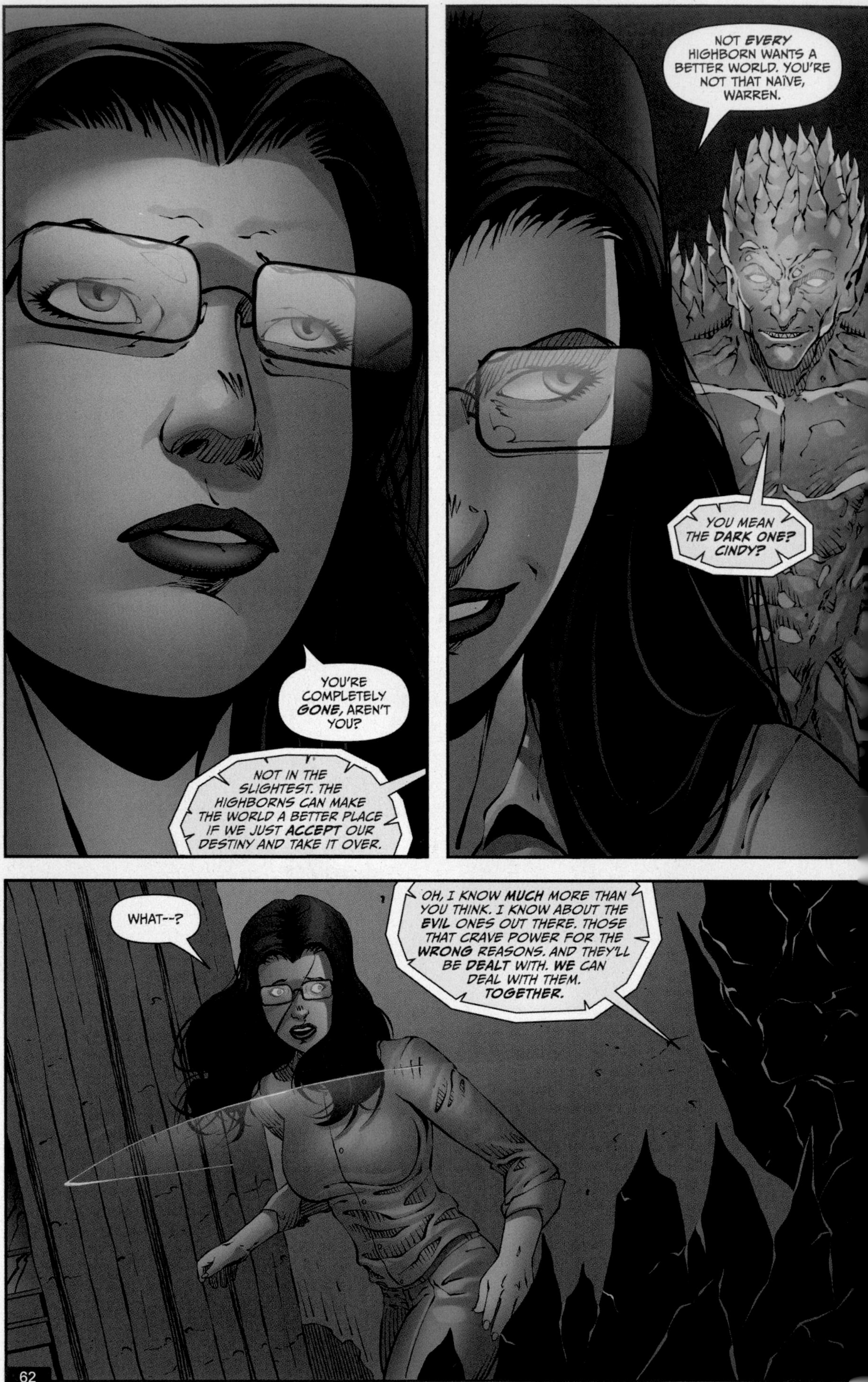
YOU'RE COMPLETELY GONE, AREN'T YOU?
NOT IN THE SLIGHTEST. THE HIGHBORNS CAN MAKE THE WORLD A BETTER PLACE IF WE JUST ACCEPT OUR DESTINY AND TAKE IT OVER.
NOT EVERY HIGHBORN WANTS A BETTER WORLD. YOU'RE NOT THAT NAÏVE, WARREN.
YOU MEAN THE DARK ONE? CINDY?
WHAT--?
OH, I KNOW MUCH MORE THAN YOU THINK. I KNOW ABOUT THE EVIL ONES OUT THERE. THOSE THAT CRAVE POWER FOR THE WRONG REASONS. AND THEY'LL BE DEALT WITH. WE CAN DEAL WITH THEM. TOGETHER.

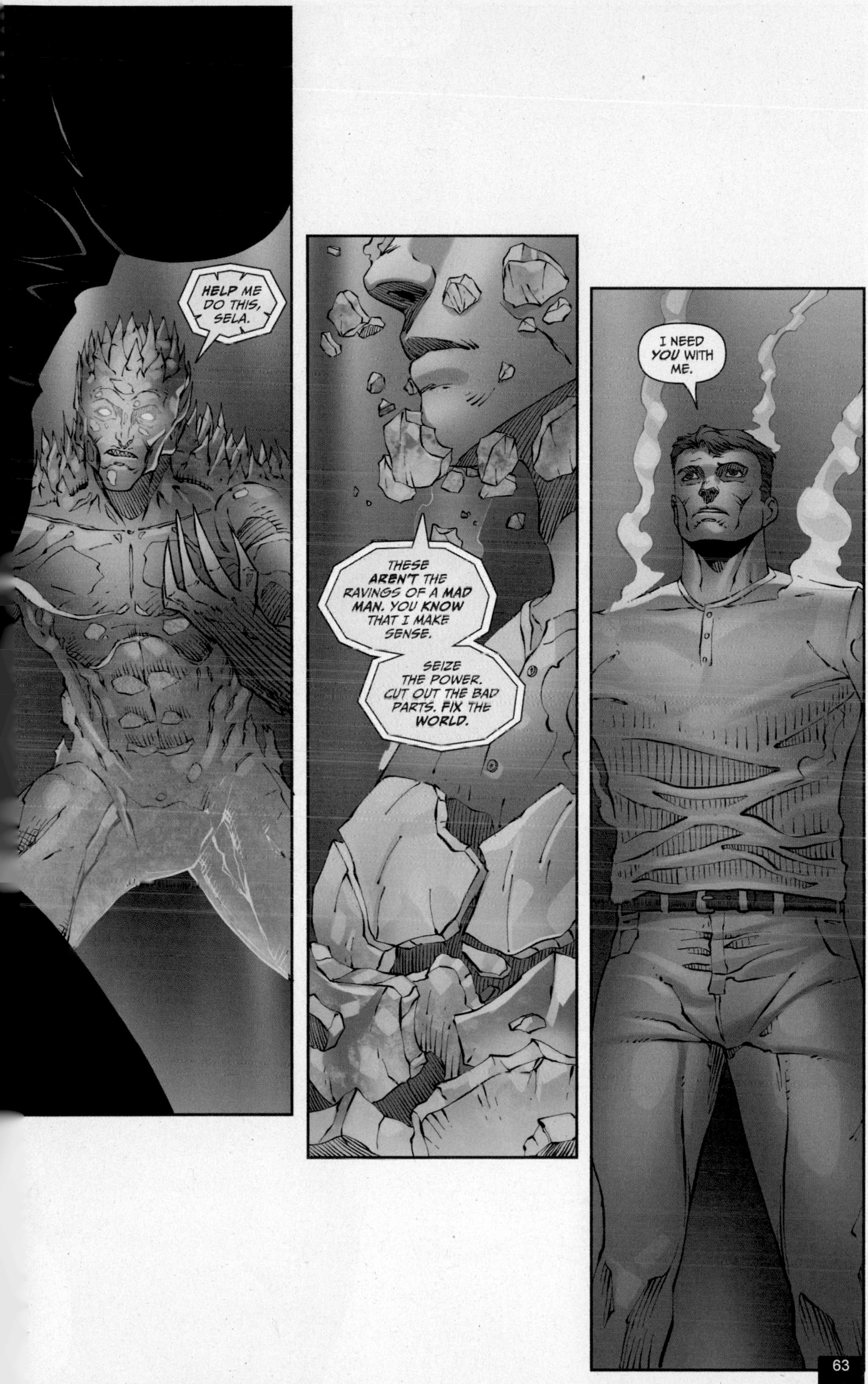
HELP ME DO THIS, SELA.
THESE AREN'T THE RAVINGS OF A MAD MAN. YOU KNOW THAT I MAKE SENSE.
SEIZE THE POWER. CUT OUT THE BAD PARTS. FIX THE WORLD.
I NEED YOU WITH ME.

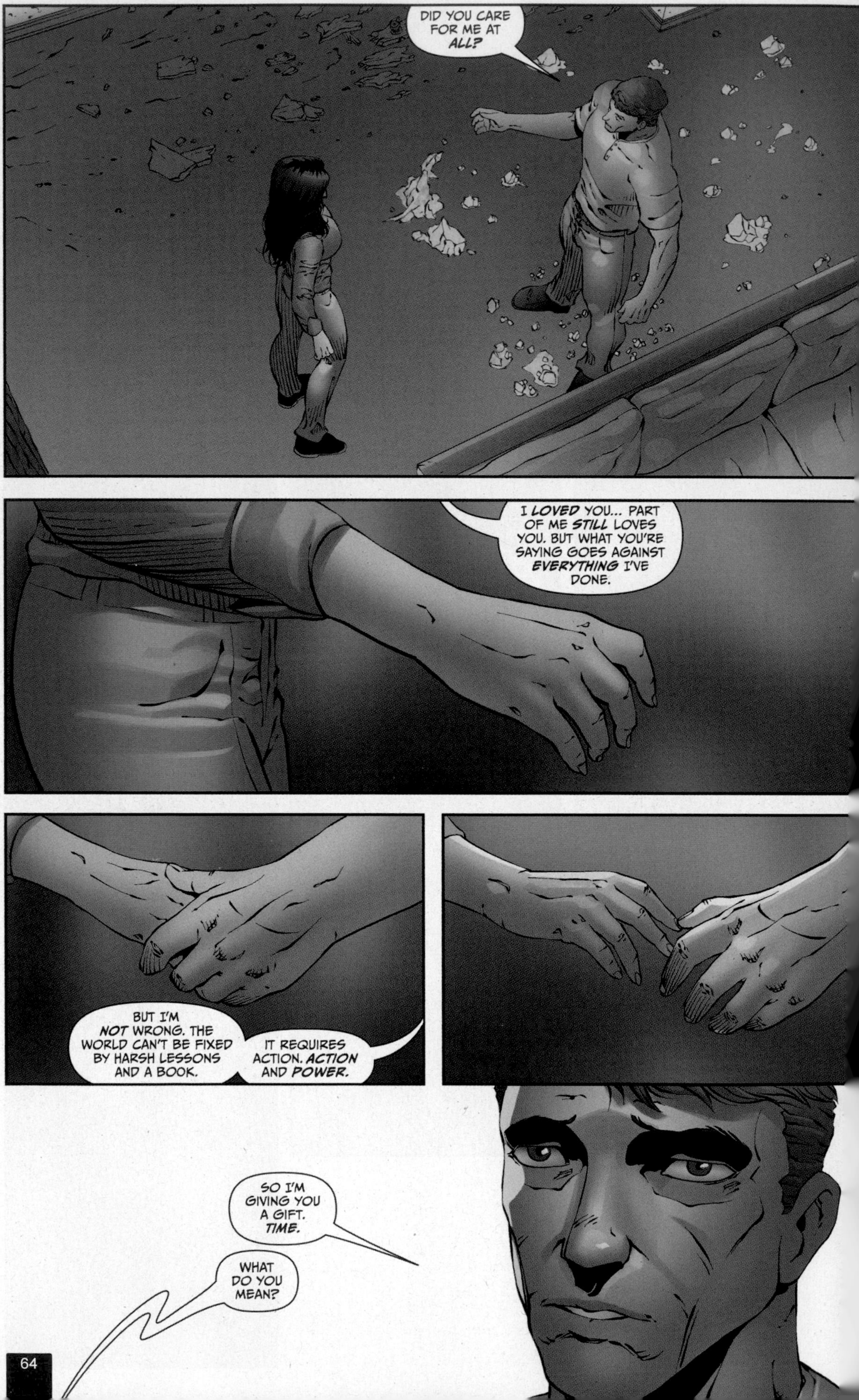
DID YOU CARE FOR ME AT ALL?
I LOVED YOU... PART OF ME STILL LOVES YOU. BUT WHAT YOU'RE SAYING GOES AGAINST EVERYTHING I'VE DONE.
BUT I'M NOT WRONG. THE WORLD CAN'T BE FIXED BY HARSH LESSONS AND A BOOK.
IT REQUIRES ACTION. ACTION AND POWER.
SO I'M GIVING YOU A GIFT. TIME.
WHAT DO YOU MEAN?

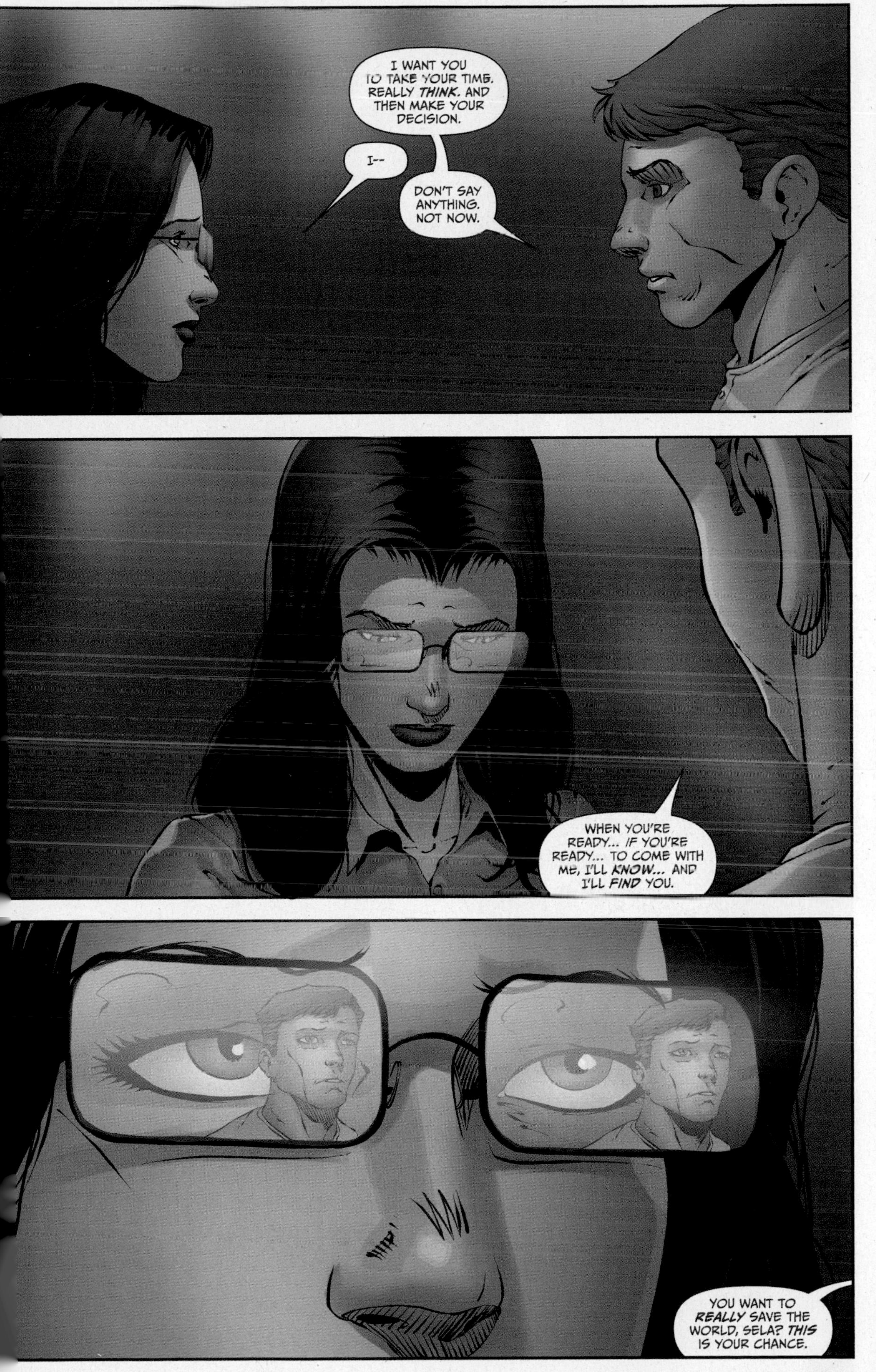
I WANT YOU TO TAKE YOUR TIME. REALLY THINK. AND THEN MAKE YOUR DECISION.
I--
DON'T SAY ANYTHING. NOT NOW.
WHEN YOU'RE READY... IF YOU'RE READY... TO COME WITH ME, I'LL KNOW... AND I'LL FIND YOU.
YOU WANT TO REALLY SAVE THE WORLD, SELA? THIS IS YOUR CHANCE.

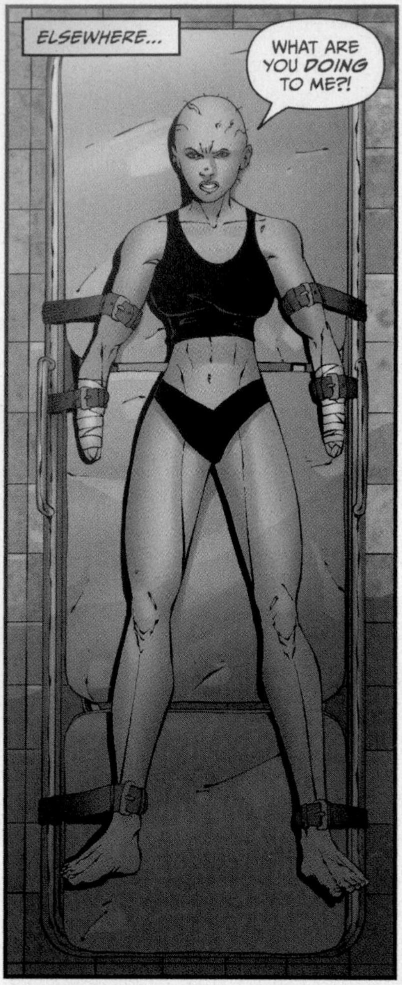
ELSEWHERE...
WHAT ARE YOU DOING TO ME?!

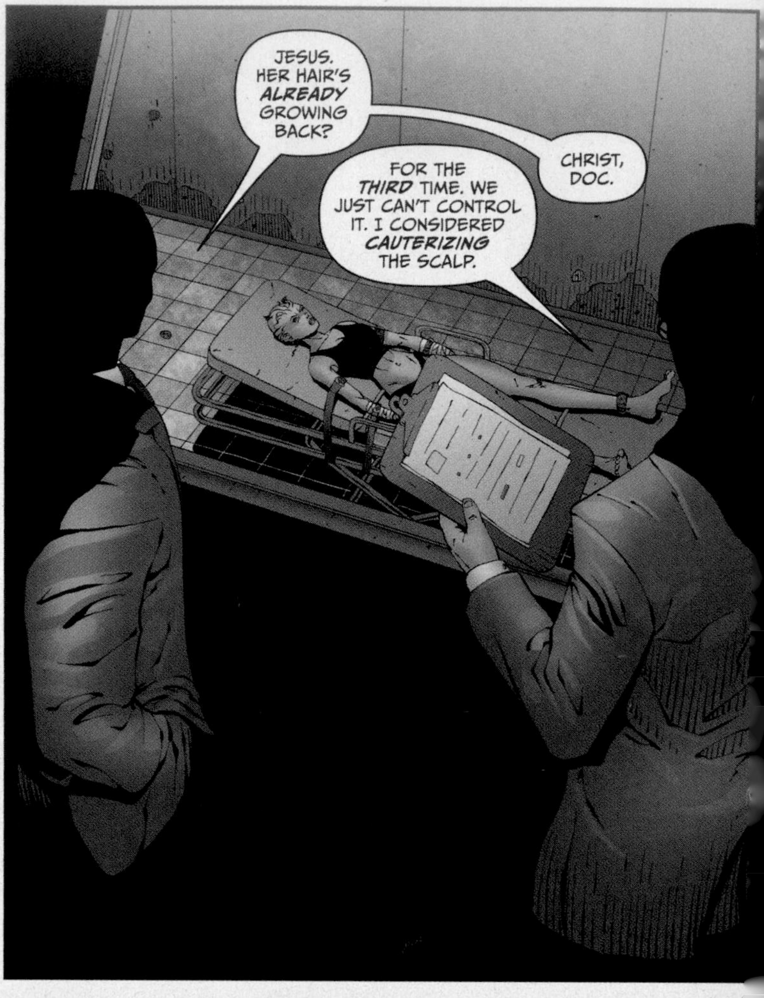
JESUS. HER HAIR'S ALREADY GROWING BACK?
CHRIST, DOC.
FOR THE THIRD TIME. WE JUST CAN'T CONTROL IT. I CONSIDERED CAUTERIZING THE SCALP.

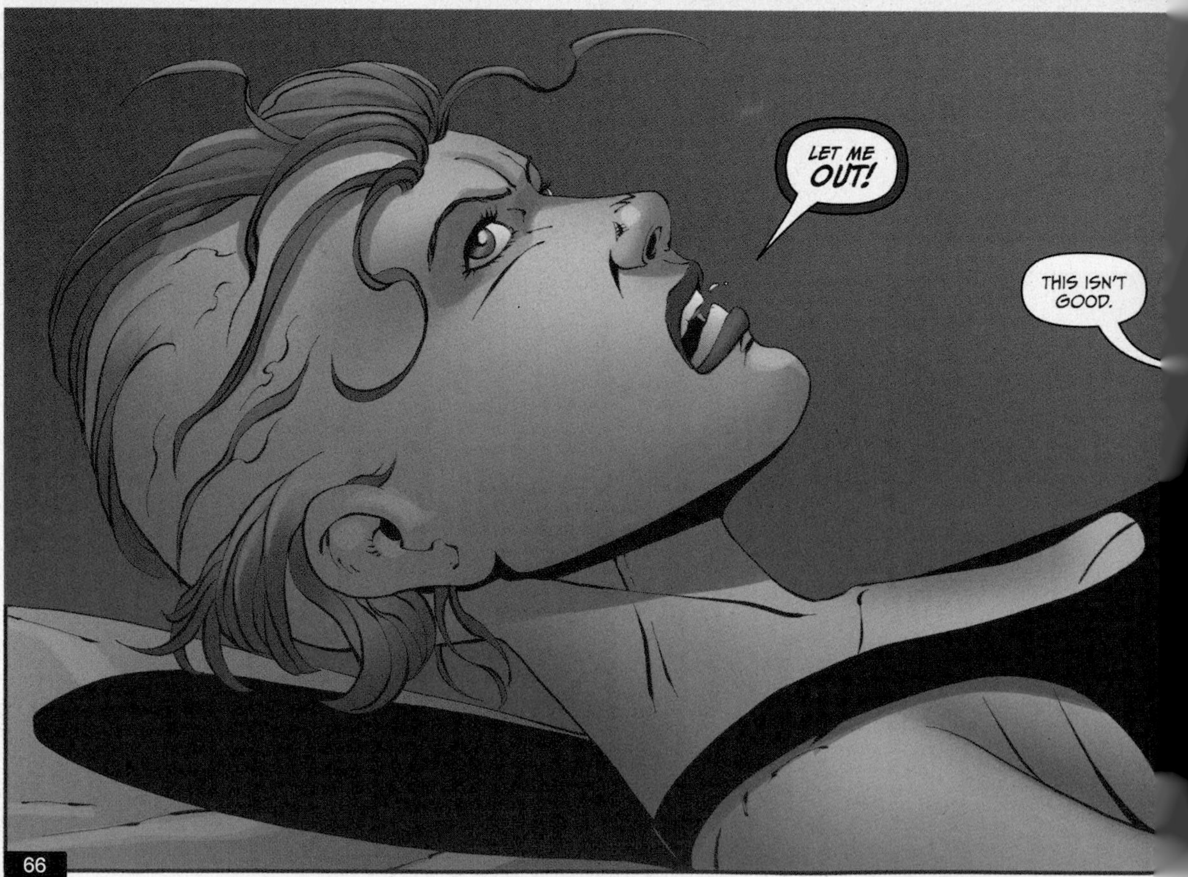
LET ME OUT!
THIS ISN'T GOOD.

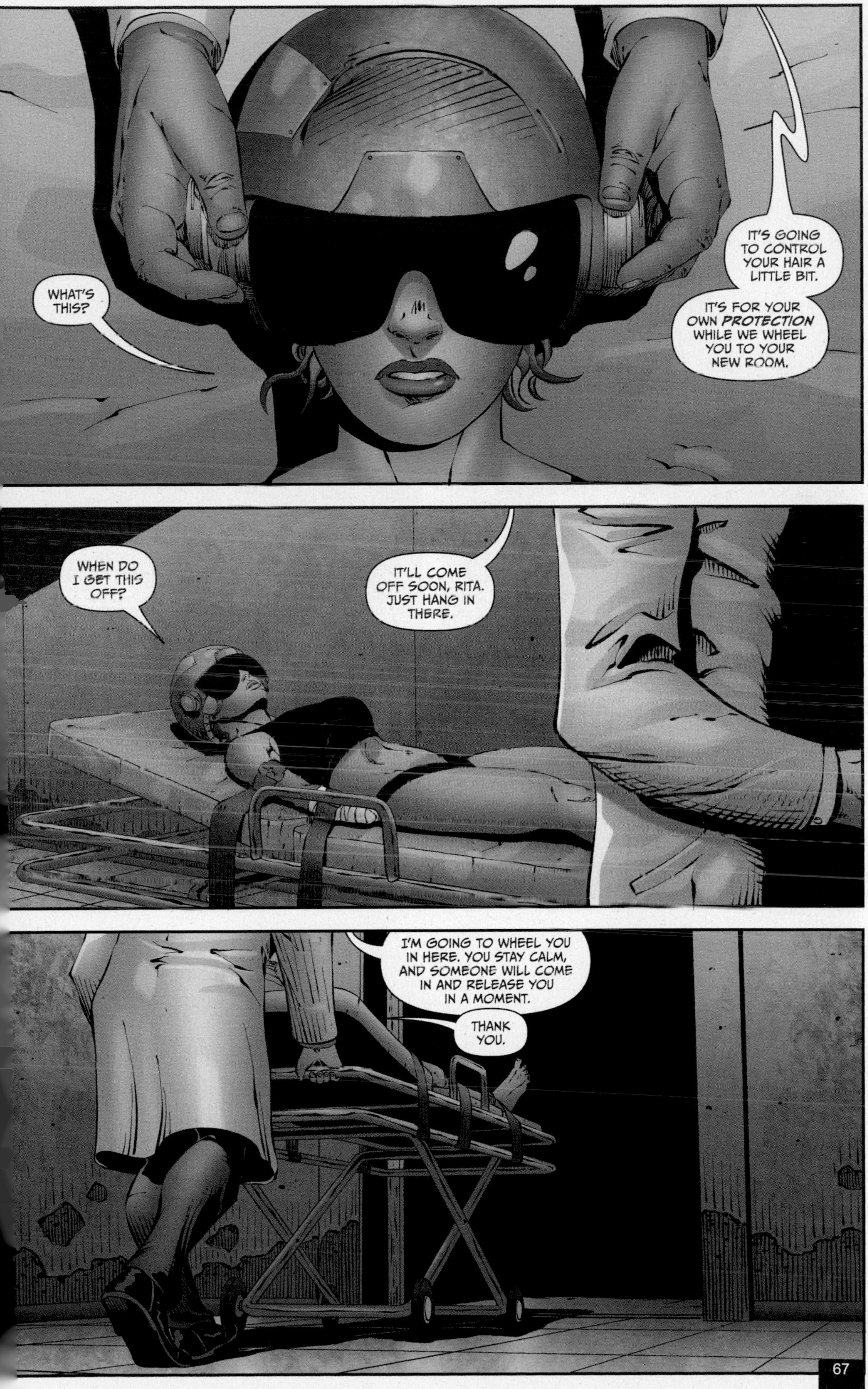
WHAT'S THIS?
IT'S GOING TO CONTROL YOUR HAIR A LITTLE BIT.
IT'S FOR YOUR OWN PROTECTION WHILE WE WHEEL YOU TO YOUR NEW ROOM.
WHEN DO I GET THIS OFF?
IT'LL COME OFF SOON, RITA. JUST HANG IN THERE.
I'M GOING TO WHEEL YOU IN HERE. YOU STAY CALM, AND SOMEONE WILL COME IN AND RELEASE YOU IN A MOMENT.
THANK YOU.

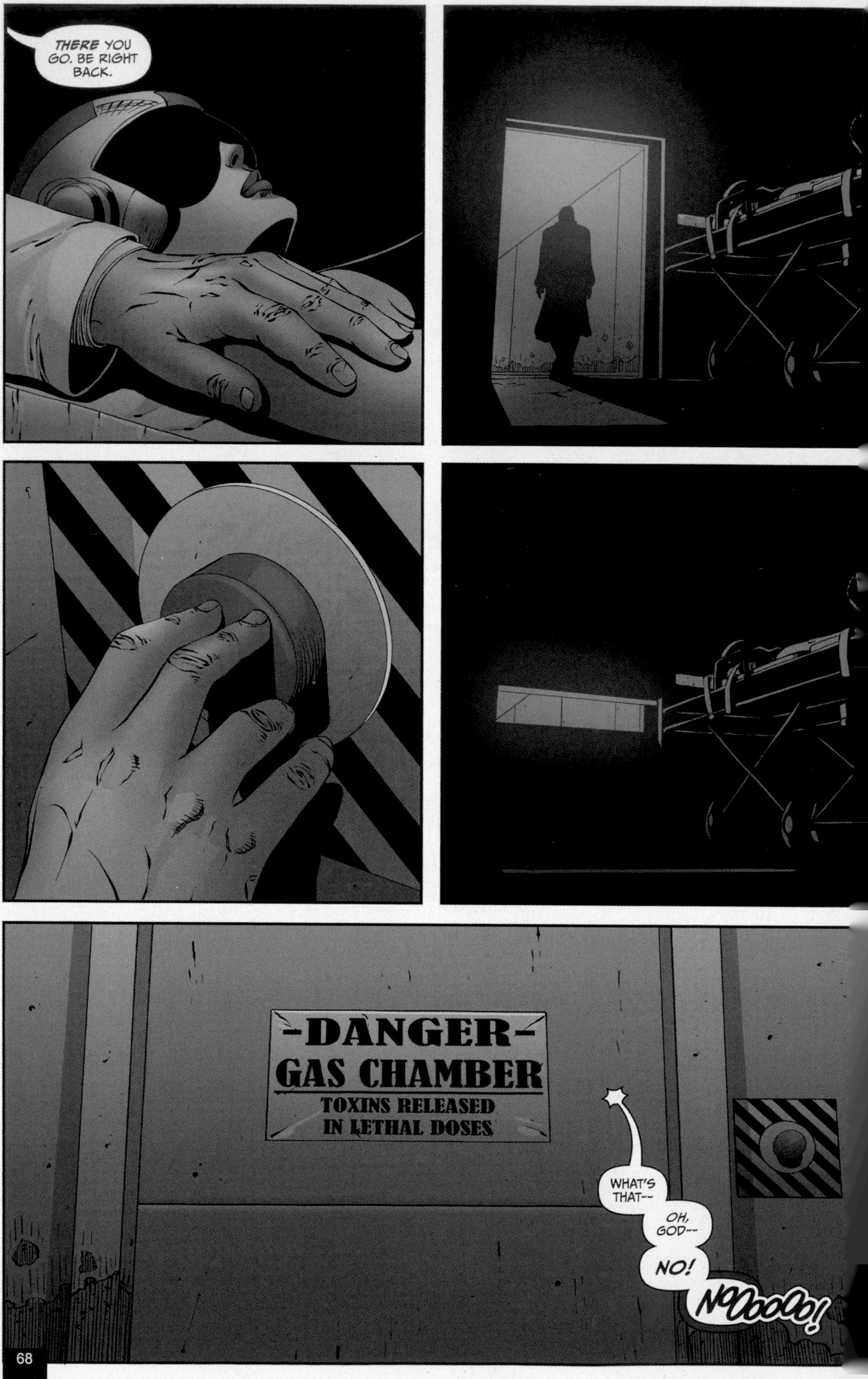
THERE YOU GO. BE RIGHT BACK.
-DANGER-
GAS CHAMBER
TOXINS RELEASED
IN LETHAL DOSES
WHAT'S THAT--
OH, GOD--
NO!
NOOOOOO!

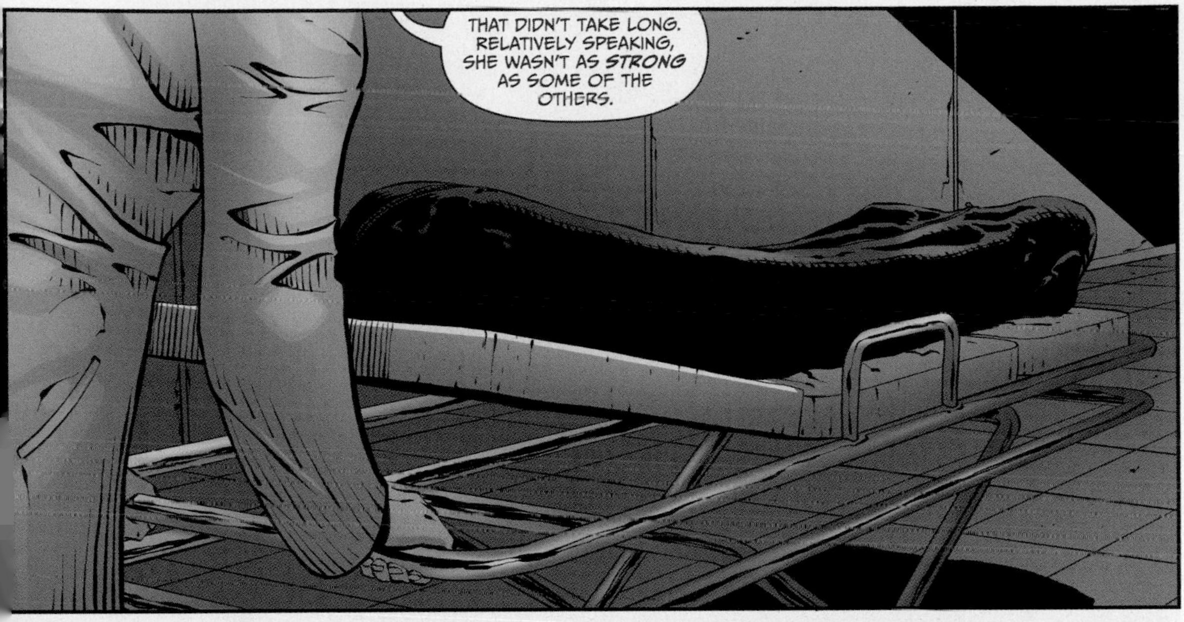
THAT DIDN'T TAKE LONG. RELATIVELY SPEAKING, SHE WASN'T AS STRONG AS SOME OF THE OTHERS.

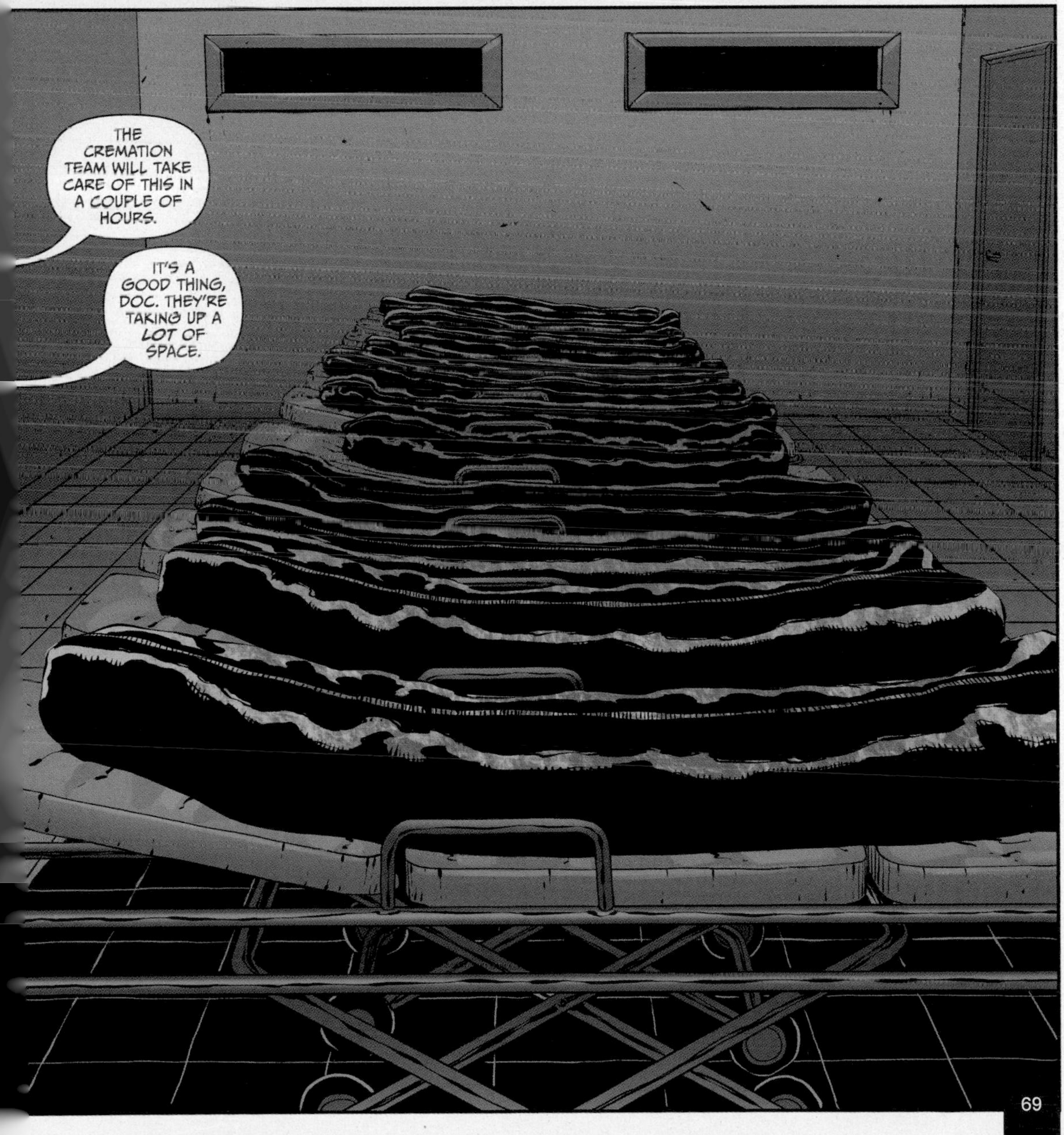
THE CREMATION TEAM WILL TAKE CARE OF THIS IN A COUPLE OF HOURS.
IT'S A GOOD THING, DOC. THEY'RE TAKING UP A LOT OF SPACE.

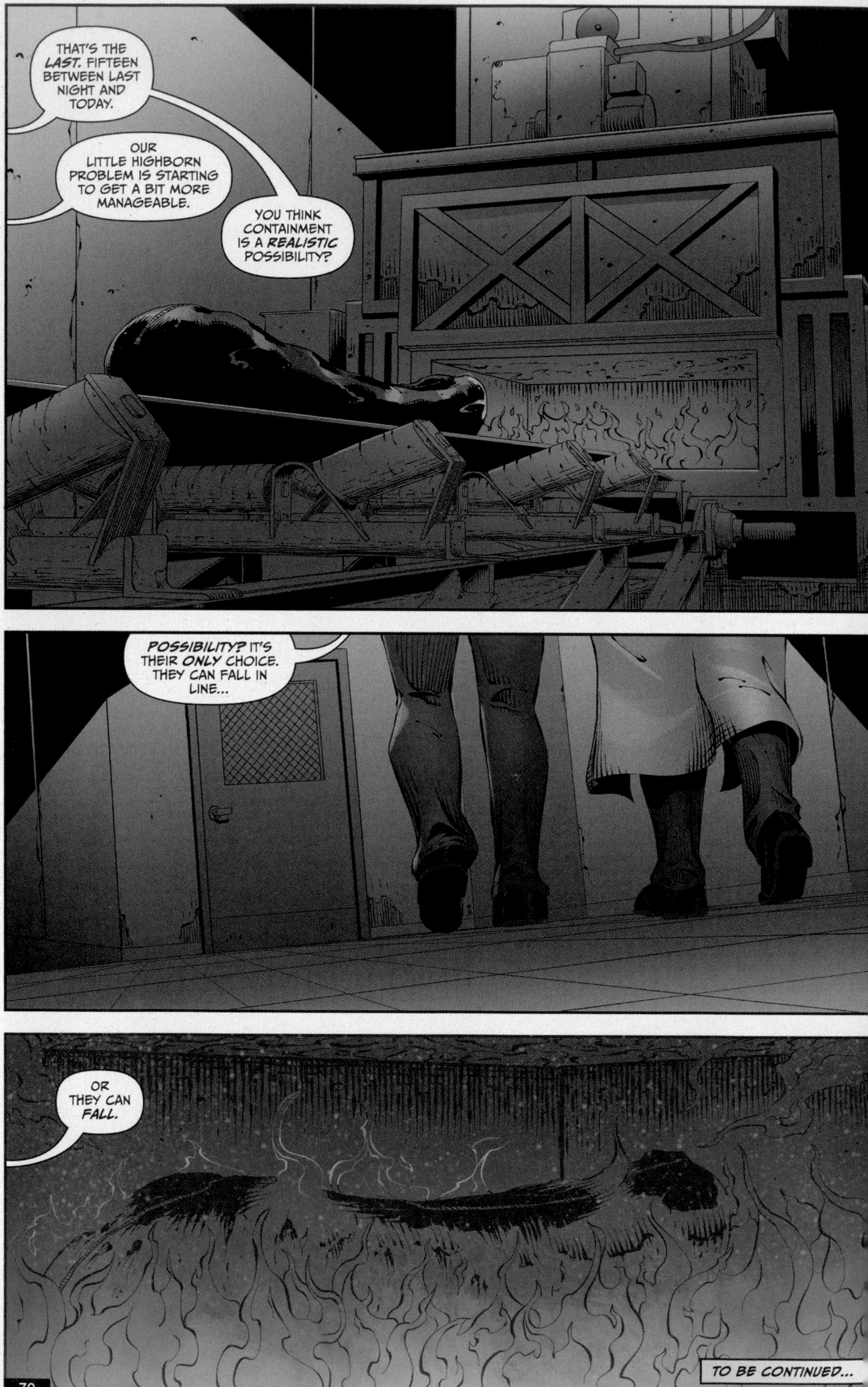
THAT'S THE *LAST.* FIFTEEN BETWEEN LAST NIGHT AND TODAY.
OUR LITTLE HIGHBORN PROBLEM IS STARTING TO GET A BIT MORE MANAGEABLE.
YOU THINK CONTAINMENT IS A *REALISTIC* POSSIBILITY?
POSSIBILITY? IT'S THEIR *ONLY* CHOICE. THEY CAN FALL IN LINE...
OR THEY CAN *FALL.*
TO BE CONTINUED...

Grimm Fairy Tales

Volume 15

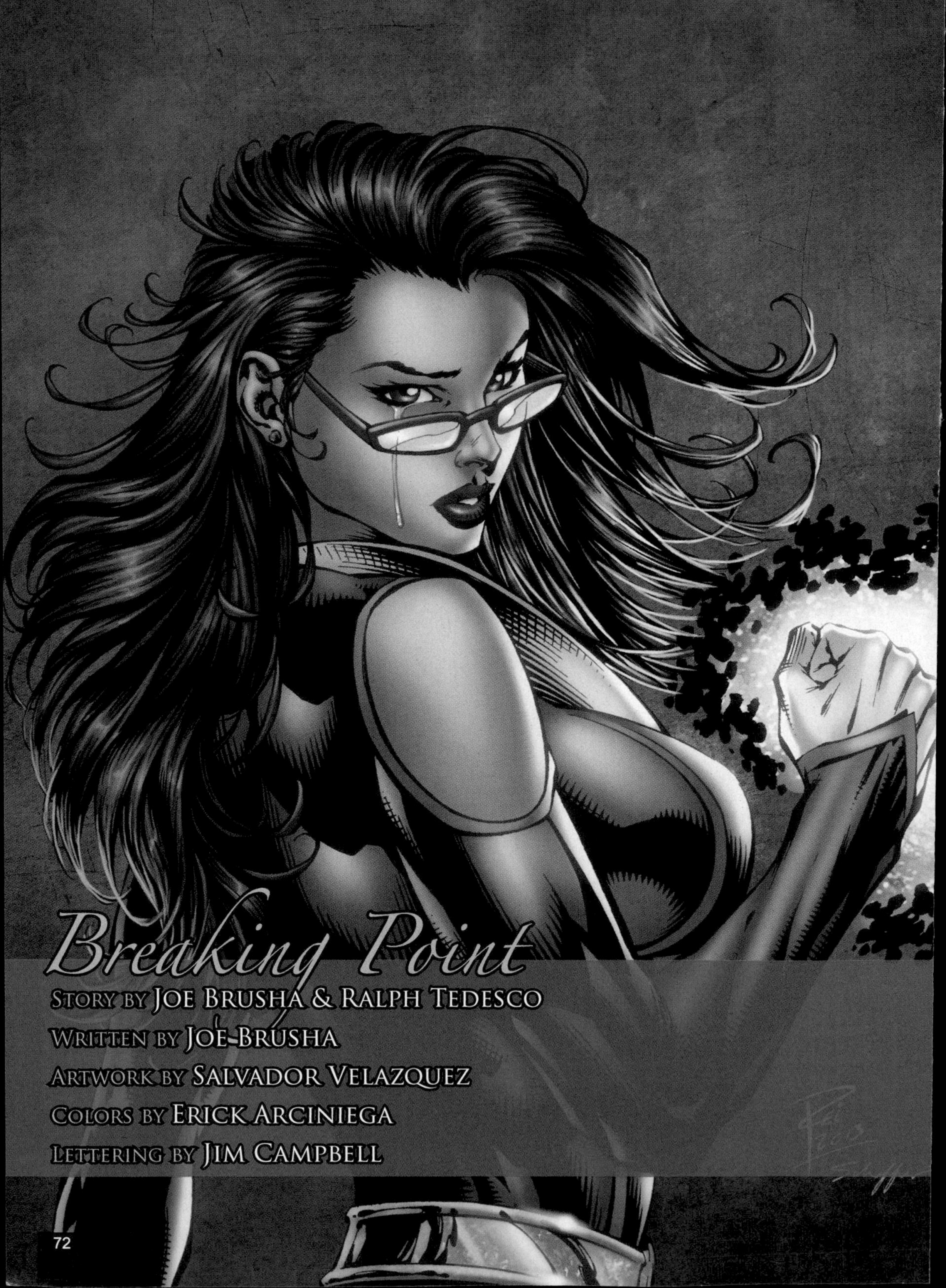

Breaking Point

Story by Joe Brusha & Ralph Tedesco

Written by Joe Brusha

Artwork by Salvador Velazquez

Colors by Erick Arciniega

Lettering by Jim Campbell

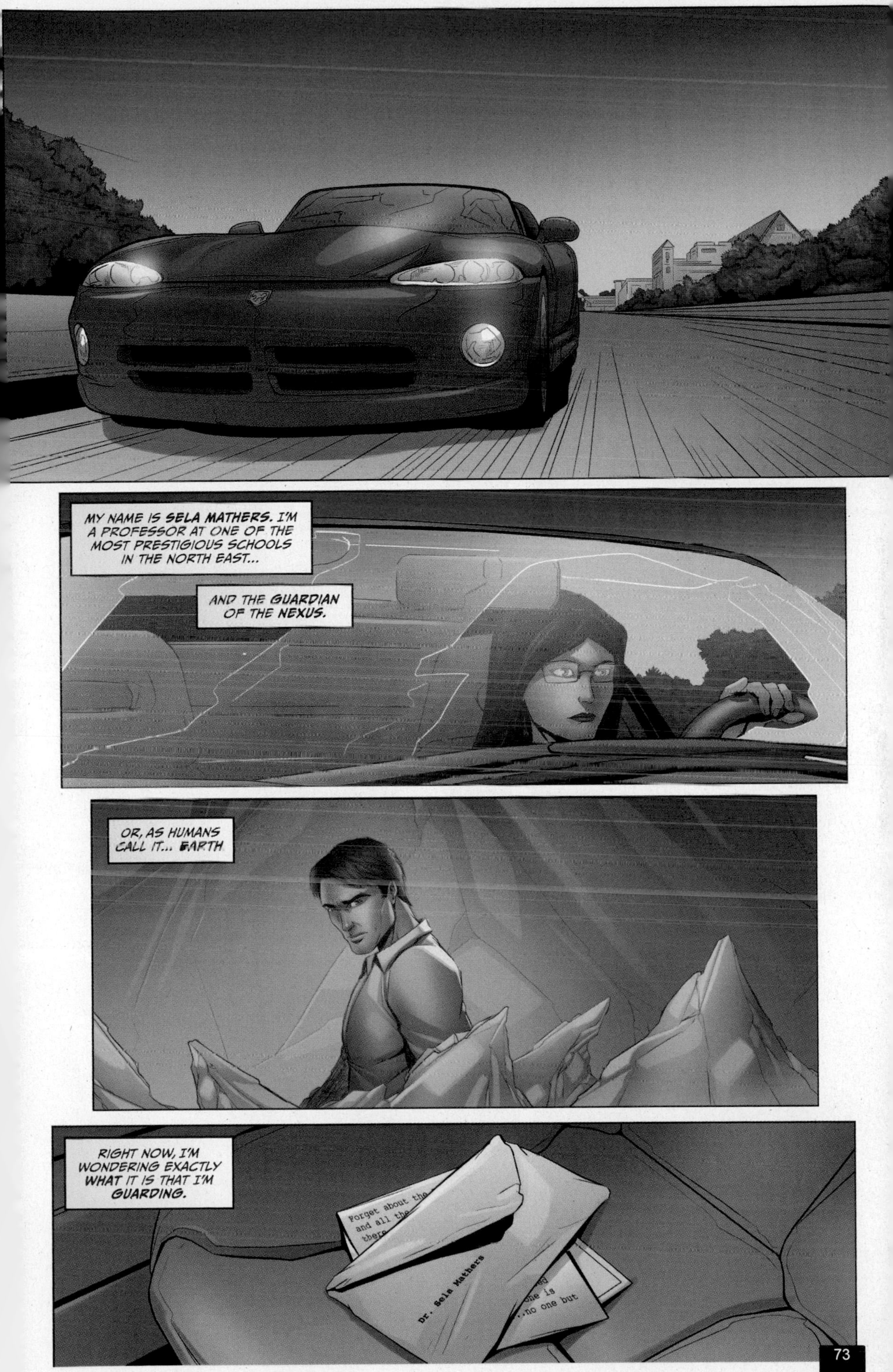
MY NAME IS SELA MATHERS. I'M A PROFESSOR AT ONE OF THE MOST PRESTIGIOUS SCHOOLS IN THE NORTH EAST...
AND THE GUARDIAN OF THE NEXUS.
OR, AS HUMANS CALL IT... EARTH
RIGHT NOW, I'M WONDERING EXACTLY WHAT IT IS THAT I'M GUARDING.
Forget about the
and all the
Dr. Sela Mathers
no one but

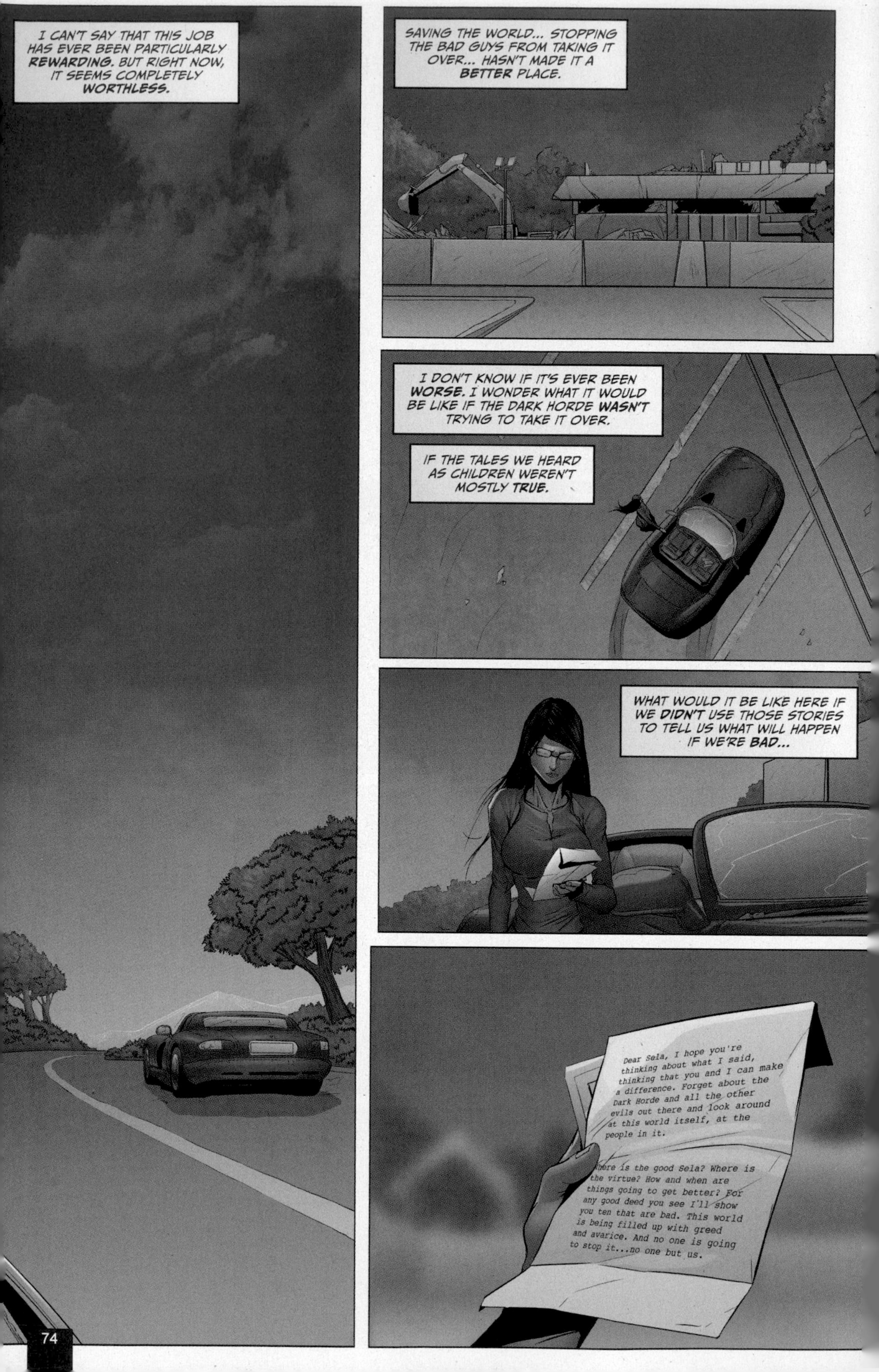
I CAN'T SAY THAT THIS JOB HAS EVER BEEN PARTICULARLY REWARDING. BUT RIGHT NOW, IT SEEMS COMPLETELY WORTHLESS.
SAVING THE WORLD... STOPPING THE BAD GUYS FROM TAKING IT OVER... HASN'T MADE IT A BETTER PLACE.
I DON'T KNOW IF IT'S EVER BEEN WORSE. I WONDER WHAT IT WOULD BE LIKE IF THE DARK HORDE WASN'T TRYING TO TAKE IT OVER.
IF THE TALES WE HEARD AS CHILDREN WEREN'T MOSTLY TRUE.
WHAT WOULD IT BE LIKE HERE IF WE DIDN'T USE THOSE STORIES TO TELL US WHAT WILL HAPPEN IF WE'RE BAD...
Dear Sela, I hope you're thinking about what I said, thinking that you and I can make a difference. Forget about the Dark Horde and all the other evils out there and look around at this world itself, at the people in it.
Where is the good Sela? Where is the virtue? How and when are things going to get better? For any good deed you see I'll show you ten that are bad. This world is being filled up with greed and avarice. And no one is going to stop it...no one but us.

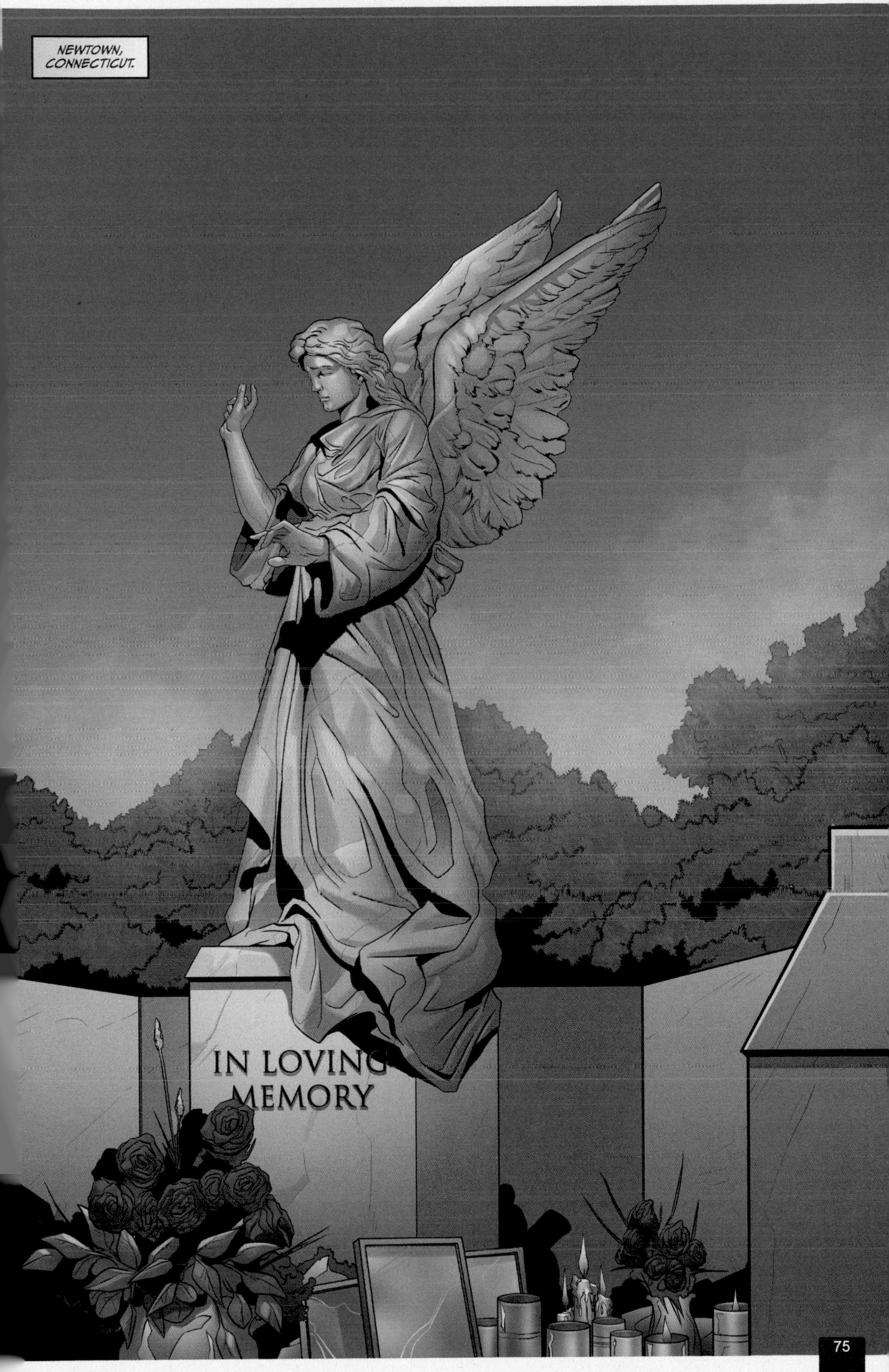
NEWTOWN, CONNECTICUT.
IN LOVING MEMORY

NOT LONG AGO, A MADMAN TOOK TWENTY-SIX INNOCENT LIVES HERE.

TWENTY OF THEM WERE CHILDREN... PRECIOUS AND BEAUTIFUL AS ANYTHING COULD BE.

HE WASN'T A MEMBER OF THE DARK HORDE. HE WASN'T SOME CRAZED HIGHBORN, BENT ON WORLD DOMINATION. HE WAS JUST AN EVIL COWARD WHO WANTED TO FEEL LIKE HE HAD POWER...

AND HE USED AN AUTOMATIC WEAPON IN A WAY TOO HORRIBLE TO COMPREHEND TO DO THAT.

THIS CAN'T BE THE WAY THE WORLD IS SUPPOSED TO BE. SOMETHING HAD TO GO WRONG ALONG THE WAY. CHILDREN CAN'T DIE LIKE THIS... THIS CAN'T BE ALLOWED TO HAPPEN.

MAYBE WARREN WAS RIGHT. IF WE RULED HUMANS, WE COULD STOP THIS FROM EVER HAPPENING AGAIN.

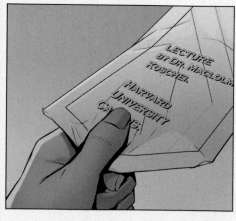

LECTURE BY DR. MACLOLM KOSCHEI.
HARVARD UNIVERSITY CAMPUS;

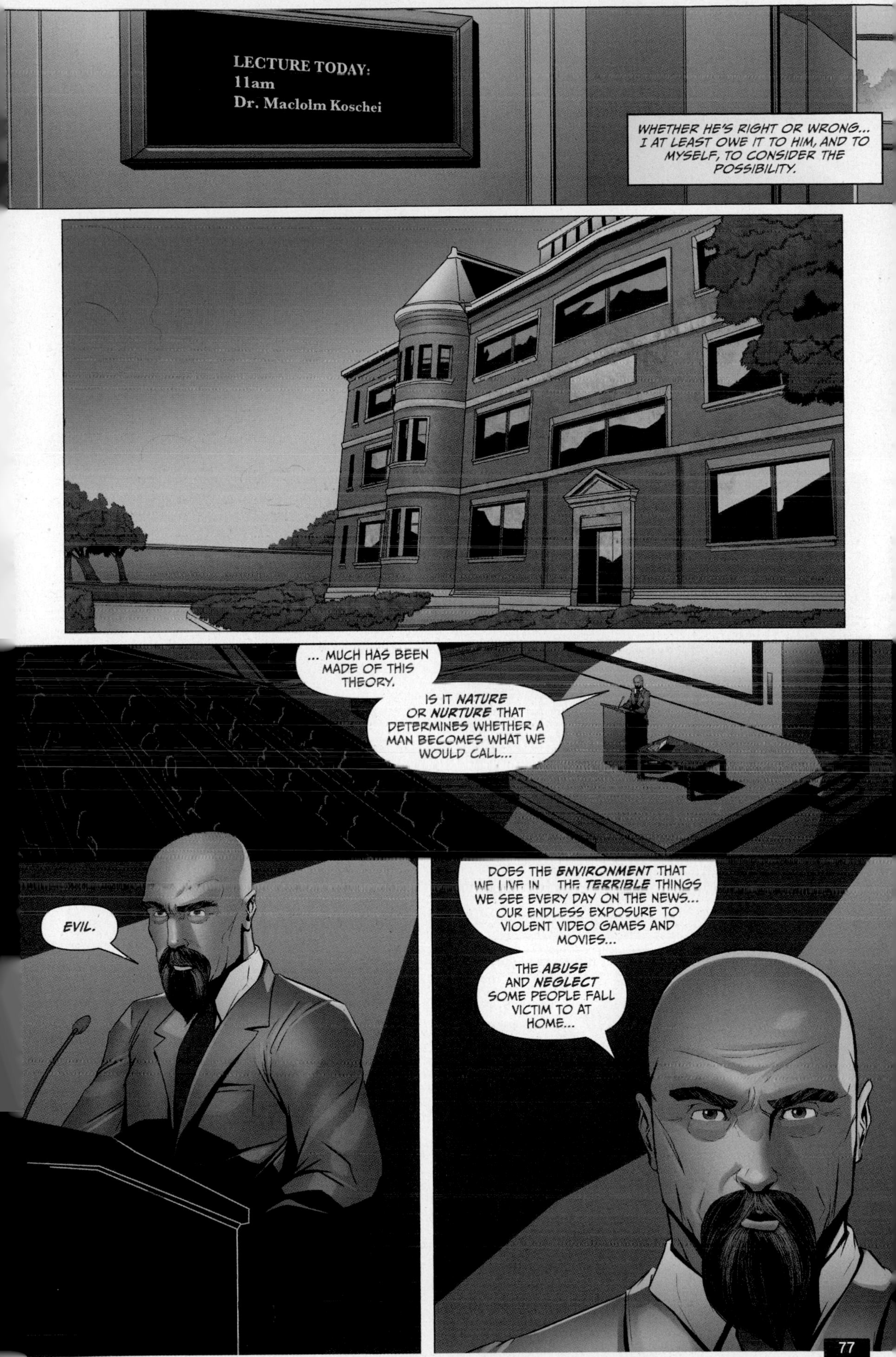
LECTURE TODAY:
11am
Dr. Maclolm Koschei
WHETHER HE'S RIGHT OR WRONG... I AT LEAST OWE IT TO HIM, AND TO MYSELF, TO CONSIDER THE POSSIBILITY.
... MUCH HAS BEEN MADE OF THIS THEORY.
IS IT NATURE OR NURTURE THAT DETERMINES WHETHER A MAN BECOMES WHAT WE WOULD CALL...
EVIL.
DOES THE ENVIRONMENT THAT WE LIVE IN... THE TERRIBLE THINGS WE SEE EVERY DAY ON THE NEWS... OUR ENDLESS EXPOSURE TO VIOLENT VIDEO GAMES AND MOVIES...
THE ABUSE AND NEGLECT SOME PEOPLE FALL VICTIM TO AT HOME...

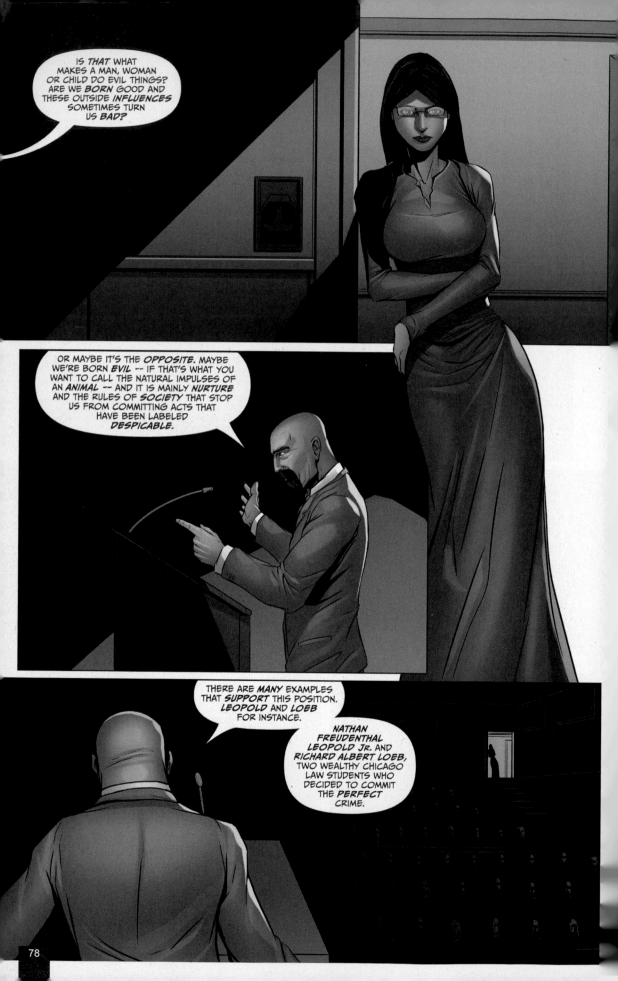

IS *THAT* WHAT MAKES A MAN, WOMAN OR CHILD DO EVIL THINGS? ARE WE *BORN* GOOD AND THESE OUTSIDE *INFLUENCES* SOMETIMES TURN US *BAD?*

OR MAYBE IT'S THE *OPPOSITE.* MAYBE WE'RE BORN *EVIL* –– IF THAT'S WHAT YOU WANT TO CALL THE NATURAL IMPULSES OF AN *ANIMAL* –– AND IT IS MAINLY *NURTURE* AND THE RULES OF *SOCIETY* THAT STOP US FROM COMMITTING ACTS THAT HAVE BEEN LABELED *DESPICABLE.*

THERE ARE *MANY* EXAMPLES THAT *SUPPORT* THIS POSITION. *LEOPOLD* AND *LOEB* FOR INSTANCE.

NATHAN FREUDENTHAL LEOPOLD Jr. AND *RICHARD ALBERT LOEB,* TWO WEALTHY CHICAGO LAW STUDENTS WHO DECIDED TO COMMIT THE *PERFECT* CRIME.

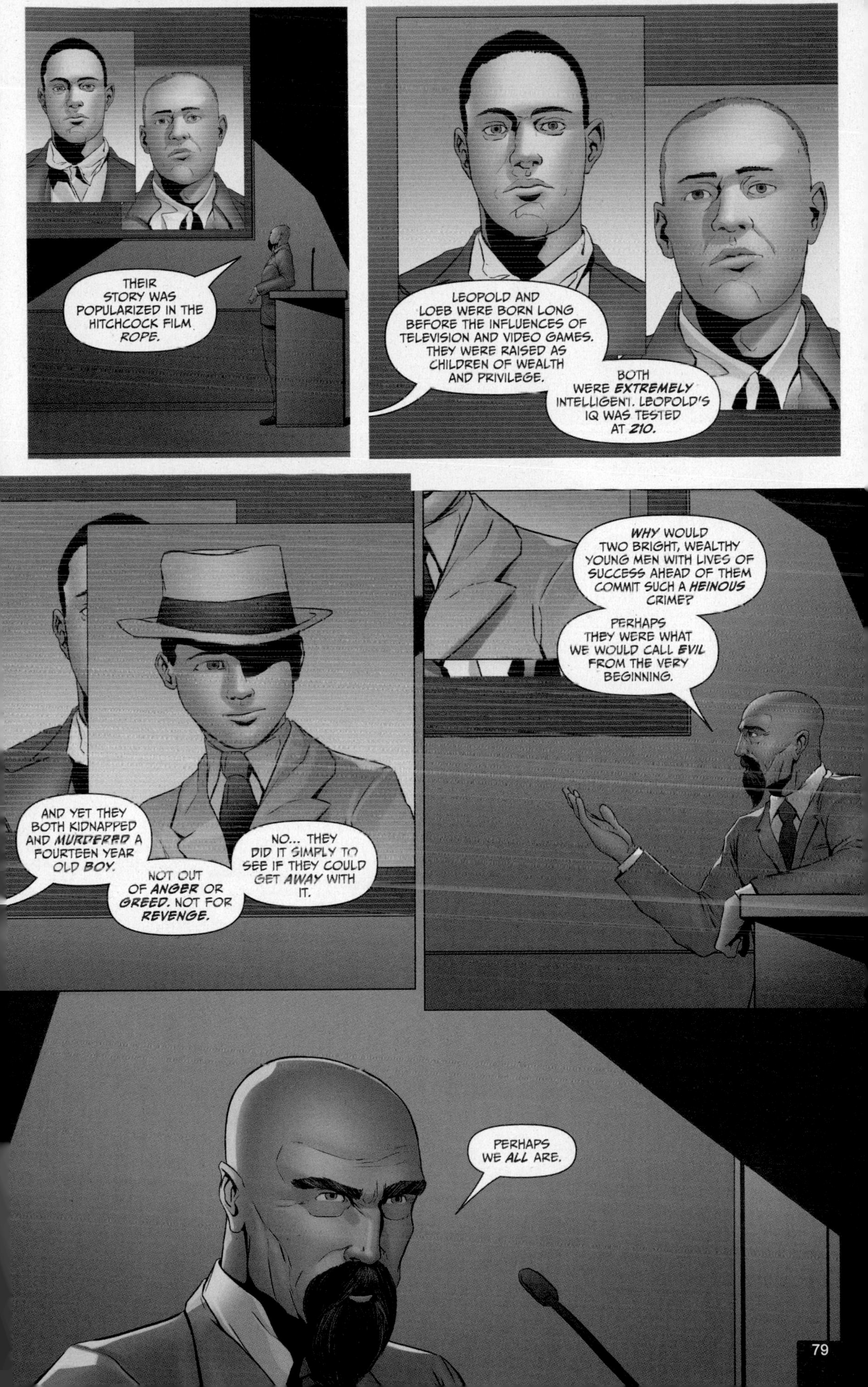

THEIR STORY WAS POPULARIZED IN THE HITCHCOCK FILM *ROPE.*
LEOPOLD AND LOEB WERE BORN LONG BEFORE THE INFLUENCES OF TELEVISION AND VIDEO GAMES. THEY WERE RAISED AS CHILDREN OF WEALTH AND PRIVILEGE.
BOTH WERE ***EXTREMELY*** INTELLIGENT. LEOPOLD'S IQ WAS TESTED AT ***210.***
AND YET THEY BOTH KIDNAPPED AND ***MURDERED*** A FOURTEEN YEAR OLD ***BOY.***
NOT OUT OF ***ANGER*** OR ***GREED.*** NOT FOR ***REVENGE.***
NO... THEY DID IT SIMPLY TO SEE IF THEY COULD GET ***AWAY*** WITH IT.
WHY WOULD TWO BRIGHT, WEALTHY YOUNG MEN WITH LIVES OF SUCCESS AHEAD OF THEM COMMIT SUCH A ***HEINOUS*** CRIME?
PERHAPS THEY WERE WHAT WE WOULD CALL ***EVIL*** FROM THE VERY BEGINNING.
PERHAPS WE ***ALL*** ARE.

DR. KOSCHEI.

YES?

I'M SELA MATHERS. A PROFESSOR AT HUXFORD ACADEMY.

HELLO. VERY NICE TO MEET YOU, PROFESSOR MATHERS.

A FRIEND OF MINE SUGGESTED THAT I SHOULD LISTEN TO YOUR LECTURE.

IT WAS QUITE INTERESTING.

THANK YOU.

DO YOU HAVE TIME TO GRAB A CUP OF COFFEE?

OF COURSE... ONE OF MY RULES OF LIFE IS TO *NEVER* REFUSE A PRETTY WOMAN.

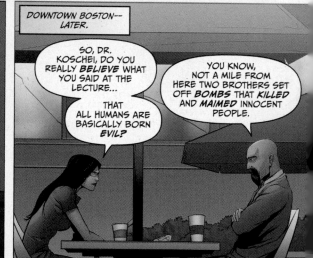

DOWNTOWN BOSTON-- LATER.

SO, DR. KOSCHEI, DO YOU REALLY *BELIEVE* WHAT YOU SAID AT THE LECTURE...

THAT ALL HUMANS ARE BASICALLY BORN *EVIL?*

YOU KNOW, NOT A MILE FROM HERE TWO BROTHERS SET OFF *BOMBS* THAT *KILLED* AND *MAIMED* INNOCENT PEOPLE.

YES. I KNOW.

WHY DID THEY DO IT?

THEY WERE *TERRORISTS.* THEY--

THEY WERE *ANGRY.* THEY WERE *POOR.* THEY WERE RAISED IN A CULTURE AND A HOME WITH NO *LOVE.*

THAT ALL MAY BE *TRUE.* BUT TELL ME *THIS...* WHY DID *CAIN* KILL *ABEL?*

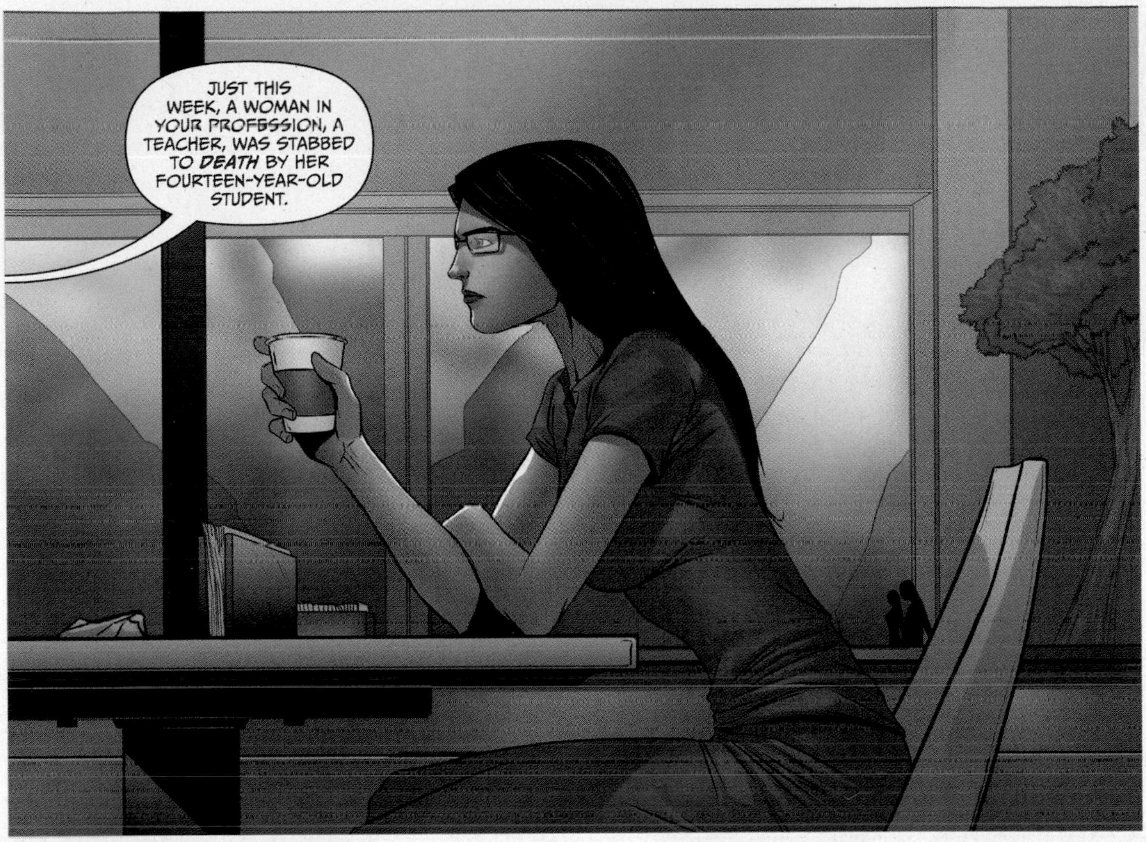
JUST THIS WEEK, A WOMAN IN YOUR PROFESSION, A TEACHER, WAS STABBED TO *DEATH* BY HER FOURTEEN-YEAR-OLD STUDENT.

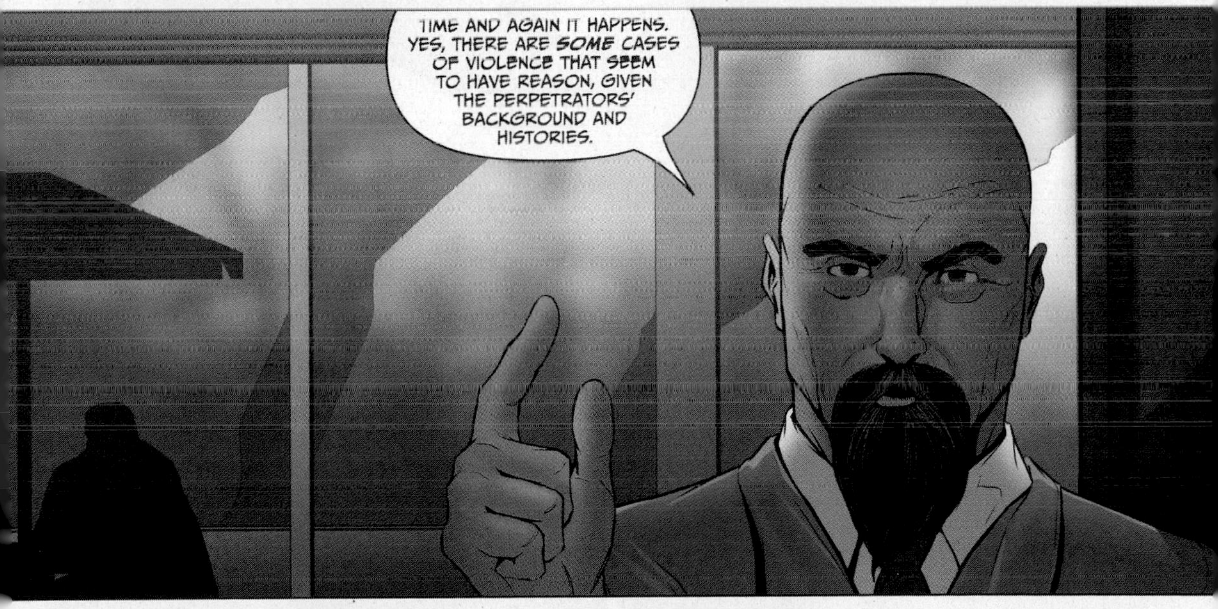
TIME AND AGAIN IT HAPPENS. YES, THERE ARE *SOME* CASES OF VIOLENCE THAT SEEM TO HAVE REASON, GIVEN THE PERPETRATORS' BACKGROUND AND HISTORIES.

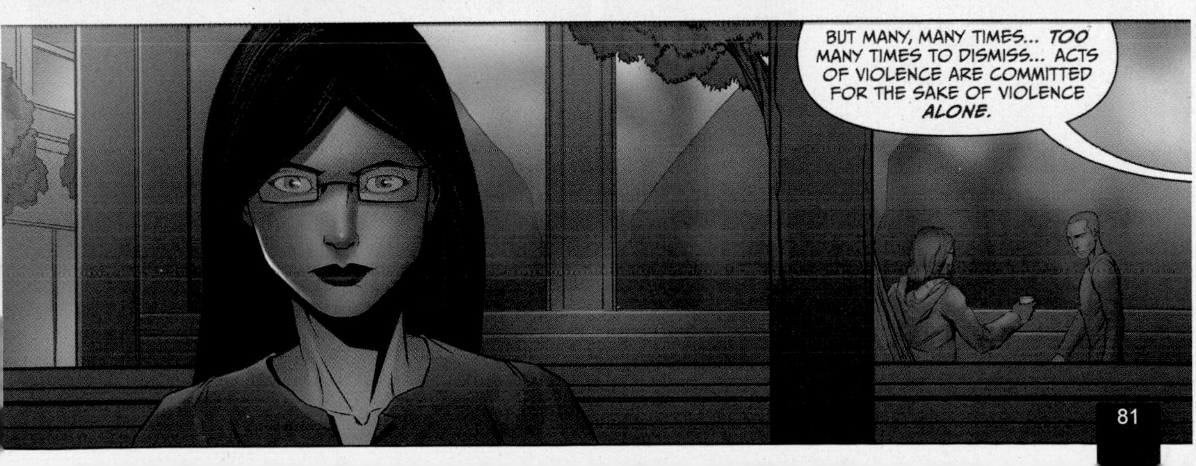
BUT MANY, MANY TIMES... *TOO* MANY TIMES TO DISMISS... ACTS OF VIOLENCE ARE COMMITTED FOR THE SAKE OF VIOLENCE *ALONE.*

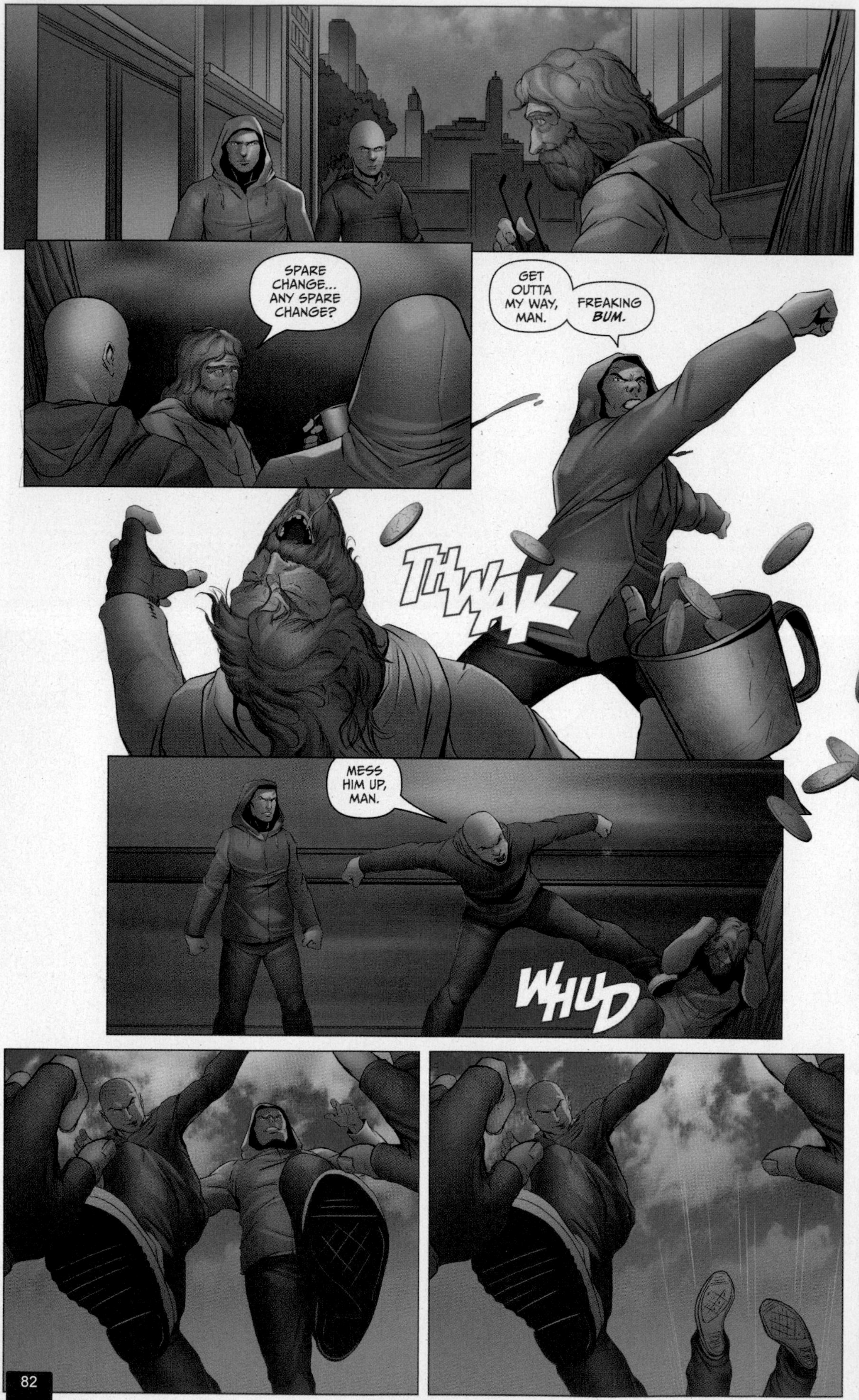
SPARE CHANGE... ANY SPARE CHANGE?
GET OUTTA MY WAY, MAN.
FREAKING *BUM.*
THWAK
MESS HIM UP, MAN.
WHUD

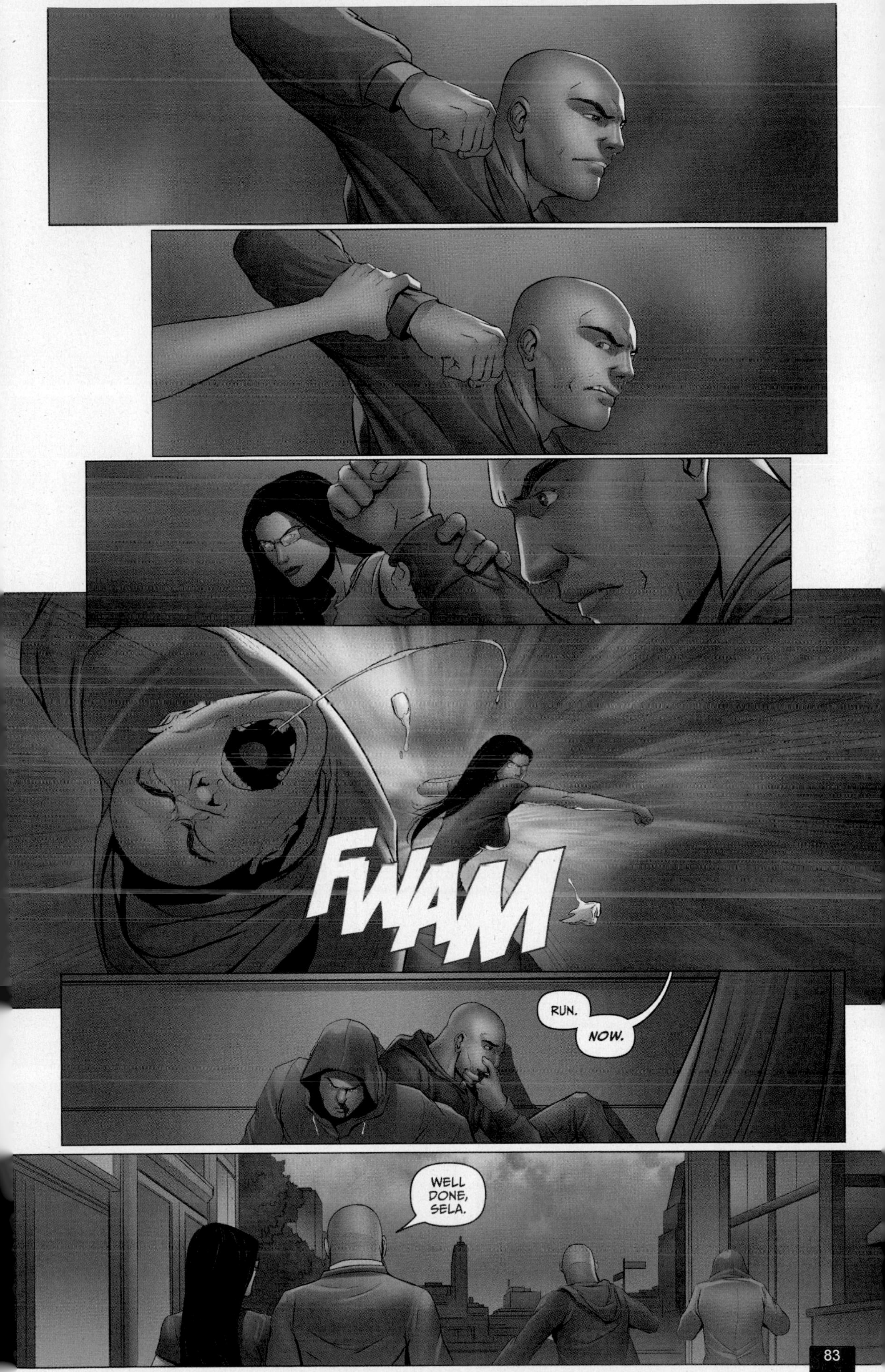
FWAM
RUN.
NOW.
WELL DONE, SELA.

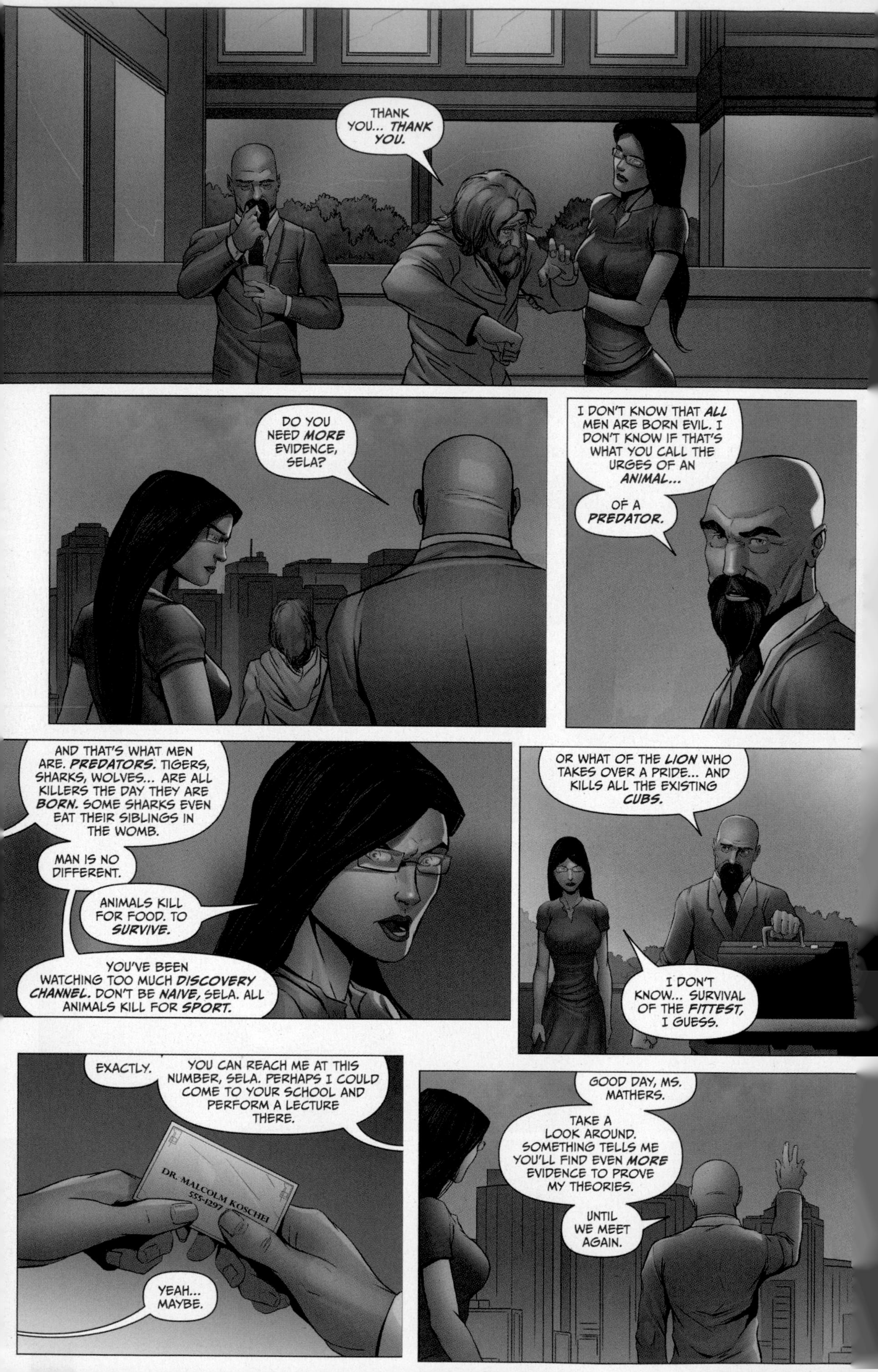
THANK YOU... THANK YOU.
DO YOU NEED MORE EVIDENCE, SELA?
I DON'T KNOW THAT ALL MEN ARE BORN EVIL. I DON'T KNOW IF THAT'S WHAT YOU CALL THE URGES OF AN ANIMAL...
OF A PREDATOR.
AND THAT'S WHAT MEN ARE. PREDATORS. TIGERS, SHARKS, WOLVES... ARE ALL KILLERS THE DAY THEY ARE BORN. SOME SHARKS EVEN EAT THEIR SIBLINGS IN THE WOMB.
MAN IS NO DIFFERENT.
ANIMALS KILL FOR FOOD. TO SURVIVE.
YOU'VE BEEN WATCHING TOO MUCH DISCOVERY CHANNEL. DON'T BE NAIVE, SELA. ALL ANIMALS KILL FOR SPORT.
OR WHAT OF THE LION WHO TAKES OVER A PRIDE... AND KILLS ALL THE EXISTING CUBS.
I DON'T KNOW... SURVIVAL OF THE FITTEST, I GUESS.
EXACTLY.
YOU CAN REACH ME AT THIS NUMBER, SELA. PERHAPS I COULD COME TO YOUR SCHOOL AND PERFORM A LECTURE THERE.
DR. MALCOLM KOSCHEI
555-1297
YEAH... MAYBE.
GOOD DAY, MS. MATHERS.
TAKE A LOOK AROUND. SOMETHING TELLS ME YOU'LL FIND EVEN MORE EVIDENCE TO PROVE MY THEORIES.
UNTIL WE MEET AGAIN.

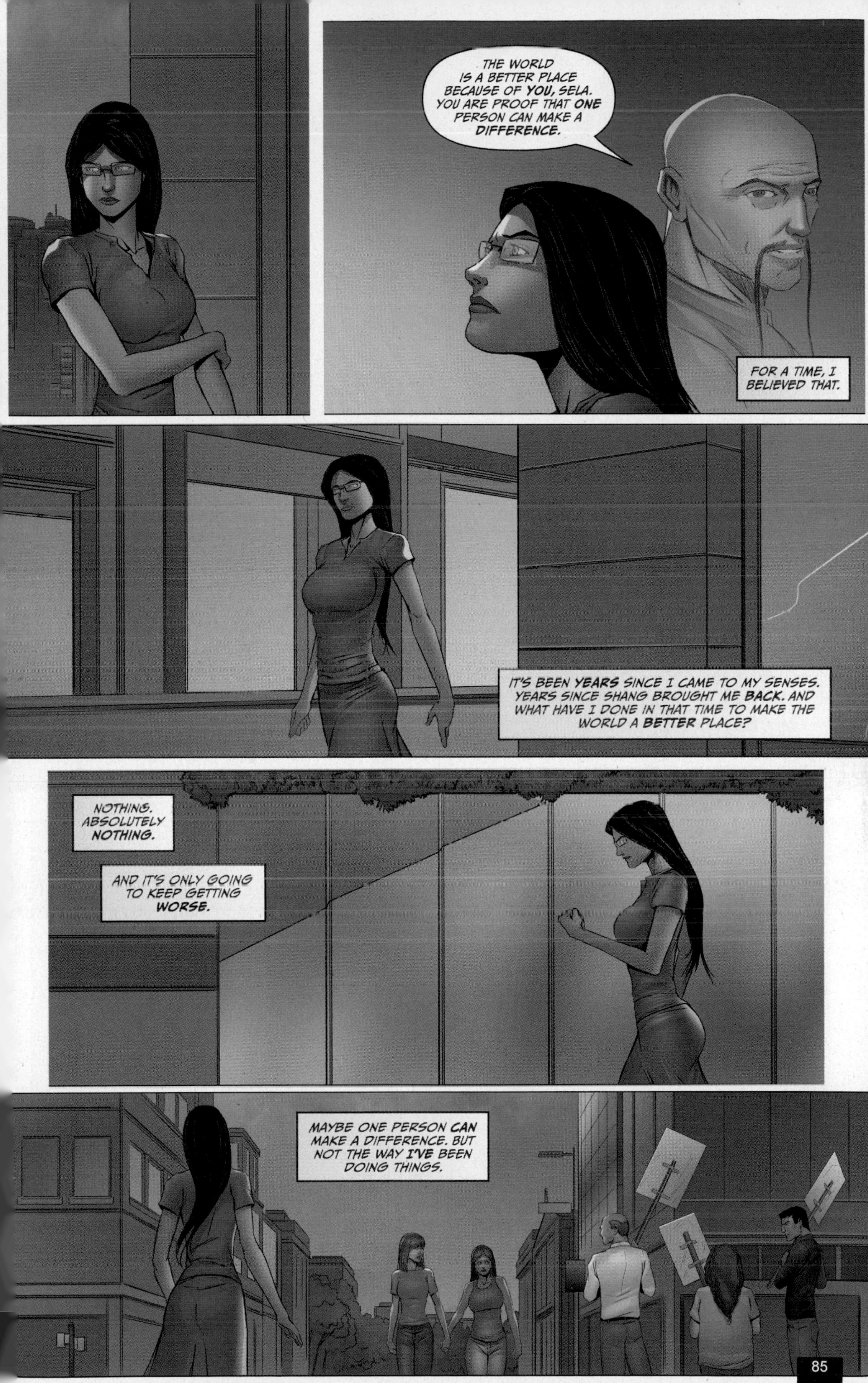
THE WORLD IS A BETTER PLACE BECAUSE OF YOU, SELA. YOU ARE PROOF THAT ONE PERSON CAN MAKE A DIFFERENCE.
FOR A TIME, I BELIEVED THAT.
IT'S BEEN YEARS SINCE I CAME TO MY SENSES. YEARS SINCE SHANG BROUGHT ME BACK. AND WHAT HAVE I DONE IN THAT TIME TO MAKE THE WORLD A BETTER PLACE?
NOTHING. ABSOLUTELY NOTHING.
AND IT'S ONLY GOING TO KEEP GETTING WORSE.
MAYBE ONE PERSON CAN MAKE A DIFFERENCE. BUT NOT THE WAY I'VE BEEN DOING THINGS.

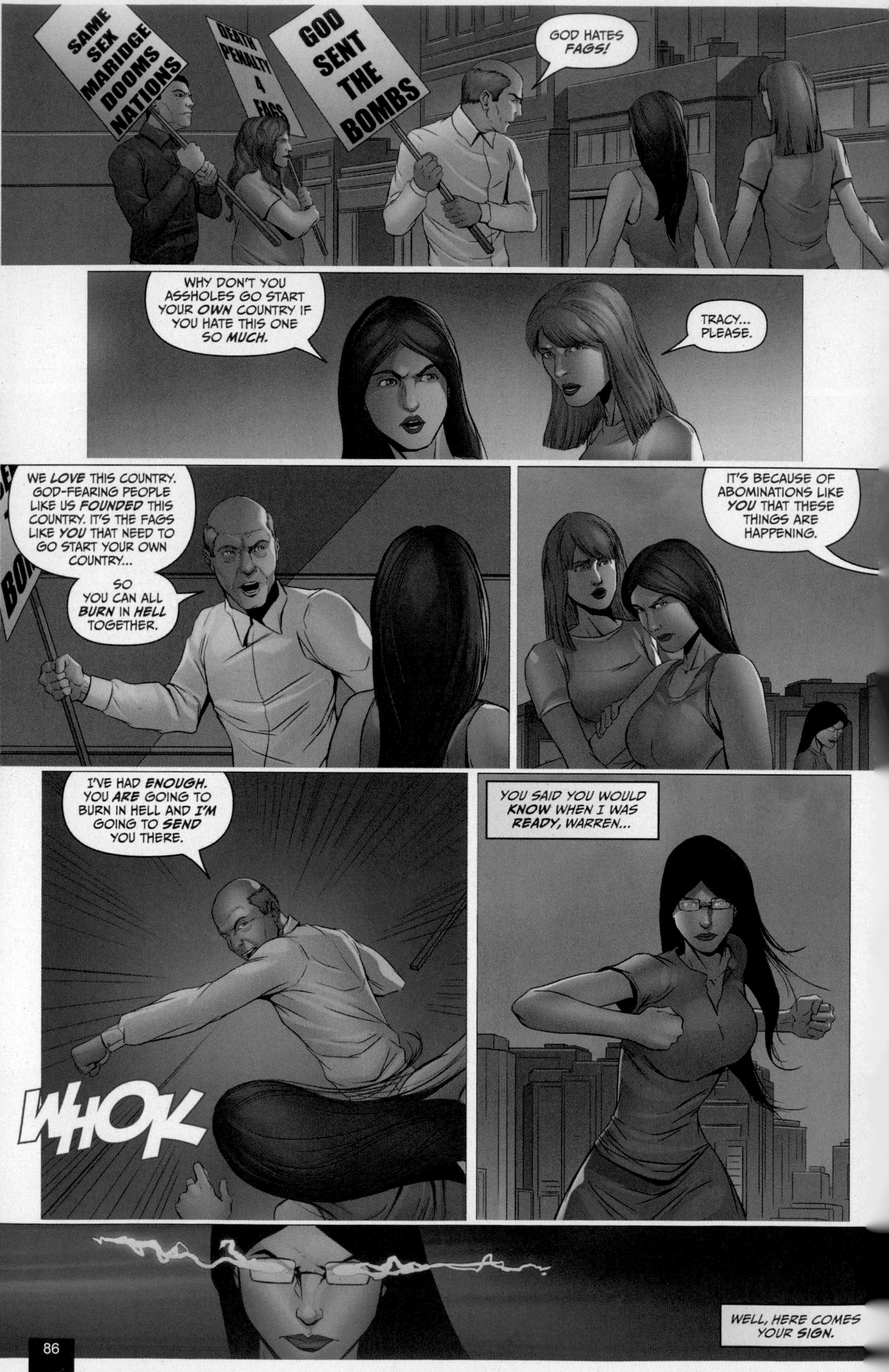
SAME SEX MARIDGE DOOMS NATIONS
DEATH PENALTY 4 FAGS
GOD SENT THE BOMBS
GOD HATES FAGS!
WHY DON'T YOU ASSHOLES GO START YOUR OWN COUNTRY IF YOU HATE THIS ONE SO MUCH.
TRACY... PLEASE.
WE LOVE THIS COUNTRY. GOD-FEARING PEOPLE LIKE US FOUNDED THIS COUNTRY. IT'S THE FAGS LIKE YOU THAT NEED TO GO START YOUR OWN COUNTRY...
SO YOU CAN ALL BURN IN HELL TOGETHER.
IT'S BECAUSE OF ABOMINATIONS LIKE YOU THAT THESE THINGS ARE HAPPENING.
I'VE HAD ENOUGH. YOU ARE GOING TO BURN IN HELL AND I'M GOING TO SEND YOU THERE.
WHOK
YOU SAID YOU WOULD KNOW WHEN I WAS READY, WARREN...
WELL, HERE COMES YOUR SIGN.

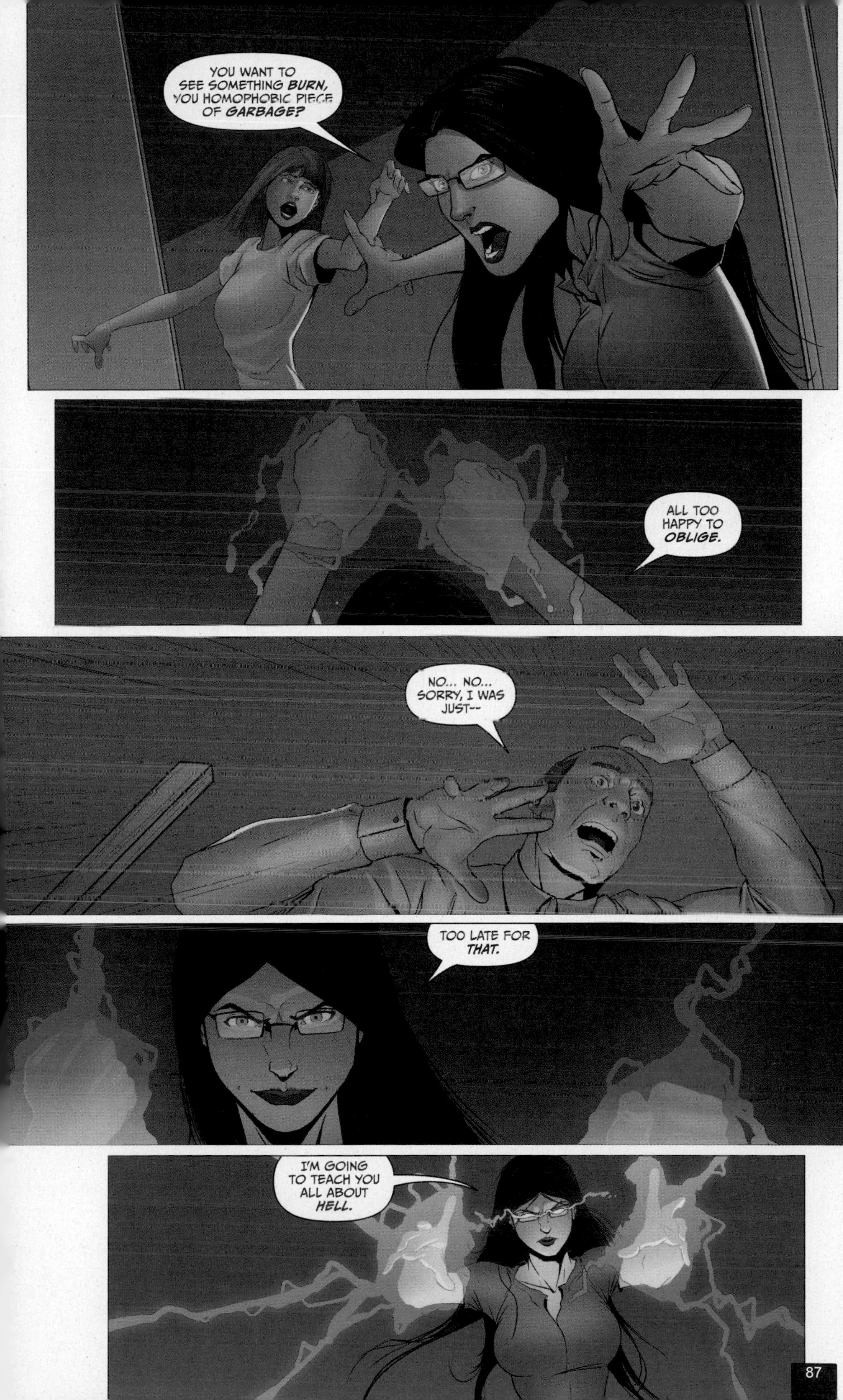
YOU WANT TO SEE SOMETHING BURN, YOU HOMOPHOBIC PIECE OF GARBAGE?
ALL TOO HAPPY TO OBLIGE.
NO... NO... SORRY, I WAS JUST--
TOO LATE FOR THAT.
I'M GOING TO TEACH YOU ALL ABOUT HELL.

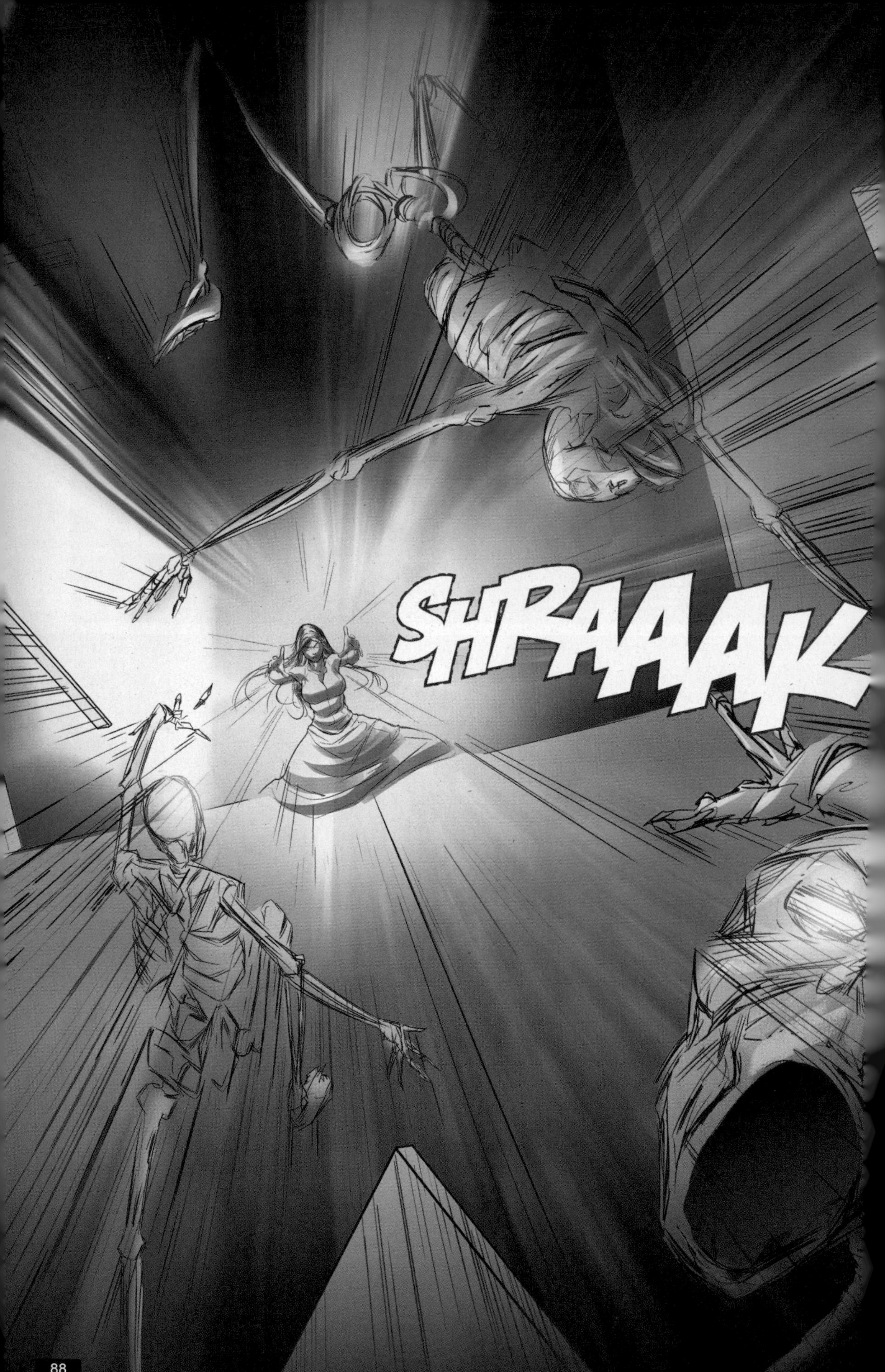
SHRAAAK

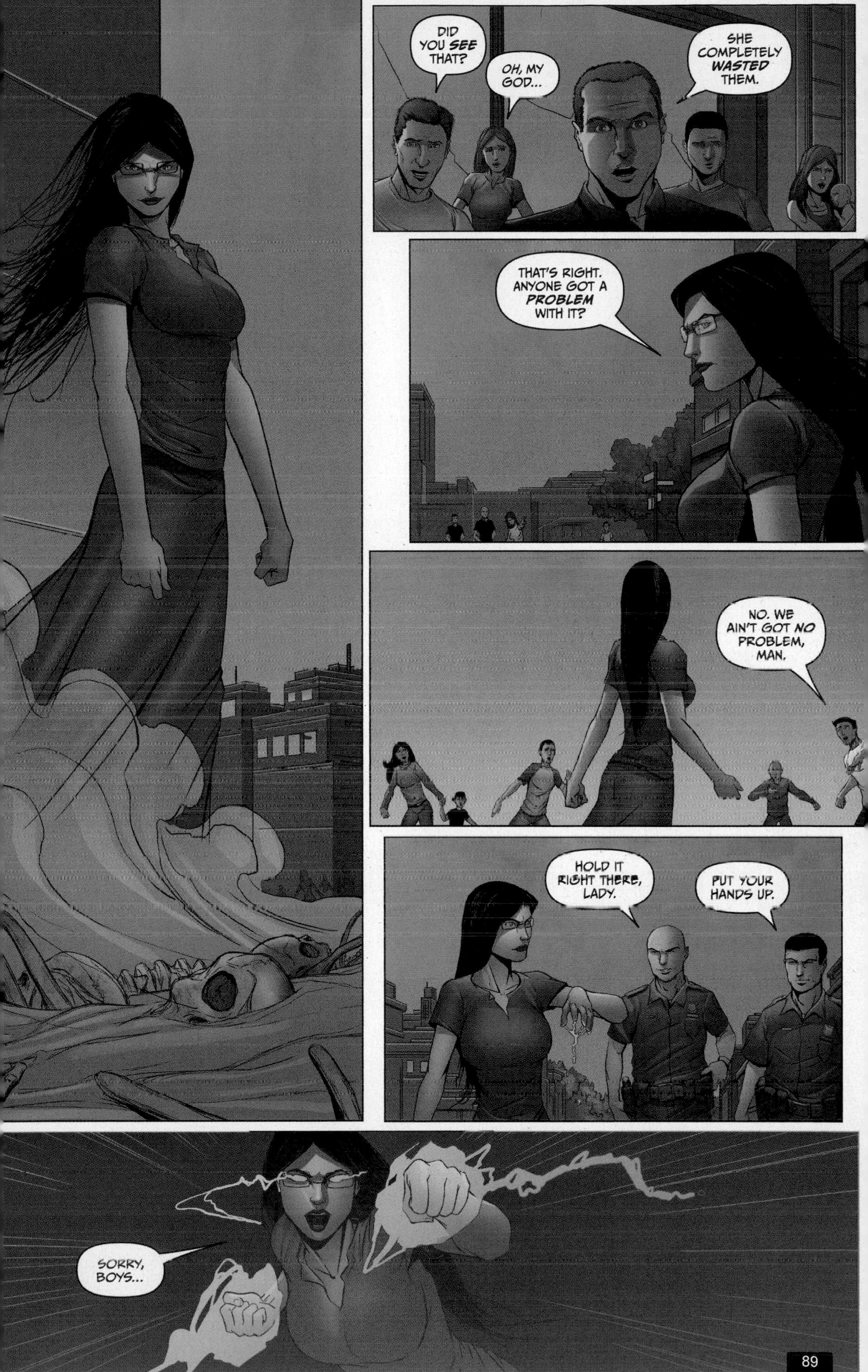
DID YOU SEE THAT?
OH, MY GOD...
SHE COMPLETELY WASTED THEM.
THAT'S RIGHT. ANYONE GOT A PROBLEM WITH IT?
NO. WE AIN'T GOT NO PROBLEM, MAN.
HOLD IT RIGHT THERE, LADY.
PUT YOUR HANDS UP.
SORRY, BOYS...

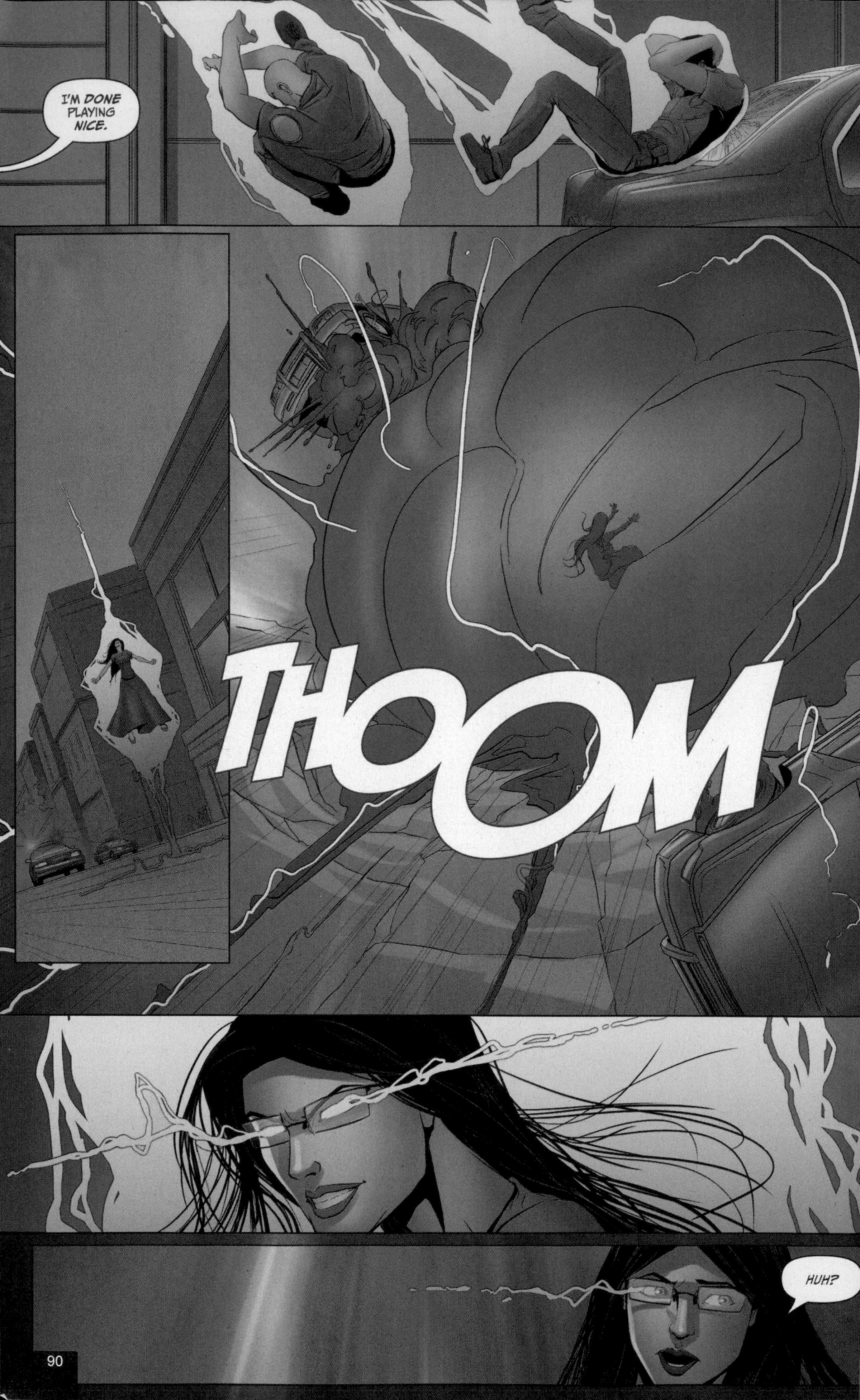
I'M DONE PLAYING NICE.
THOOM
HUH?

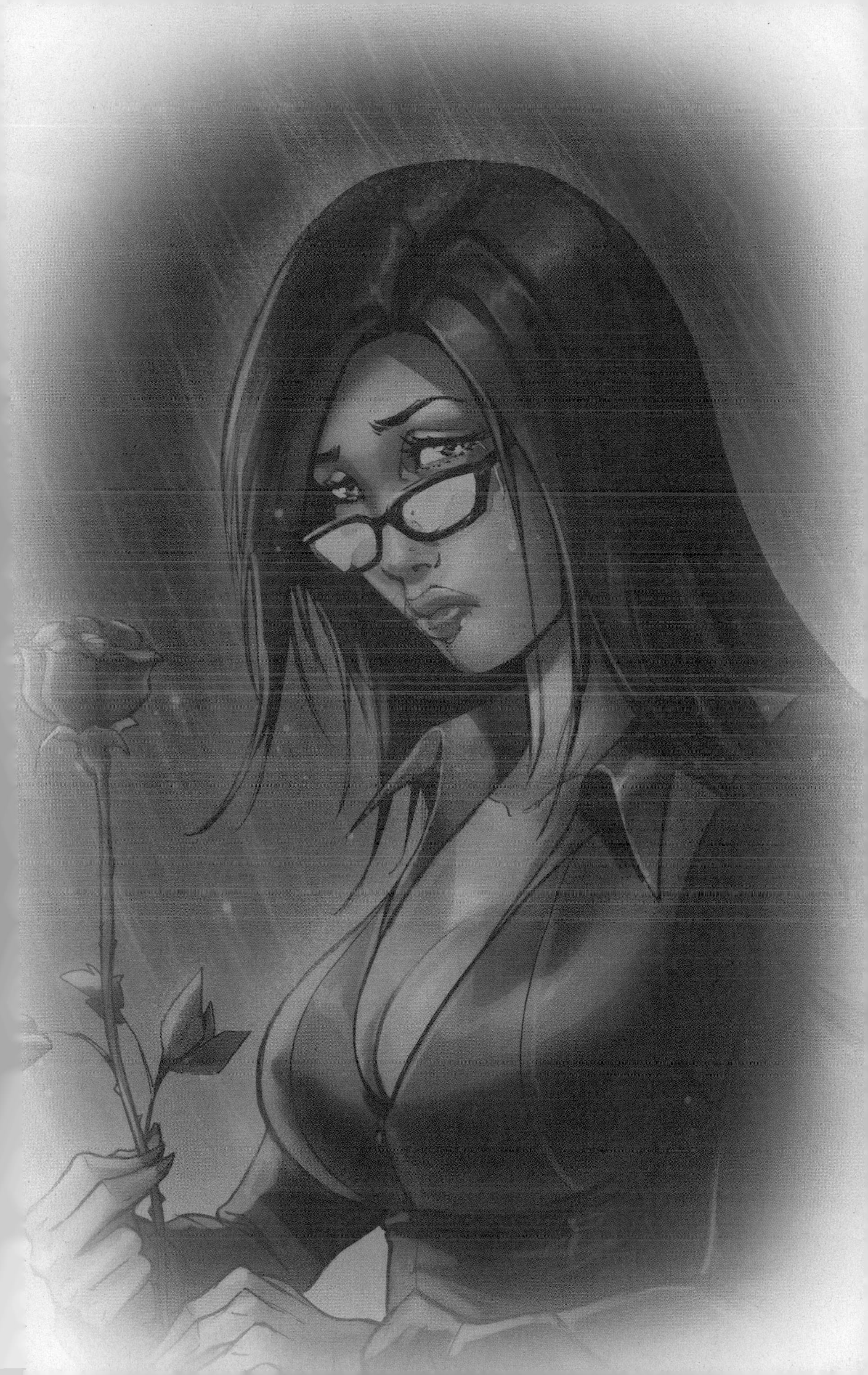

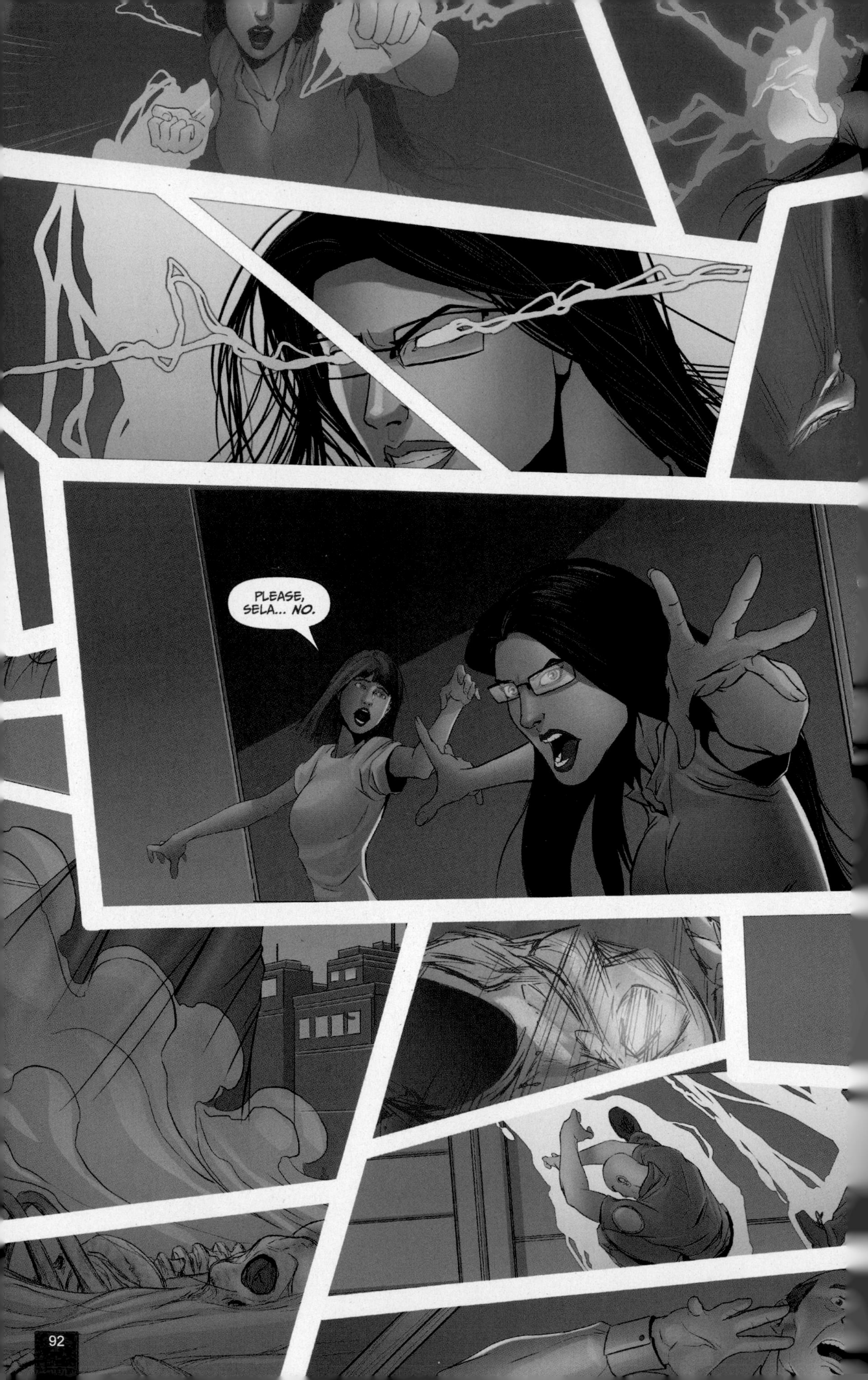
PLEASE, SELA... NO.

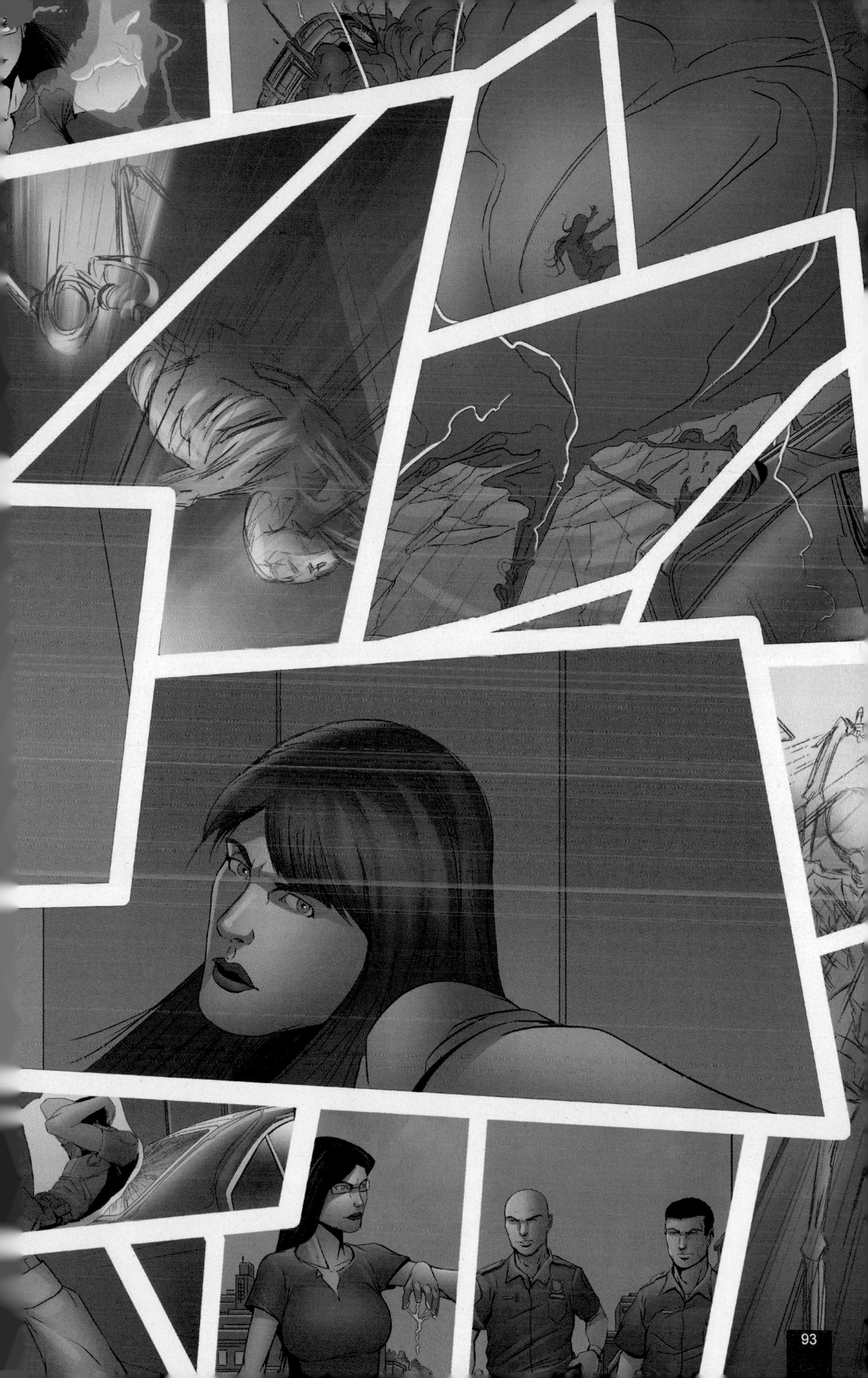

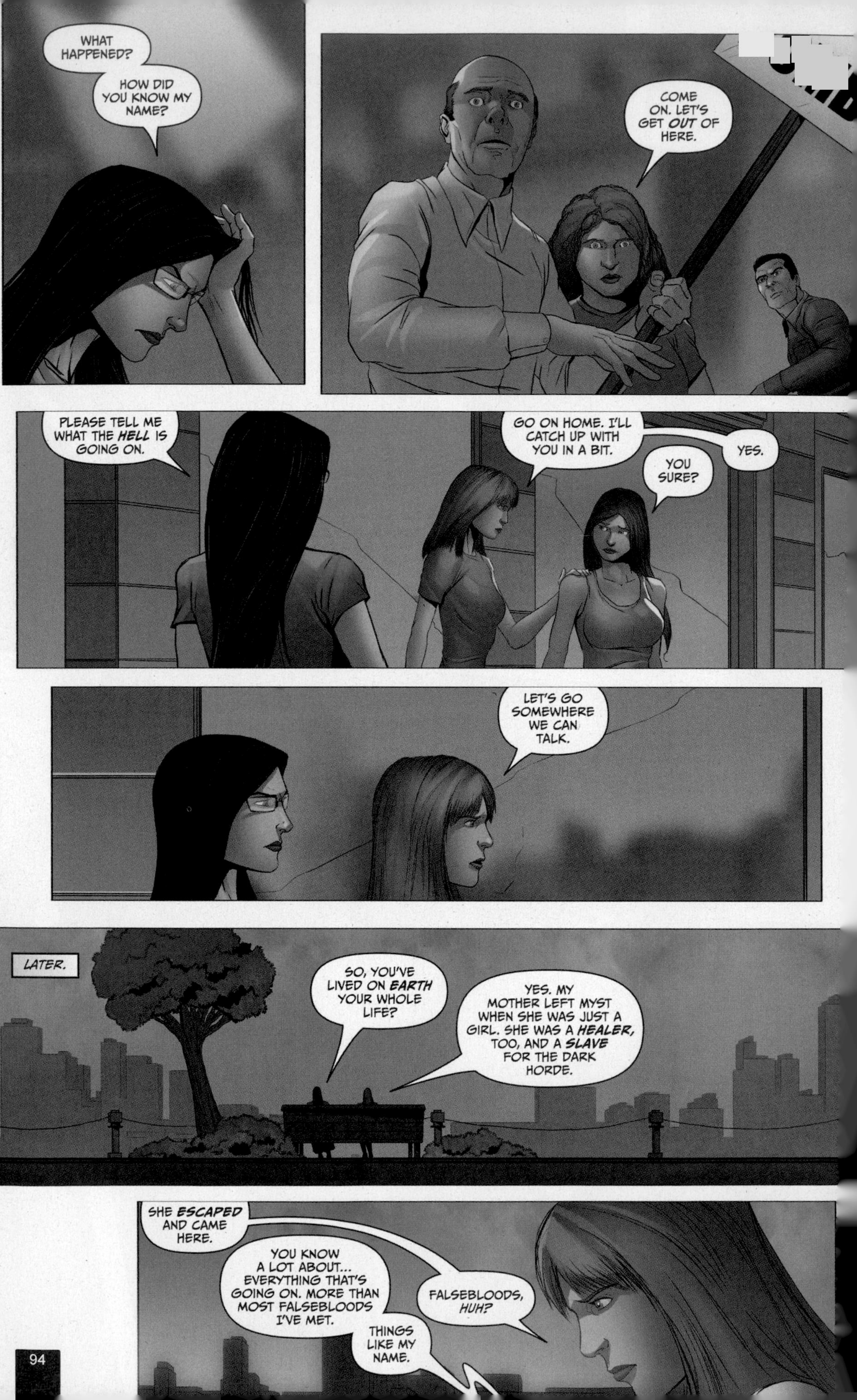
WHAT HAPPENED?
HOW DID YOU KNOW MY NAME?
COME ON. LET'S GET OUT OF HERE.
PLEASE TELL ME WHAT THE HELL IS GOING ON.
GO ON HOME. I'LL CATCH UP WITH YOU IN A BIT.
YOU SURE?
YES.
LET'S GO SOMEWHERE WE CAN TALK.
LATER.
SO, YOU'VE LIVED ON EARTH YOUR WHOLE LIFE?
YES. MY MOTHER LEFT MYST WHEN SHE WAS JUST A GIRL. SHE WAS A HEALER, TOO, AND A SLAVE FOR THE DARK HORDE.
SHE ESCAPED AND CAME HERE.
YOU KNOW A LOT ABOUT... EVERYTHING THAT'S GOING ON. MORE THAN MOST FALSEBLOODS I'VE MET.
FALSEBLOODS, HUH?
THINGS LIKE MY NAME.

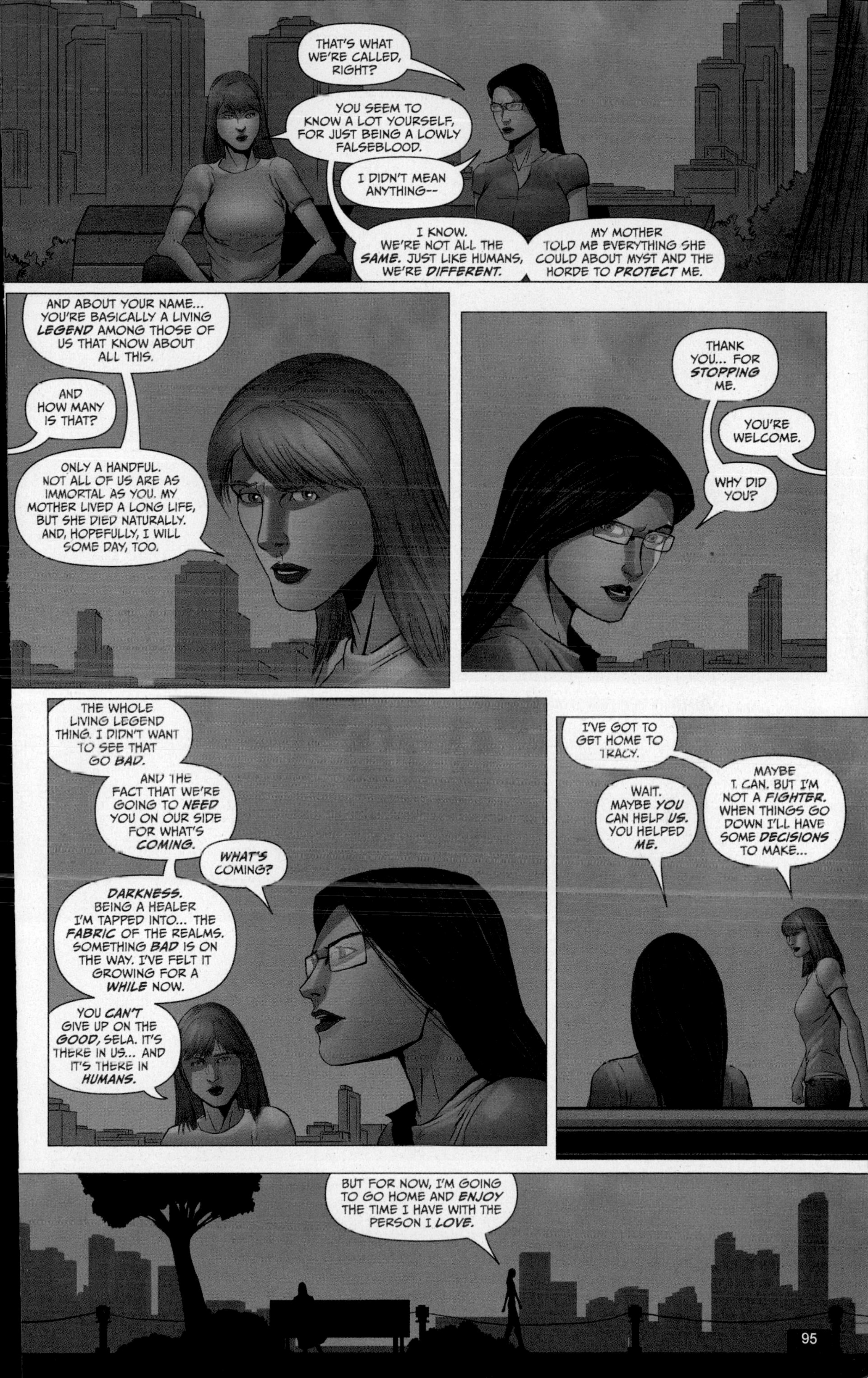

THAT'S WHAT WE'RE CALLED, RIGHT?
YOU SEEM TO KNOW A LOT YOURSELF, FOR JUST BEING A LOWLY FALSEBLOOD.
I DIDN'T MEAN ANYTHING--
I KNOW. WE'RE NOT ALL THE SAME. JUST LIKE HUMANS, WE'RE DIFFERENT.
MY MOTHER TOLD ME EVERYTHING SHE COULD ABOUT MYST AND THE HORDE TO PROTECT ME.
AND ABOUT YOUR NAME... YOU'RE BASICALLY A LIVING LEGEND AMONG THOSE OF US THAT KNOW ABOUT ALL THIS.
AND HOW MANY IS THAT?
ONLY A HANDFUL. NOT ALL OF US ARE AS IMMORTAL AS YOU. MY MOTHER LIVED A LONG LIFE, BUT SHE DIED NATURALLY. AND, HOPEFULLY, I WILL SOME DAY, TOO.
THANK YOU... FOR STOPPING ME.
YOU'RE WELCOME.
WHY DID YOU?
THE WHOLE LIVING LEGEND THING. I DIDN'T WANT TO SEE THAT GO BAD.
AND THE FACT THAT WE'RE GOING TO NEED YOU ON OUR SIDE FOR WHAT'S COMING.
WHAT'S COMING?
DARKNESS. BEING A HEALER I'M TAPPED INTO... THE FABRIC OF THE REALMS. SOMETHING BAD IS ON THE WAY. I'VE FELT IT GROWING FOR A WHILE NOW.
YOU CAN'T GIVE UP ON THE GOOD, SELA. IT'S THERE IN US... AND IT'S THERE IN HUMANS.
I'VE GOT TO GET HOME TO TRACY.
WAIT. MAYBE YOU CAN HELP US. YOU HELPED ME.
MAYBE I CAN. BUT I'M NOT A FIGHTER. WHEN THINGS GO DOWN I'LL HAVE SOME DECISIONS TO MAKE...
BUT FOR NOW, I'M GOING TO GO HOME AND ENJOY THE TIME I HAVE WITH THE PERSON I LOVE.

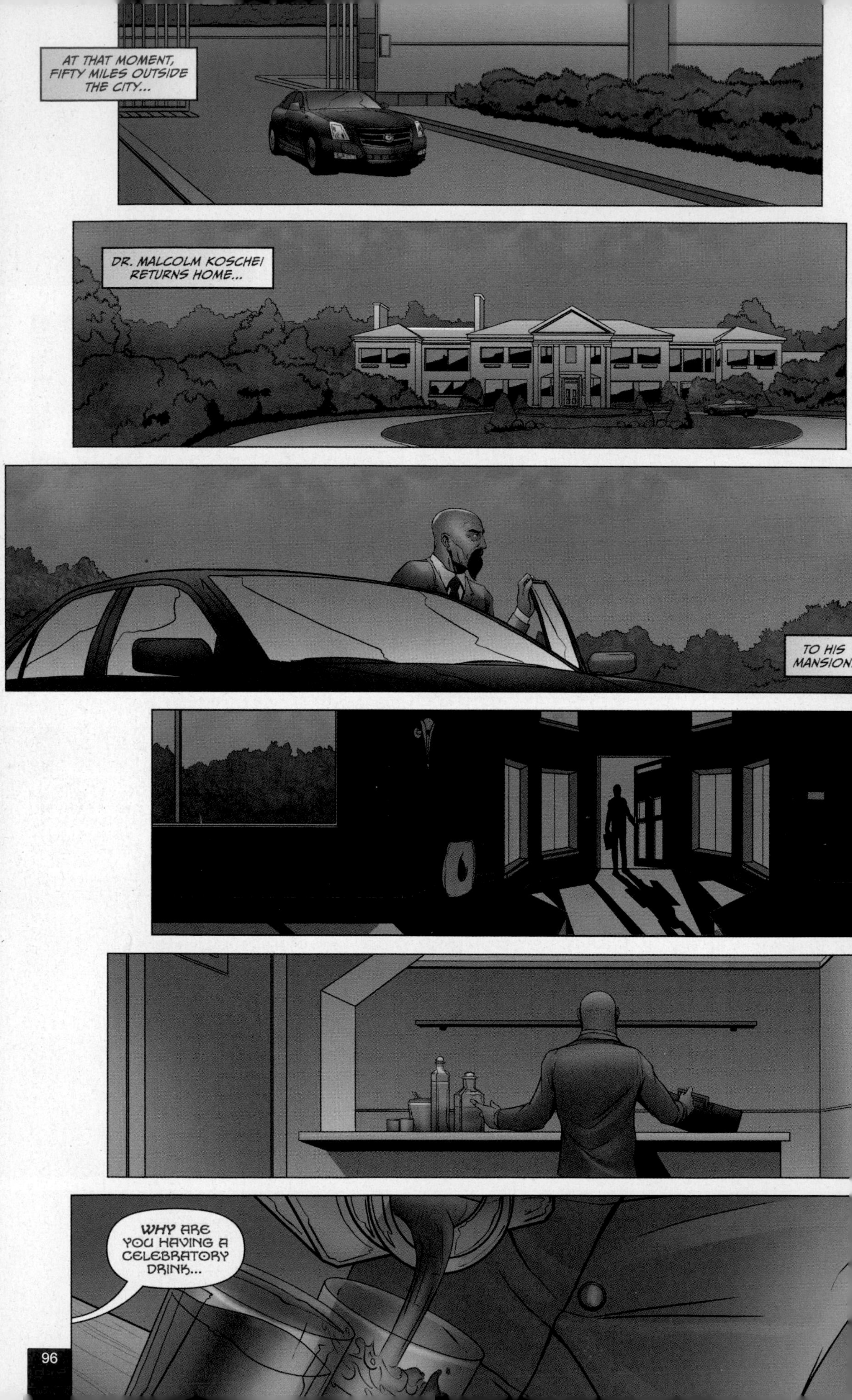
AT THAT MOMENT, FIFTY MILES OUTSIDE THE CITY...
DR. MALCOLM KOSCHEI RETURNS HOME...
TO HIS MANSION.
WHY ARE YOU HAVING A CELEBRATORY DRINK...

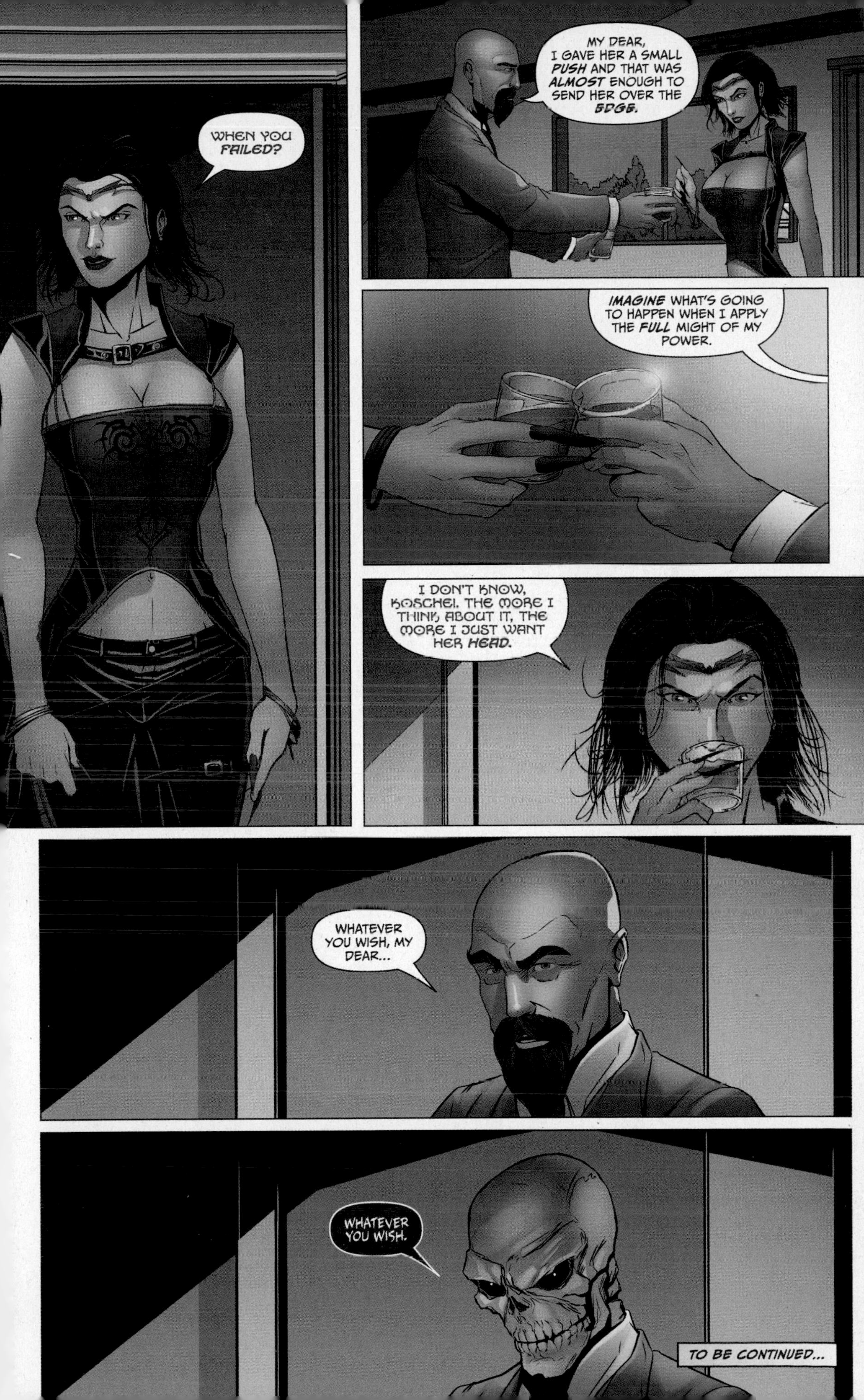
WHEN YOU FAILED?
MY DEAR, I GAVE HER A SMALL PUSH AND THAT WAS ALMOST ENOUGH TO SEND HER OVER THE EDGE.
IMAGINE WHAT'S GOING TO HAPPEN WHEN I APPLY THE FULL MIGHT OF MY POWER.
I DON'T KNOW, KOSCHEI. THE MORE I THINK ABOUT IT, THE MORE I JUST WANT HER HEAD.
WHATEVER YOU WISH, MY DEAR...
WHATEVER YOU WISH.
TO BE CONTINUED...

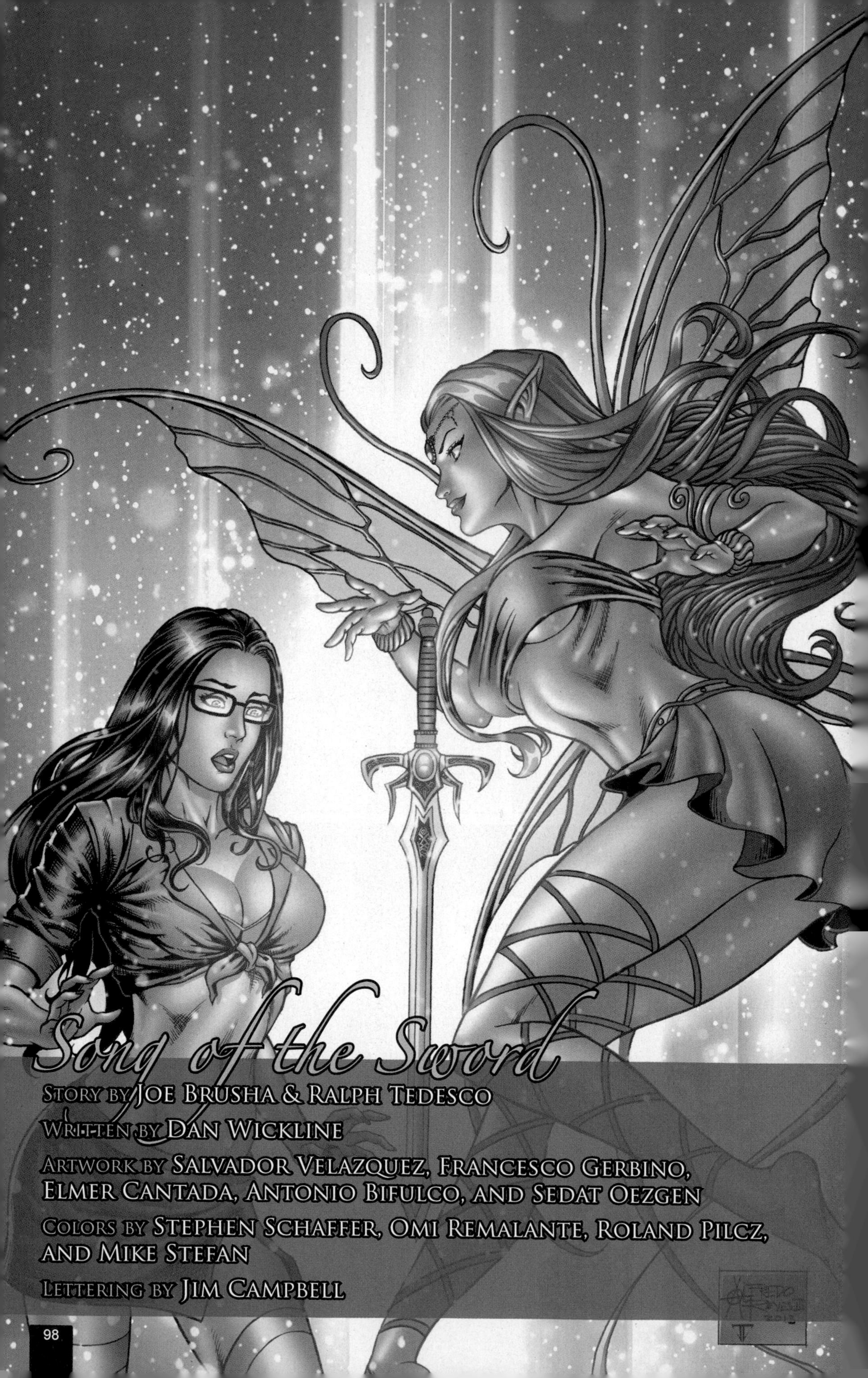

Song of the Sword

STORY BY JOE BRUSHA & RALPH TEDESCO

WRITTEN BY DAN WICKLINE

ARTWORK BY SALVADOR VELAZQUEZ, FRANCESCO GERBINO, ELMER CANTADA, ANTONIO BIFULCO, AND SEDAT OEZGEN

COLORS BY STEPHEN SCHAFFER, OMI REMALANTE, ROLAND PILCZ, AND MIKE STEFAN

LETTERING BY JIM CAMPBELL

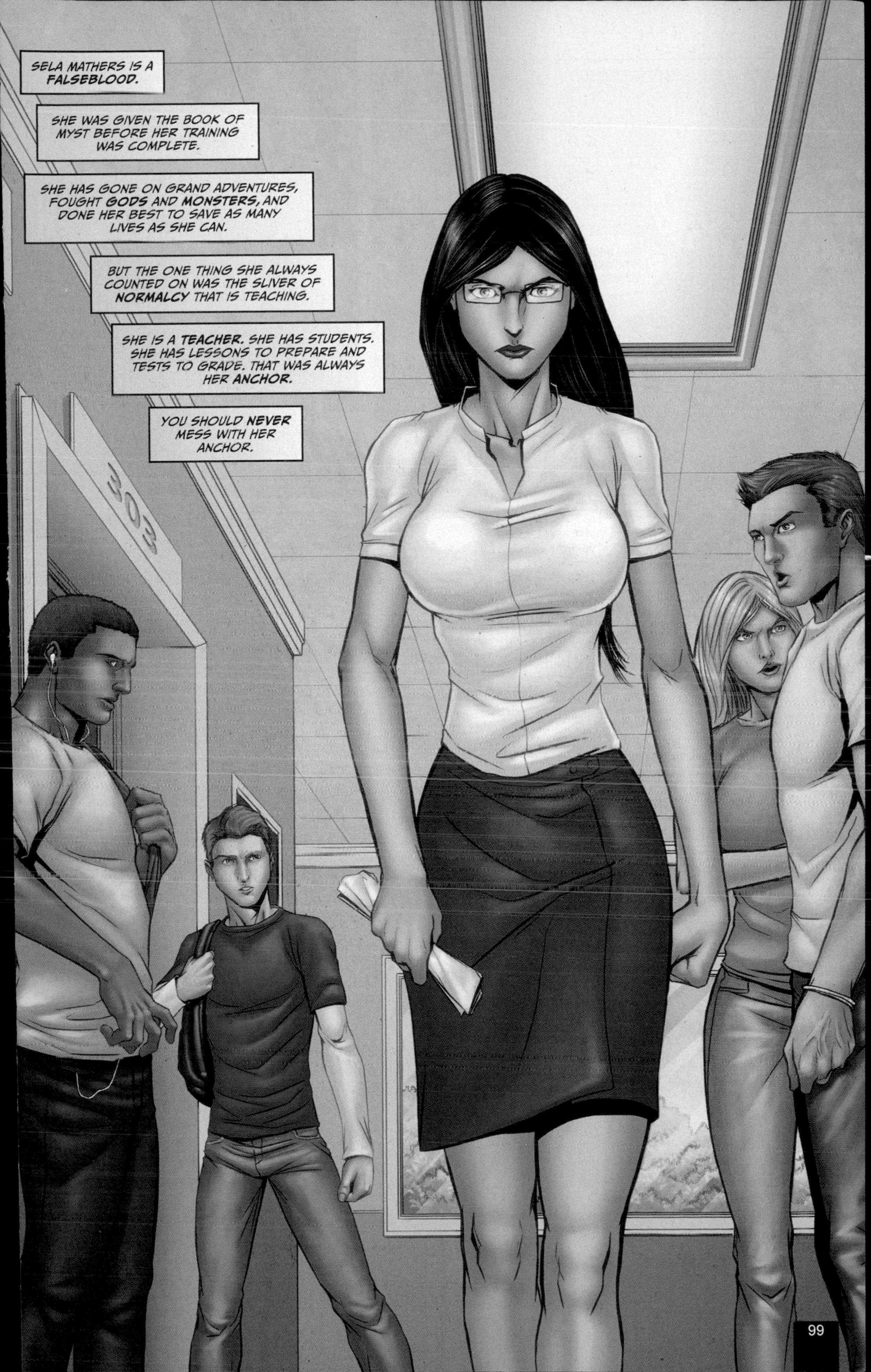
SELA MATHERS IS A FALSEBLOOD.
SHE WAS GIVEN THE BOOK OF MYST BEFORE HER TRAINING WAS COMPLETE.
SHE HAS GONE ON GRAND ADVENTURES, FOUGHT GODS AND MONSTERS, AND DONE HER BEST TO SAVE AS MANY LIVES AS SHE CAN.
BUT THE ONE THING SHE ALWAYS COUNTED ON WAS THE SLIVER OF NORMALCY THAT IS TEACHING.
SHE IS A TEACHER. SHE HAS STUDENTS. SHE HAS LESSONS TO PREPARE AND TESTS TO GRADE. THAT WAS ALWAYS HER ANCHOR.
YOU SHOULD NEVER MESS WITH HER ANCHOR.
303

I'M SORRY, MISS MATHERS, BUT DEAN CAMERON IS ON AN IMPORTANT CONFERENCE CALL AND CAN'T BE DISTURBED.

THIS WILL JUST TAKE A MOMENT.

GRAEME HENDERSON
Dean of Humanities

WHAT THE HELL?!

OH, MISS MATHERS...

IS THIS LETTER SUPPOSED TO BE SOME KIND OF JOKE?

GRAEME HENDERSON
Dean of Humanities

THAT REALLY DEPENDS ON WHAT YOU ARE TALKING ABOUT.

ACCORDING TO THIS, I'M REQUIRED TO TAKE A CLASS CALLED HISTORY OF MYTHICAL WEAPONS TO KEEP MY TEACHING CREDENTIAL!

AND I HAVE TO START THE COURSE TODAY!

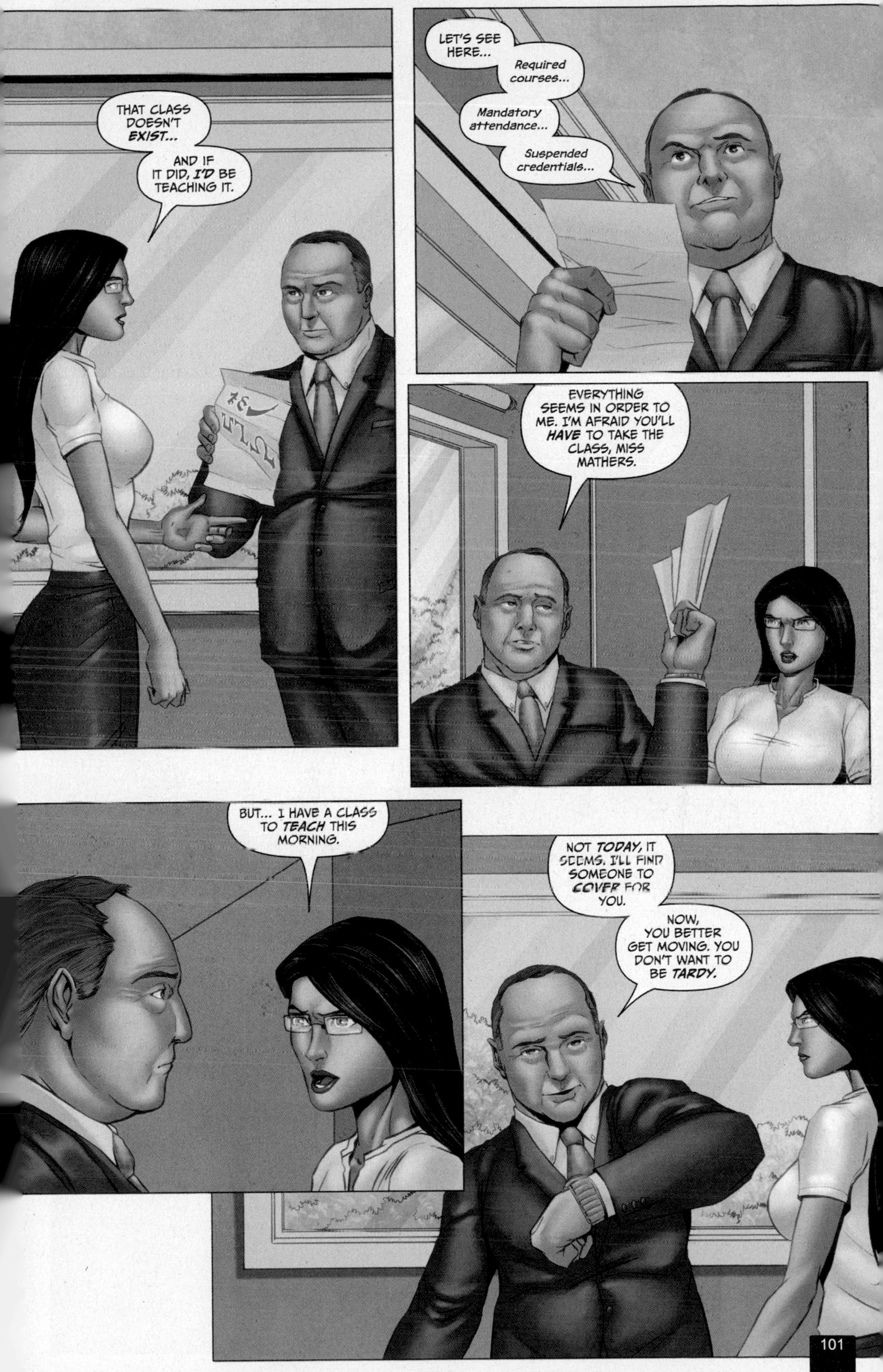

THAT CLASS DOESN'T *EXIST...*
AND IF IT DID, *I'D* BE TEACHING IT.
LET'S SEE HERE...
Required courses...
Mandatory attendance...
Suspended credentials...
EVERYTHING SEEMS IN ORDER TO ME. I'M AFRAID YOU'LL *HAVE* TO TAKE THE CLASS, MISS MATHERS.
BUT... I HAVE A CLASS TO *TEACH* THIS MORNING.
NOT *TODAY,* IT SEEMS. I'LL FIND SOMEONE TO *COVER* FOR YOU.
NOW, YOU BETTER GET MOVING. YOU DON'T WANT TO BE *TARDY.*

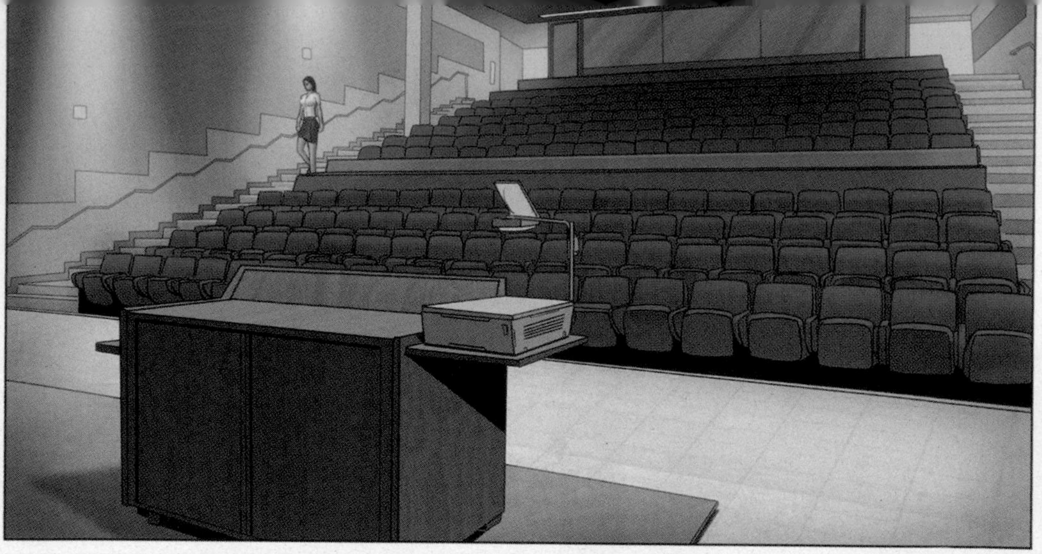

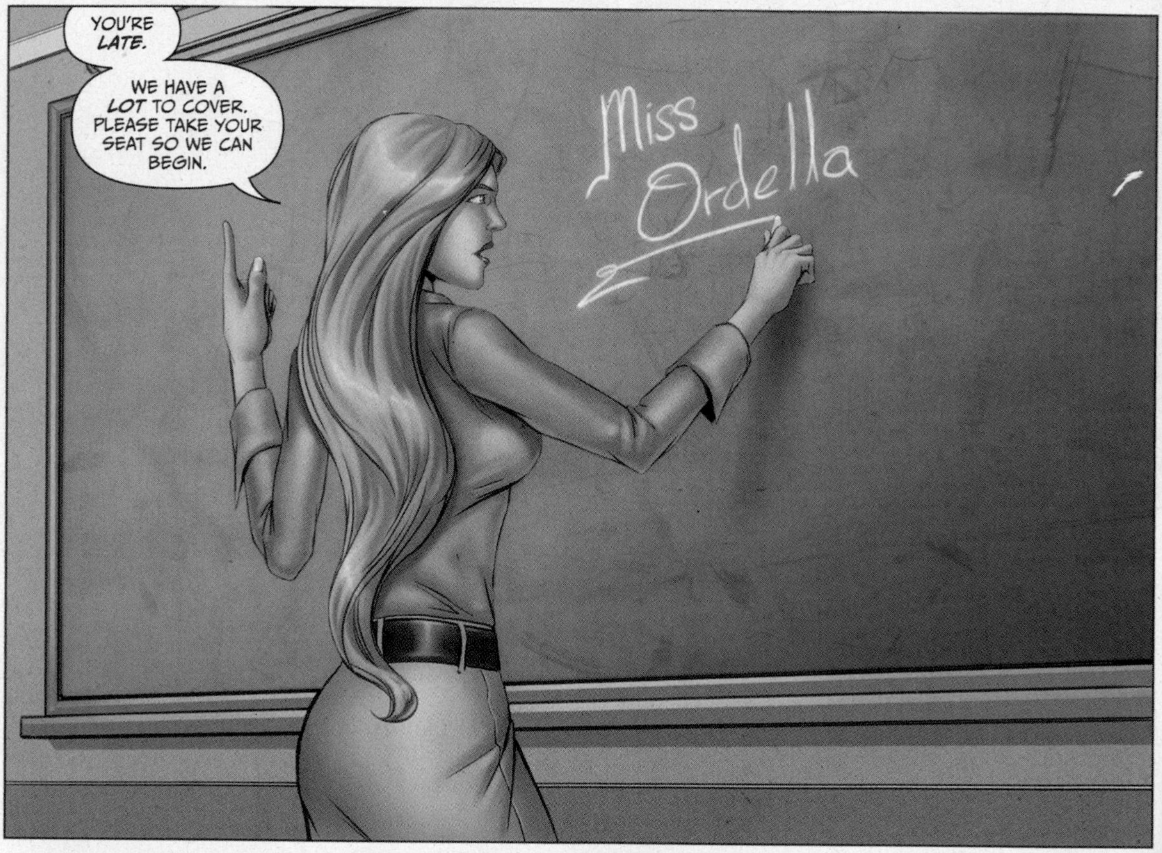

YOU'RE *LATE.*
WE HAVE A *LOT* TO COVER. PLEASE TAKE YOUR SEAT SO WE CAN BEGIN.
Miss Ordella

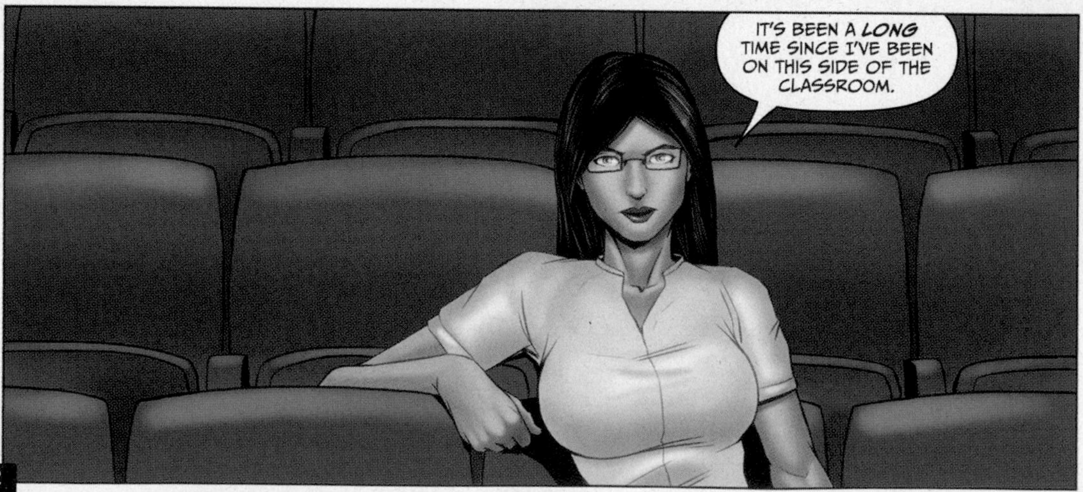

IT'S BEEN A *LONG* TIME SINCE I'VE BEEN ON THIS SIDE OF THE CLASSROOM.

MY NAME IS MISS **ORDELLA** AND YOU ARE HERE TO LEARN ABOUT THE **SWORDS** OF MYTHS AND LEGENDS.

NOW, YOU MAY **THINK** YOU KNOW EVERYTHING ABOUT THE SUBJECT... HOWEVER, THE DAY YOU **THINK** YOU KNOW **EVERYTHING** IS THE DAY YOU KNOW **NOTHING.**

THAT **BOOK**... WHERE DID YOU GET IT?

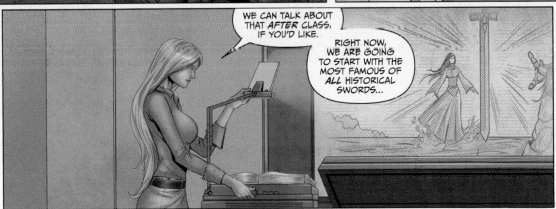

WE CAN TALK ABOUT THAT **AFTER CLASS,** IF YOU'D LIKE.

RIGHT NOW, WE ARE GOING TO START WITH THE MOST FAMOUS OF **ALL** HISTORICAL SWORDS...

"THE SWORD THAT UNITED A KINGDOM."

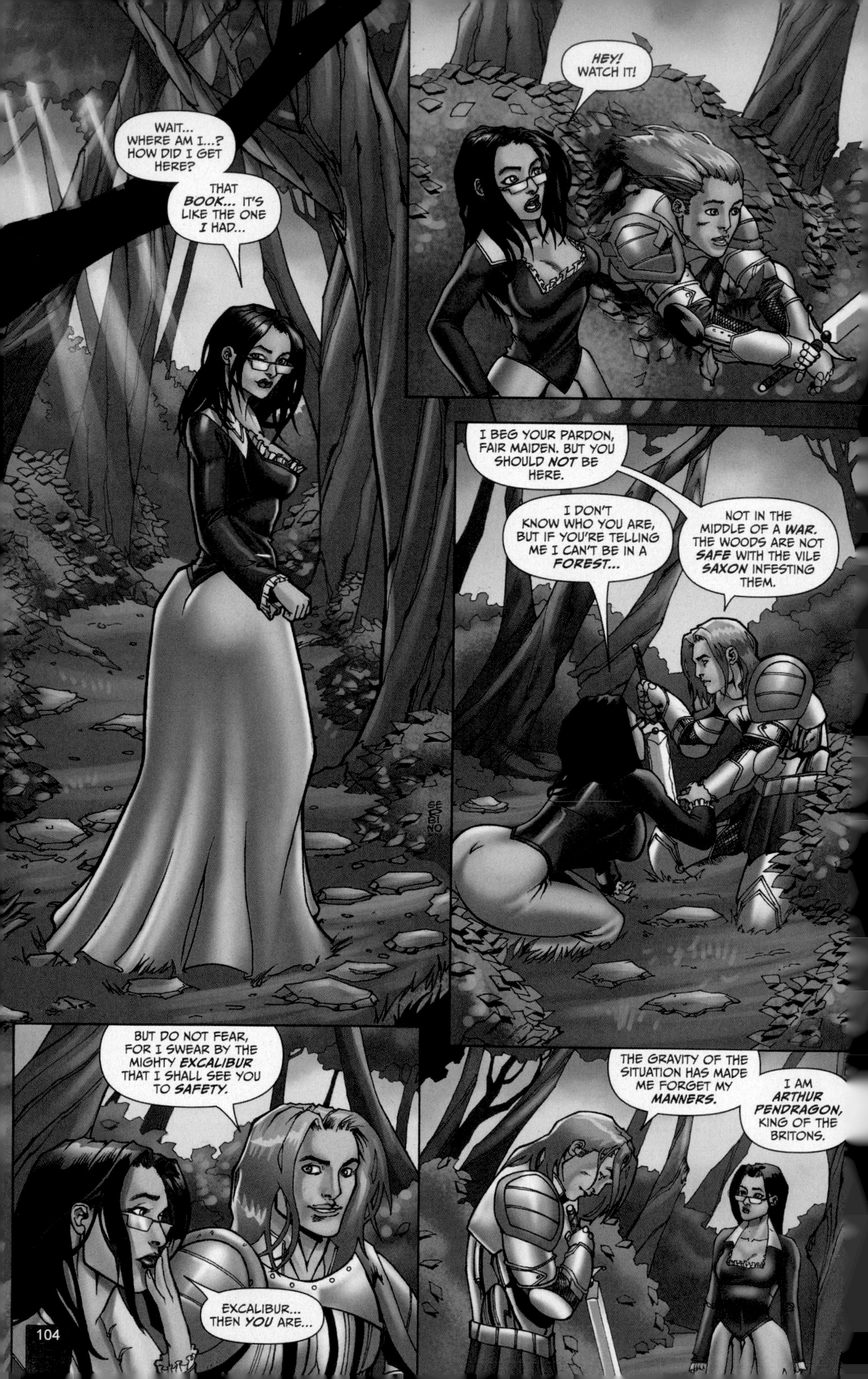
WAIT... WHERE AM I...? HOW DID I GET HERE?
THAT BOOK... IT'S LIKE THE ONE I HAD...
HEY! WATCH IT!
I BEG YOUR PARDON, FAIR MAIDEN. BUT YOU SHOULD NOT BE HERE.
I DON'T KNOW WHO YOU ARE, BUT IF YOU'RE TELLING ME I CAN'T BE IN A FOREST...
NOT IN THE MIDDLE OF A WAR. THE WOODS ARE NOT SAFE WITH THE VILE SAXON INFESTING THEM.
BUT DO NOT FEAR, FOR I SWEAR BY THE MIGHTY EXCALIBUR THAT I SHALL SEE YOU TO SAFETY.
EXCALIBUR... THEN YOU ARE...
THE GRAVITY OF THE SITUATION HAS MADE ME FORGET MY MANNERS.
I AM ARTHUR PENDRAGON, KING OF THE BRITONS.

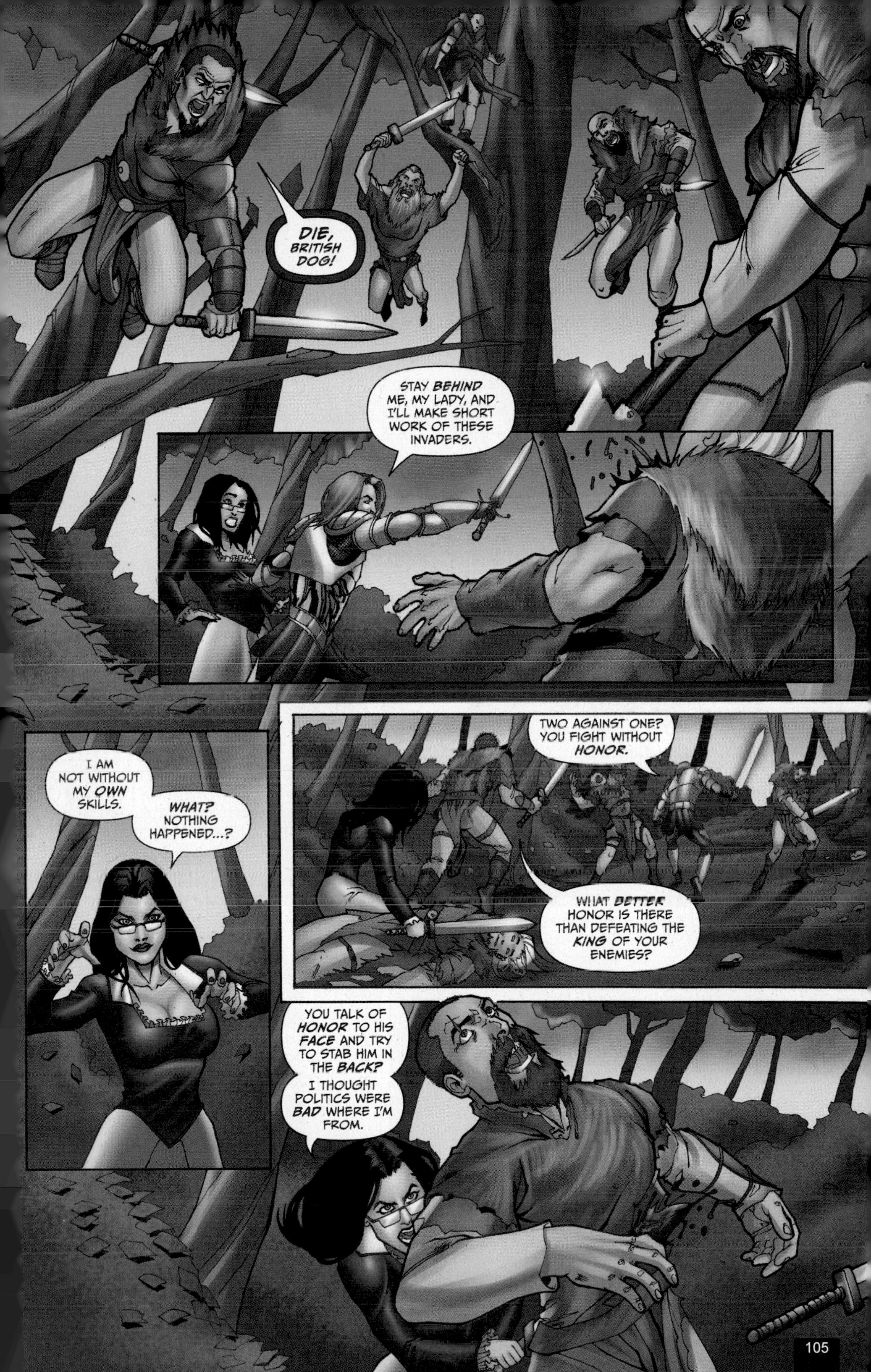

DIE, BRITISH DOG!
STAY BEHIND ME, MY LADY, AND I'LL MAKE SHORT WORK OF THESE INVADERS.
TWO AGAINST ONE? YOU FIGHT WITHOUT HONOR.
WHAT BETTER HONOR IS THERE THAN DEFEATING THE KING OF YOUR ENEMIES?
I AM NOT WITHOUT MY OWN SKILLS.
WHAT? NOTHING HAPPENED...?
YOU TALK OF HONOR TO HIS FACE AND TRY TO STAB HIM IN THE BACK?
I THOUGHT POLITICS WERE BAD WHERE I'M FROM.

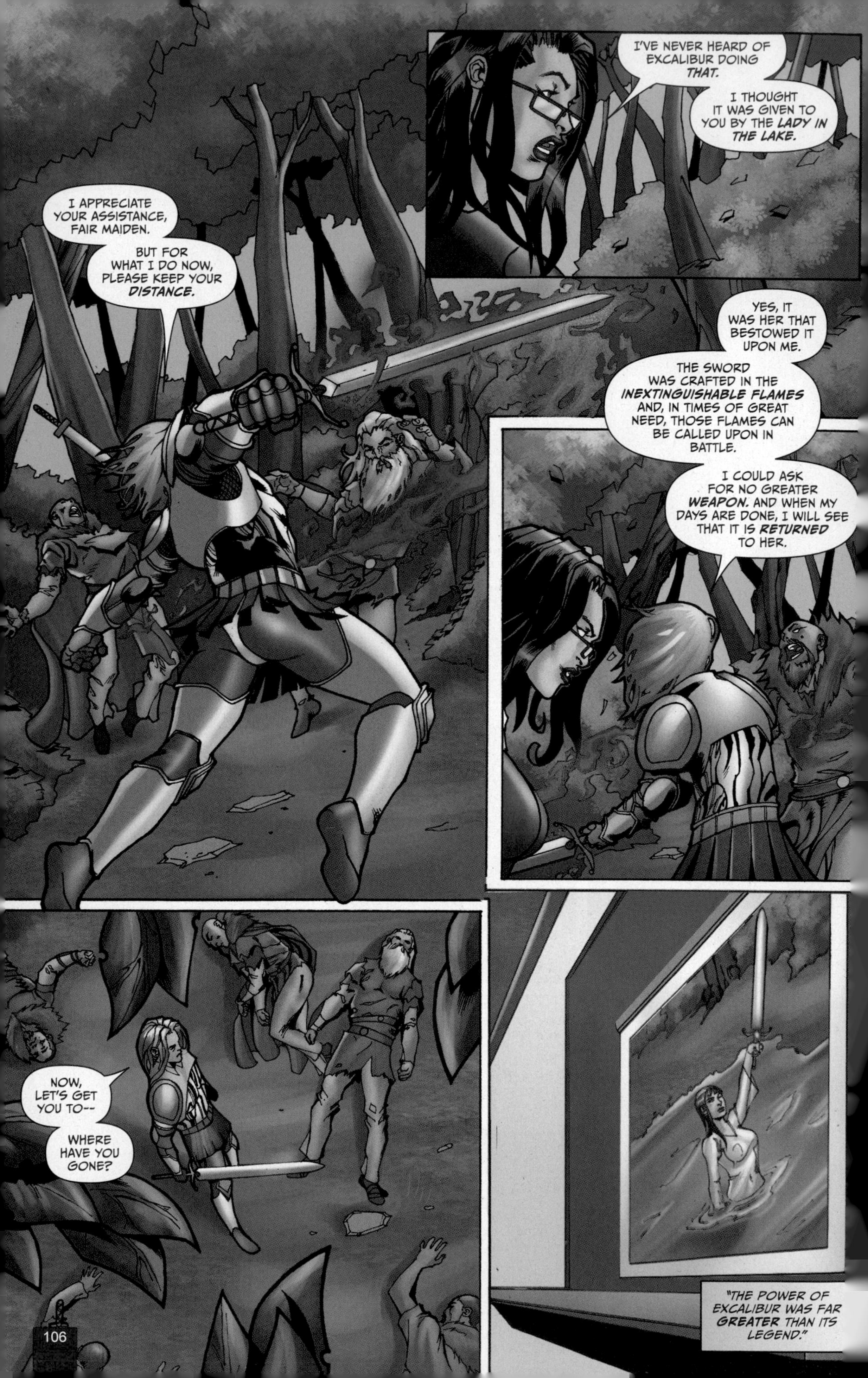
I'VE NEVER HEARD OF EXCALIBUR DOING THAT.
I THOUGHT IT WAS GIVEN TO YOU BY THE LADY IN THE LAKE.
I APPRECIATE YOUR ASSISTANCE, FAIR MAIDEN.
BUT FOR WHAT I DO NOW, PLEASE KEEP YOUR DISTANCE.
YES, IT WAS HER THAT BESTOWED IT UPON ME.
THE SWORD WAS CRAFTED IN THE INEXTINGUISHABLE FLAMES AND, IN TIMES OF GREAT NEED, THOSE FLAMES CAN BE CALLED UPON IN BATTLE.
I COULD ASK FOR NO GREATER WEAPON. AND WHEN MY DAYS ARE DONE, I WILL SEE THAT IT IS RETURNED TO HER.
NOW, LET'S GET YOU TO--
WHERE HAVE YOU GONE?
"THE POWER OF EXCALIBUR WAS FAR GREATER THAN ITS LEGEND."

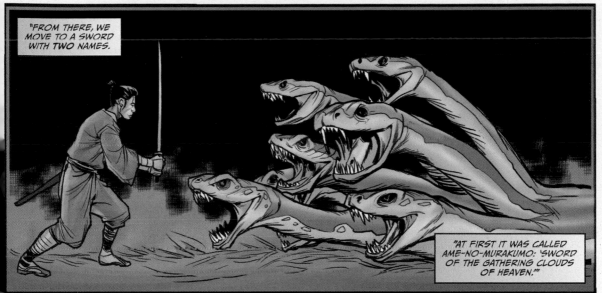

"FROM THERE, WE MOVE TO A SWORD WITH *TWO* NAMES."

"AT FIRST IT WAS CALLED AME-NO-MURAKUMO: 'SWORD OF THE GATHERING CLOUDS OF HEAVEN.'"

I'M BEING BOUNCED AROUND FROM PLACE TO PLACE... BUT *HOW?*

THAT BOOK IS ACTING LIKE MINE DID, BUT THESE AREN'T *FAIRY TALES.*

STEADY THERE, GIRL... JUST KEEP GOING...

NEEEEAAAAAAAAAA

THWOK

NO!

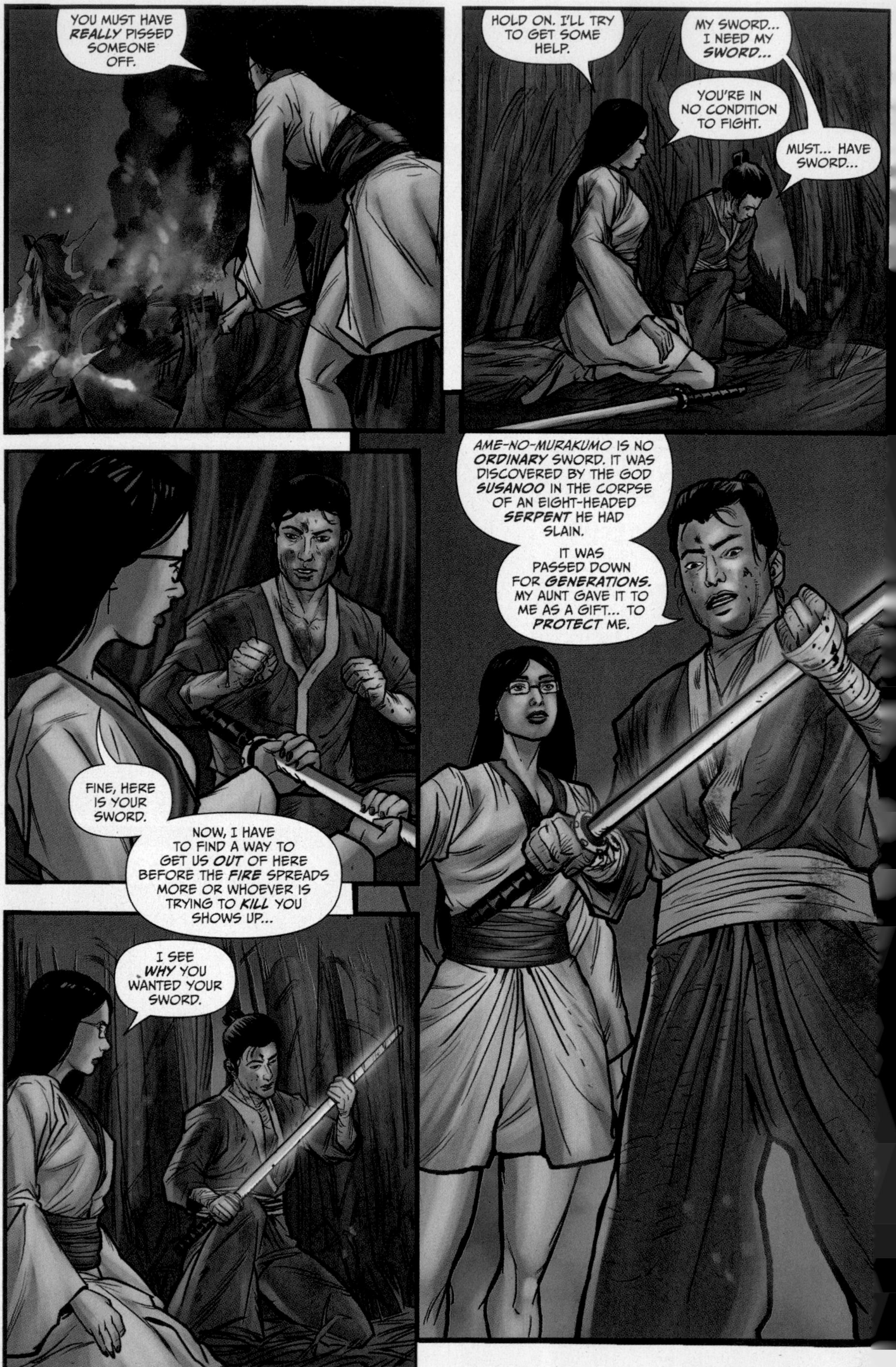

YOU MUST HAVE REALLY PISSED SOMEONE OFF.
HOLD ON. I'LL TRY TO GET SOME HELP.
MY SWORD... I NEED MY SWORD...
YOU'RE IN NO CONDITION TO FIGHT.
MUST... HAVE SWORD...
FINE, HERE IS YOUR SWORD.
NOW, I HAVE TO FIND A WAY TO GET US OUT OF HERE BEFORE THE FIRE SPREADS MORE OR WHOEVER IS TRYING TO KILL YOU SHOWS UP...
I SEE WHY YOU WANTED YOUR SWORD.
AME-NO-MURAKUMO IS NO ORDINARY SWORD. IT WAS DISCOVERED BY THE GOD SUSANOO IN THE CORPSE OF AN EIGHT-HEADED SERPENT HE HAD SLAIN.
IT WAS PASSED DOWN FOR GENERATIONS. MY AUNT GAVE IT TO ME AS A GIFT... TO PROTECT ME.

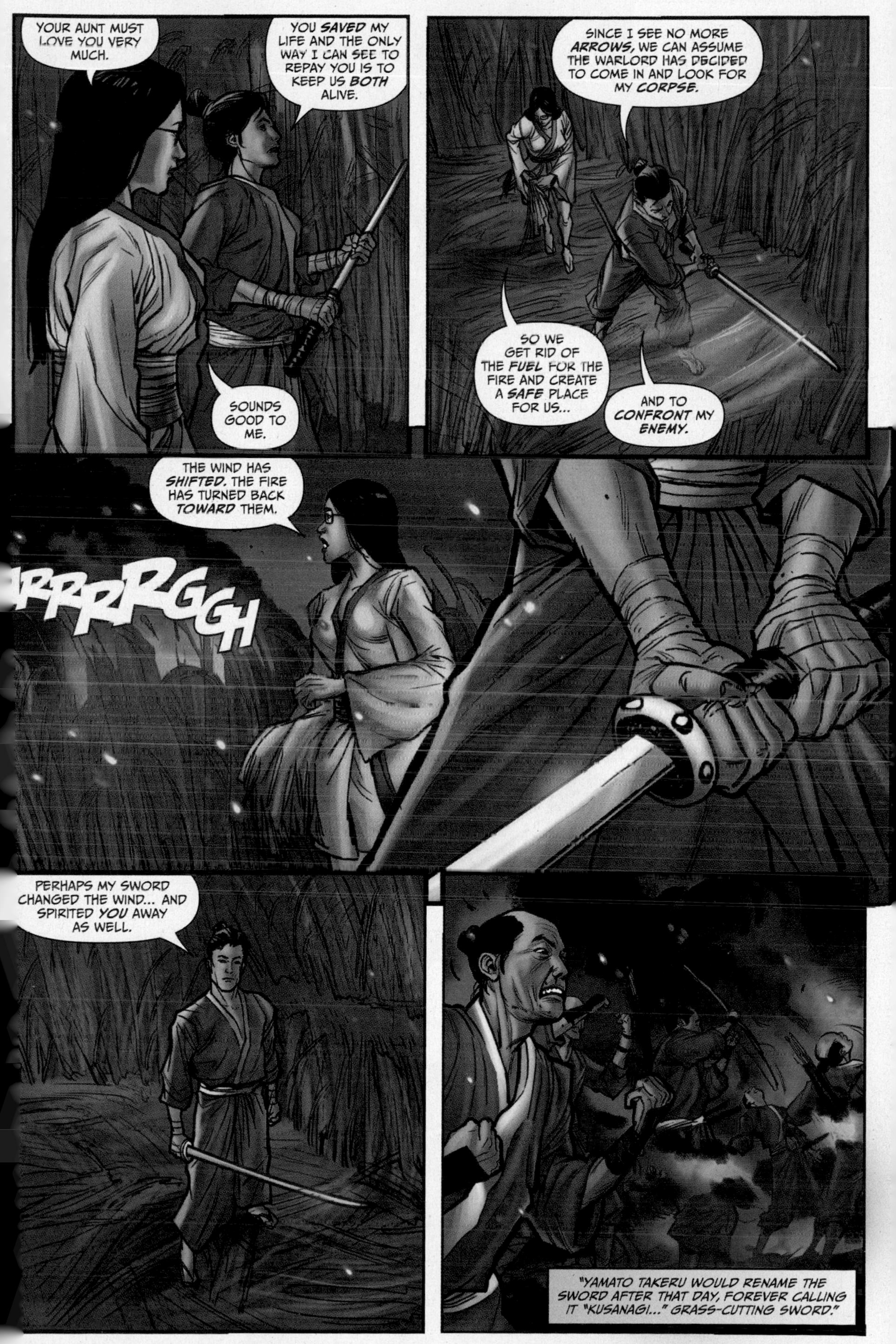
YOUR AUNT MUST LOVE YOU VERY MUCH.
YOU SAVED MY LIFE AND THE ONLY WAY I CAN SEE TO REPAY YOU IS TO KEEP US BOTH ALIVE.
SOUNDS GOOD TO ME.
SINCE I SEE NO MORE ARROWS, WE CAN ASSUME THE WARLORD HAS DECIDED TO COME IN AND LOOK FOR MY CORPSE.
SO WE GET RID OF THE FUEL FOR THE FIRE AND CREATE A SAFE PLACE FOR US...
AND TO CONFRONT MY ENEMY.
THE WIND HAS SHIFTED. THE FIRE HAS TURNED BACK TOWARD THEM.
RRRRGGH
PERHAPS MY SWORD CHANGED THE WIND... AND SPIRITED YOU AWAY AS WELL.
"YAMATO TAKERU WOULD RENAME THE SWORD AFTER THAT DAY, FOREVER CALLING IT "KUSANAGI..." GRASS-CUTTING SWORD."

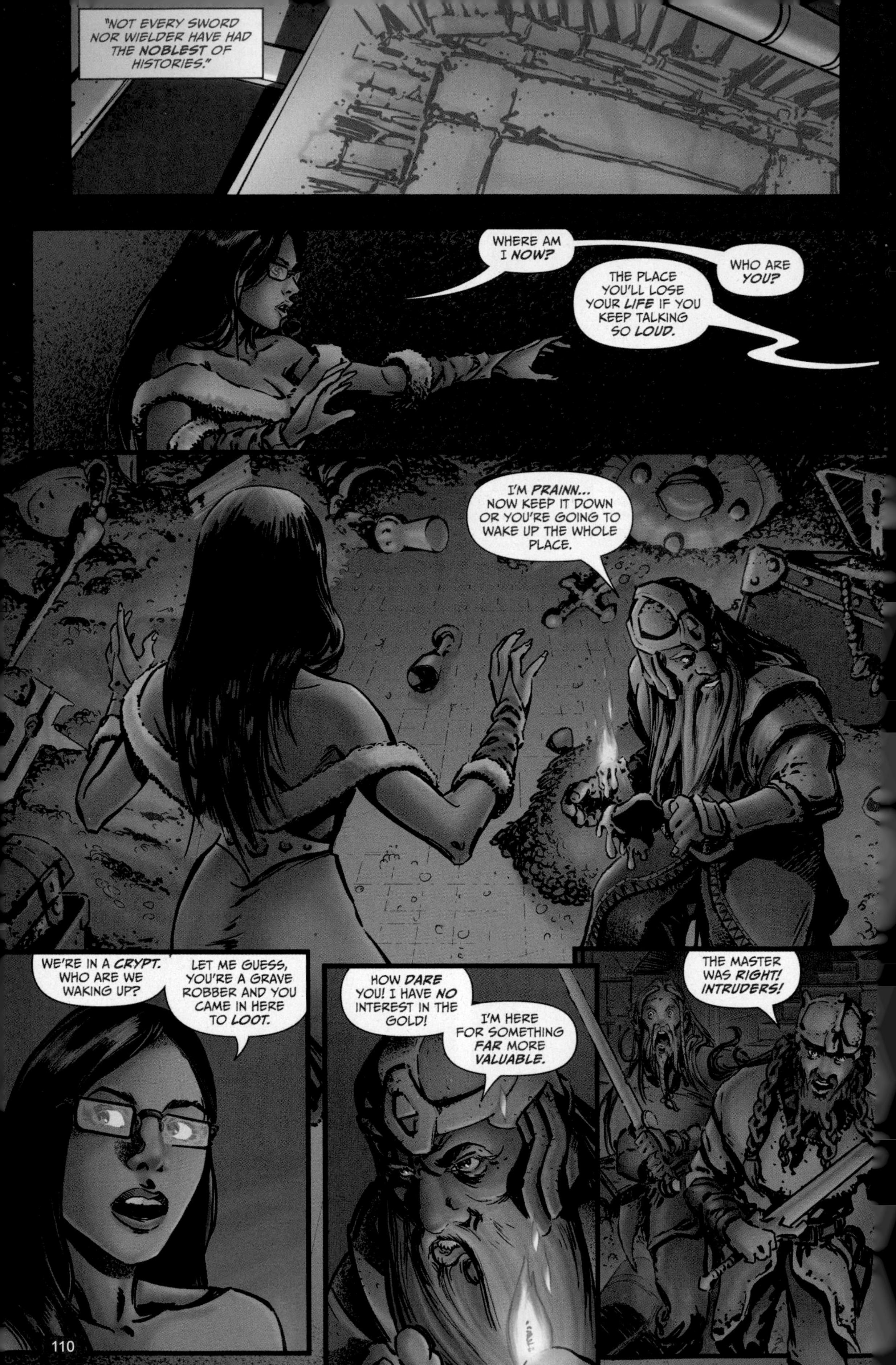

"NOT EVERY SWORD NOR WIELDER HAVE HAD THE NOBLEST OF HISTORIES."
WHERE AM I NOW?
WHO ARE YOU?
THE PLACE YOU'LL LOSE YOUR LIFE IF YOU KEEP TALKING SO LOUD.
I'M PRAINN... NOW KEEP IT DOWN OR YOU'RE GOING TO WAKE UP THE WHOLE PLACE.
WE'RE IN A CRYPT. WHO ARE WE WAKING UP?
LET ME GUESS, YOU'RE A GRAVE ROBBER AND YOU CAME IN HERE TO LOOT.
HOW DARE YOU! I HAVE NO INTEREST IN THE GOLD!
I'M HERE FOR SOMETHING FAR MORE VALUABLE.
THE MASTER WAS RIGHT! INTRUDERS!

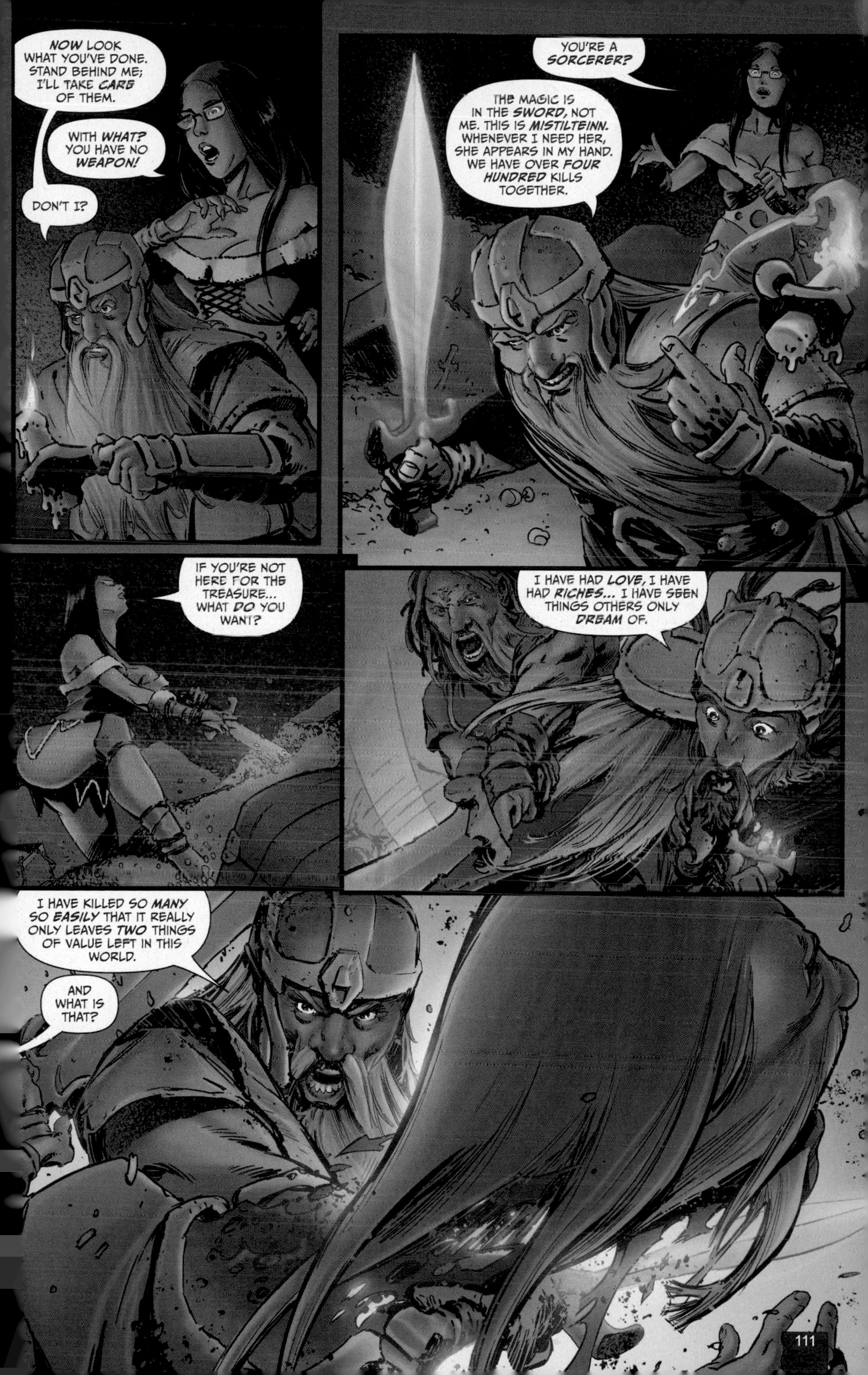
NOW LOOK WHAT YOU'VE DONE. STAND BEHIND ME; I'LL TAKE CARE OF THEM.
WITH WHAT? YOU HAVE NO WEAPON!
DON'T I?
YOU'RE A SORCERER?
THE MAGIC IS IN THE SWORD, NOT ME. THIS IS MISTILTEINN. WHENEVER I NEED HER, SHE APPEARS IN MY HAND. WE HAVE OVER FOUR HUNDRED KILLS TOGETHER.
IF YOU'RE NOT HERE FOR THE TREASURE... WHAT DO YOU WANT?
I HAVE HAD LOVE, I HAVE HAD RICHES... I HAVE SEEN THINGS OTHERS ONLY DREAM OF.
I HAVE KILLED SO MANY SO EASILY THAT IT REALLY ONLY LEAVES TWO THINGS OF VALUE LEFT IN THIS WORLD.
AND WHAT IS THAT?

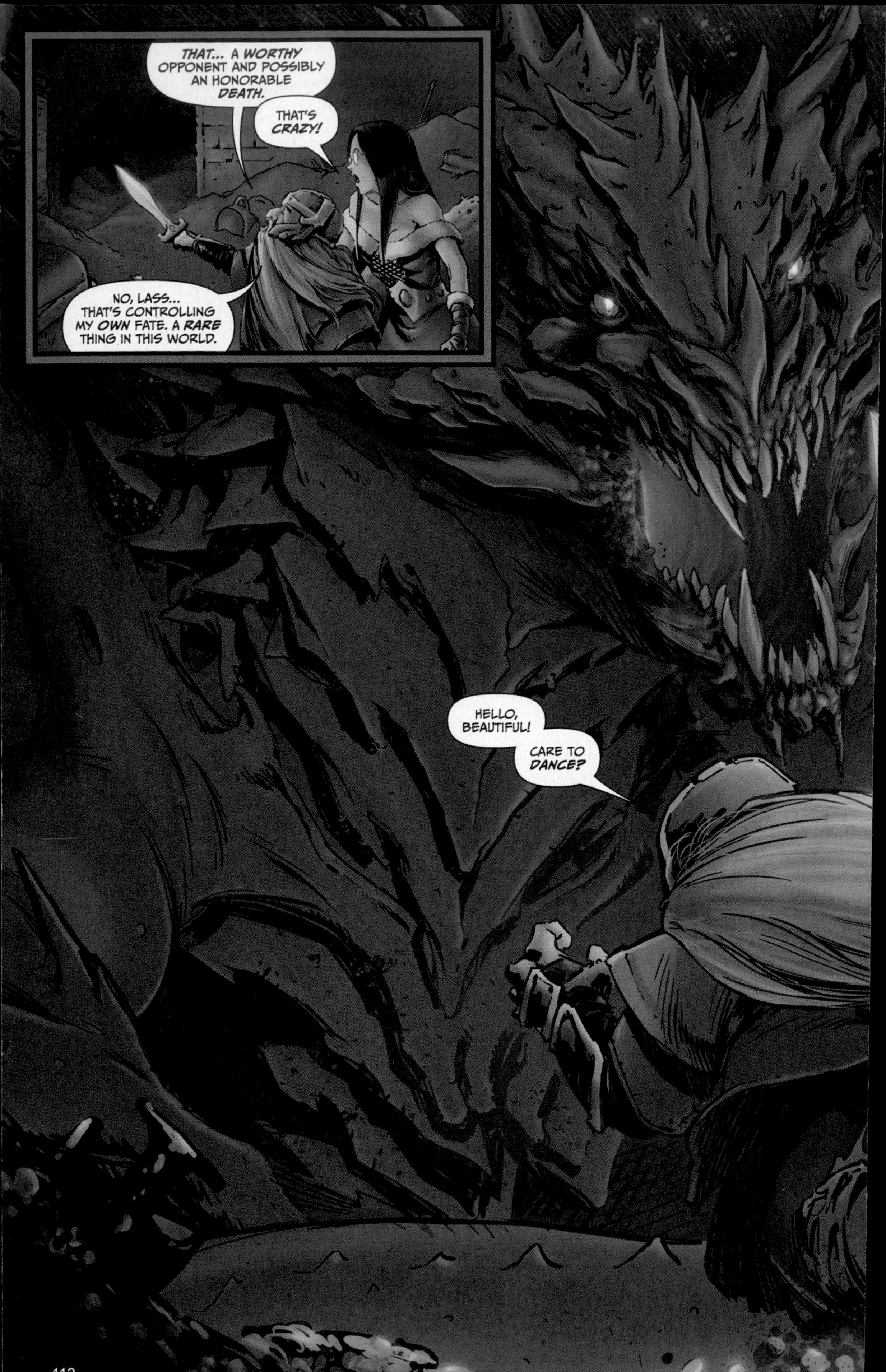
THAT... A WORTHY OPPONENT AND POSSIBLY AN HONORABLE DEATH.
THAT'S CRAZY!
NO, LASS... THAT'S CONTROLLING MY OWN FATE. A RARE THING IN THIS WORLD.
HELLO, BEAUTIFUL!
CARE TO DANCE?

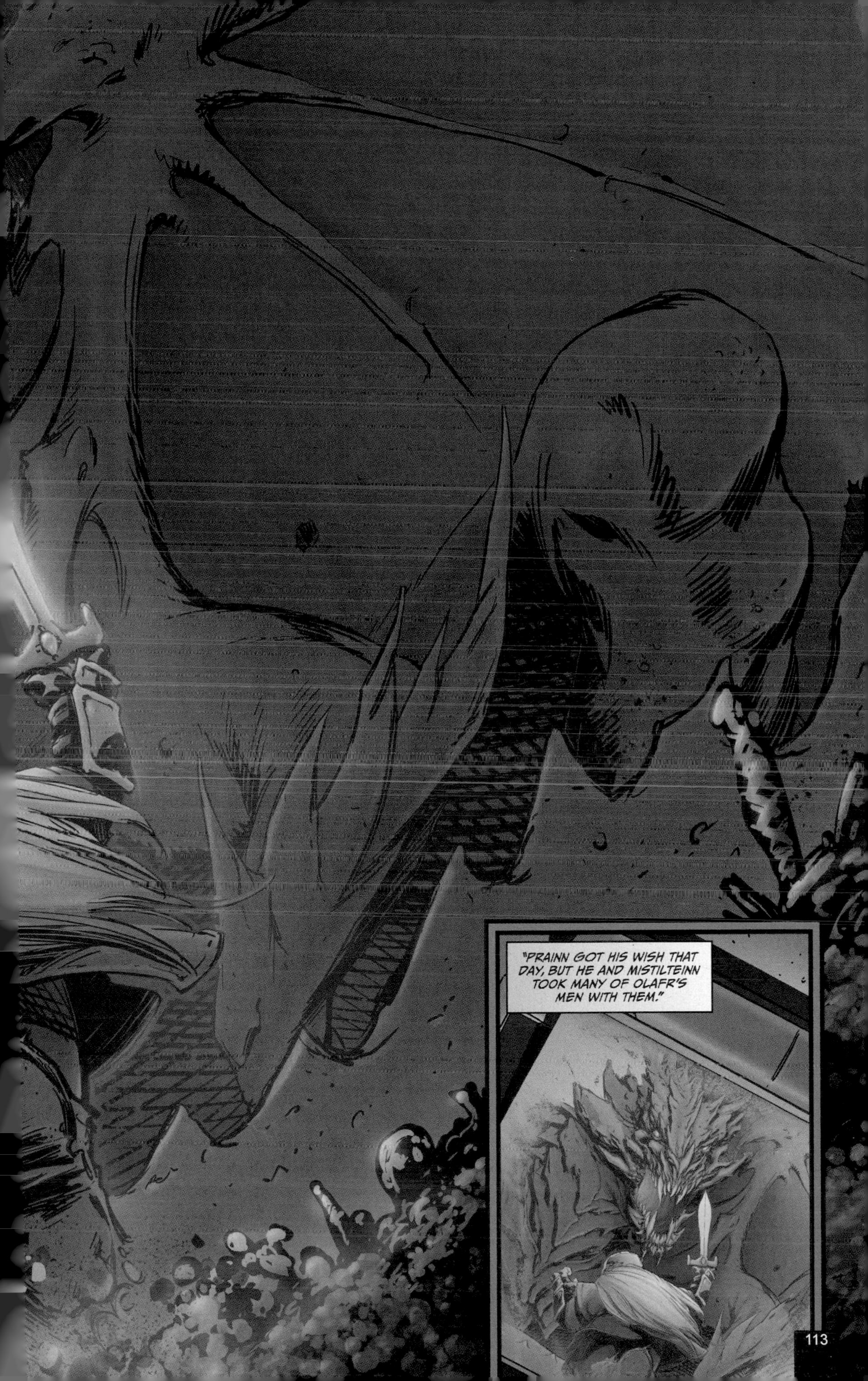
"PRAINN GOT HIS WISH THAT DAY, BUT HE AND MISTILTEINN TOOK MANY OF OLAFR'S MEN WITH THEM."

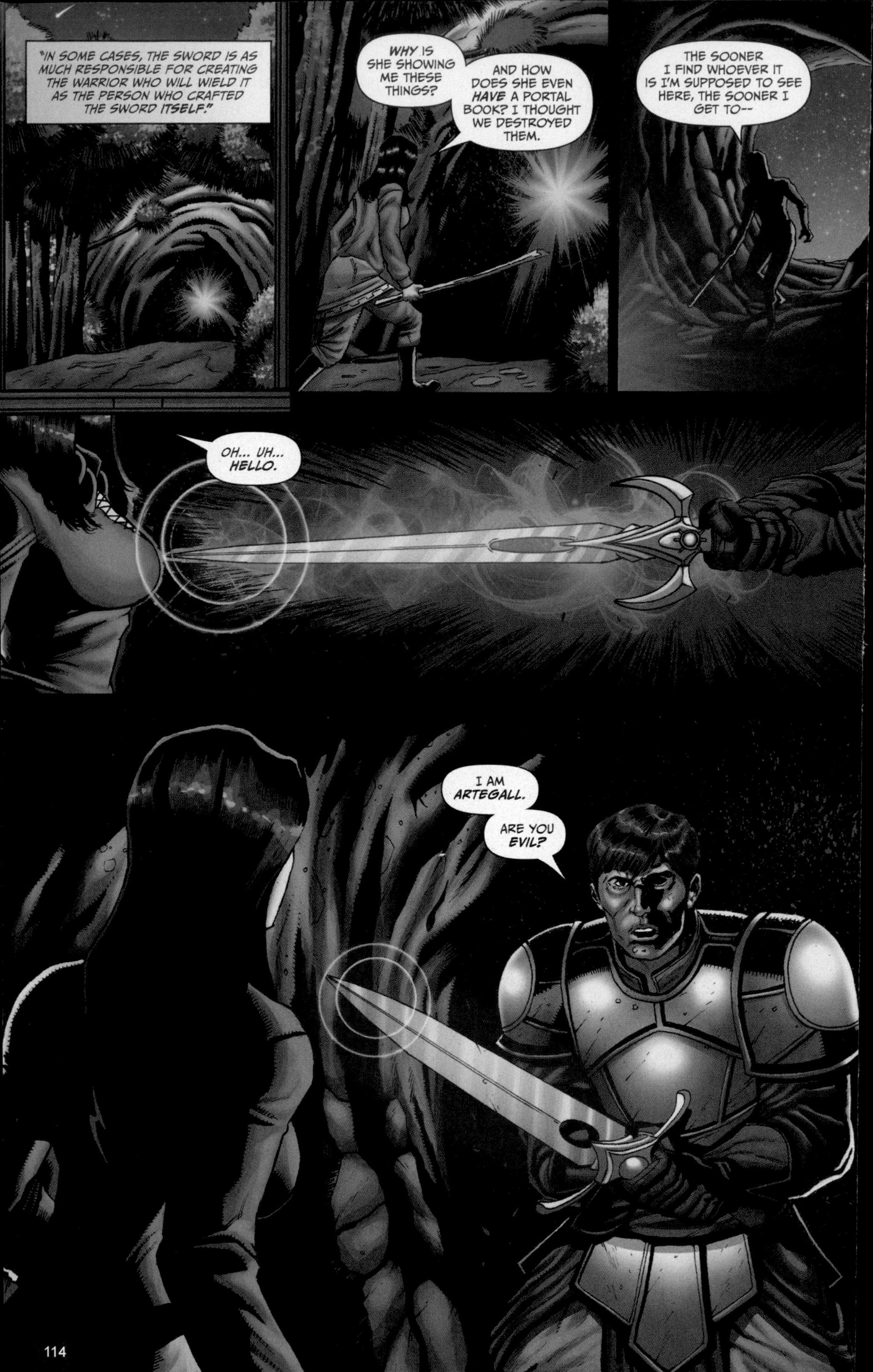
"IN SOME CASES, THE SWORD IS AS MUCH RESPONSIBLE FOR CREATING THE WARRIOR WHO WILL WIELD IT AS THE PERSON WHO CRAFTED THE SWORD ITSELF."
WHY IS SHE SHOWING ME THESE THINGS?
AND HOW DOES SHE EVEN HAVE A PORTAL BOOK? I THOUGHT WE DESTROYED THEM.
THE SOONER I FIND WHOEVER IT IS I'M SUPPOSED TO SEE HERE, THE SOONER I GET TO--
OH... UH... HELLO.
I AM ARTEGALL.
ARE YOU EVIL?

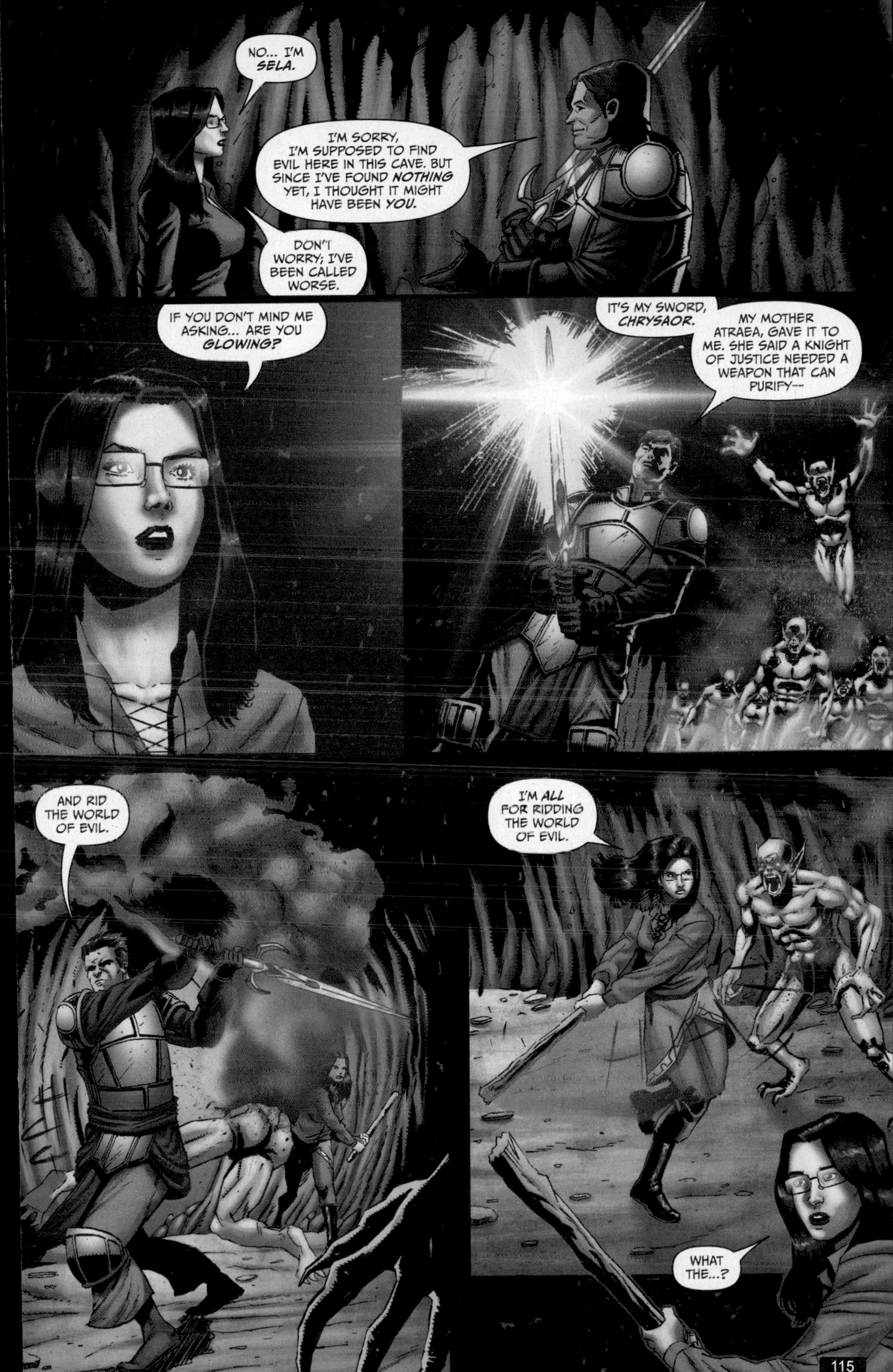
NO... I'M SELA.
I'M SORRY, I'M SUPPOSED TO FIND EVIL HERE IN THIS CAVE. BUT SINCE I'VE FOUND NOTHING YET, I THOUGHT IT MIGHT HAVE BEEN YOU.
DON'T WORRY; I'VE BEEN CALLED WORSE.
IF YOU DON'T MIND ME ASKING... ARE YOU GLOWING?
IT'S MY SWORD, CHRYSAOR.
MY MOTHER ATRAEA, GAVE IT TO ME. SHE SAID A KNIGHT OF JUSTICE NEEDED A WEAPON THAT CAN PURIFY--
AND RID THE WORLD OF EVIL.
I'M ALL FOR RIDDING THE WORLD OF EVIL.
WHAT THE...?

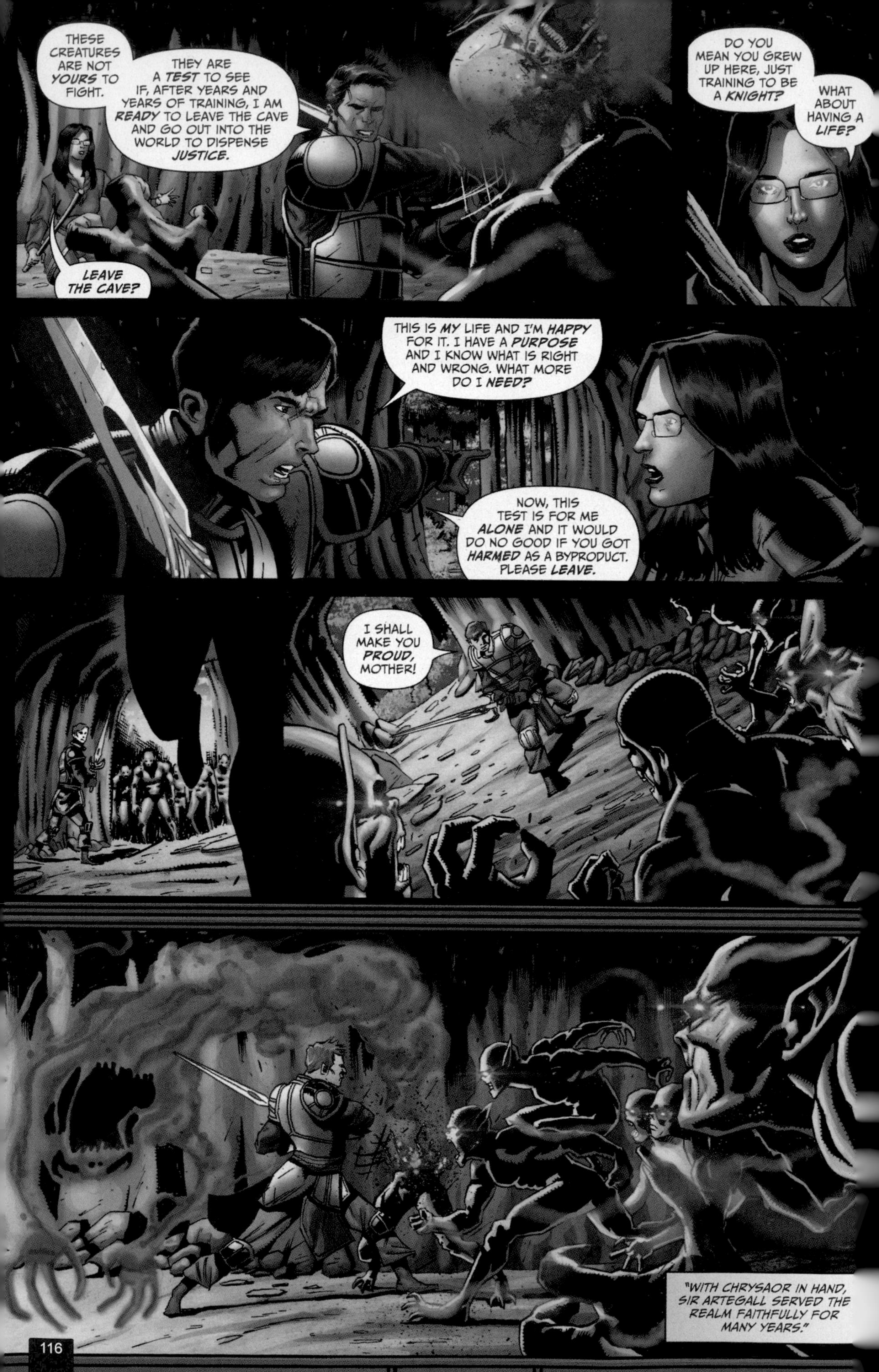

THESE CREATURES ARE NOT YOURS TO FIGHT.
THEY ARE A TEST TO SEE IF, AFTER YEARS AND YEARS OF TRAINING, I AM READY TO LEAVE THE CAVE AND GO OUT INTO THE WORLD TO DISPENSE JUSTICE.
LEAVE THE CAVE?
DO YOU MEAN YOU GREW UP HERE, JUST TRAINING TO BE A KNIGHT?
WHAT ABOUT HAVING A LIFE?
THIS IS MY LIFE AND I'M HAPPY FOR IT. I HAVE A PURPOSE AND I KNOW WHAT IS RIGHT AND WRONG. WHAT MORE DO I NEED?
NOW, THIS TEST IS FOR ME ALONE AND IT WOULD DO NO GOOD IF YOU GOT HARMED AS A BYPRODUCT. PLEASE LEAVE.
I SHALL MAKE YOU PROUD, MOTHER!
"WITH CHRYSAOR IN HAND, SIR ARTEGALL SERVED THE REALM FAITHFULLY FOR MANY YEARS."

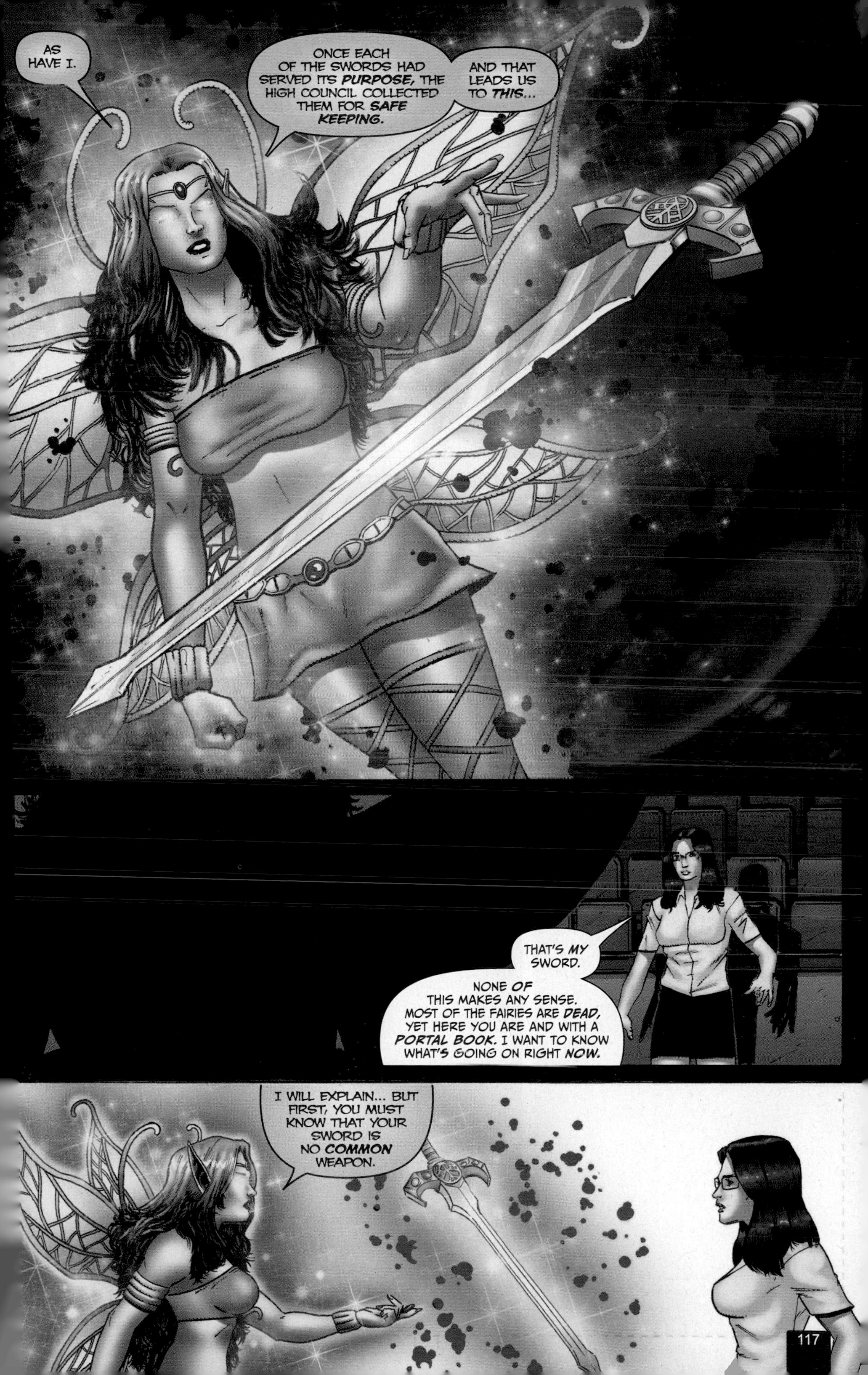
AS HAVE I.
ONCE EACH OF THE SWORDS HAD SERVED ITS PURPOSE, THE HIGH COUNCIL COLLECTED THEM FOR SAFE KEEPING.
AND THAT LEADS US TO THIS...
THAT'S MY SWORD.
NONE OF THIS MAKES ANY SENSE. MOST OF THE FAIRIES ARE DEAD, YET HERE YOU ARE AND WITH A PORTAL BOOK. I WANT TO KNOW WHAT'S GOING ON RIGHT NOW.
I WILL EXPLAIN... BUT FIRST, YOU MUST KNOW THAT YOUR SWORD IS NO COMMON WEAPON.

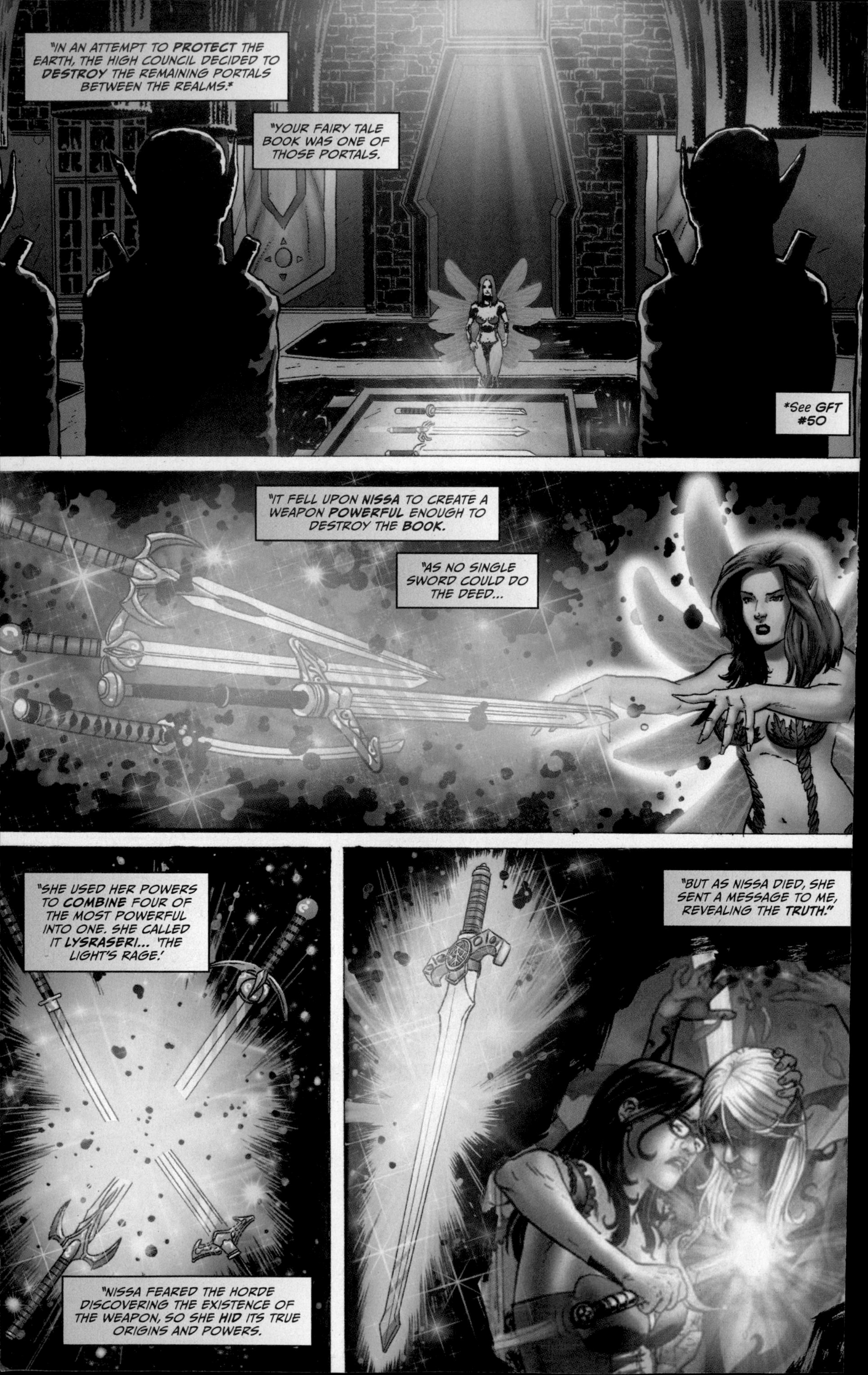
"IN AN ATTEMPT TO PROTECT THE EARTH, THE HIGH COUNCIL DECIDED TO DESTROY THE REMAINING PORTALS BETWEEN THE REALMS.*
"YOUR FAIRY TALE BOOK WAS ONE OF THOSE PORTALS.
*See GFT #50
"IT FELL UPON NISSA TO CREATE A WEAPON POWERFUL ENOUGH TO DESTROY THE BOOK.
"AS NO SINGLE SWORD COULD DO THE DEED...
"SHE USED HER POWERS TO COMBINE FOUR OF THE MOST POWERFUL INTO ONE. SHE CALLED IT LYSRASERI... 'THE LIGHT'S RAGE.'
"NISSA FEARED THE HORDE DISCOVERING THE EXISTENCE OF THE WEAPON, SO SHE HID ITS TRUE ORIGINS AND POWERS.
"BUT AS NISSA DIED, SHE SENT A MESSAGE TO ME, REVEALING THE TRUTH."

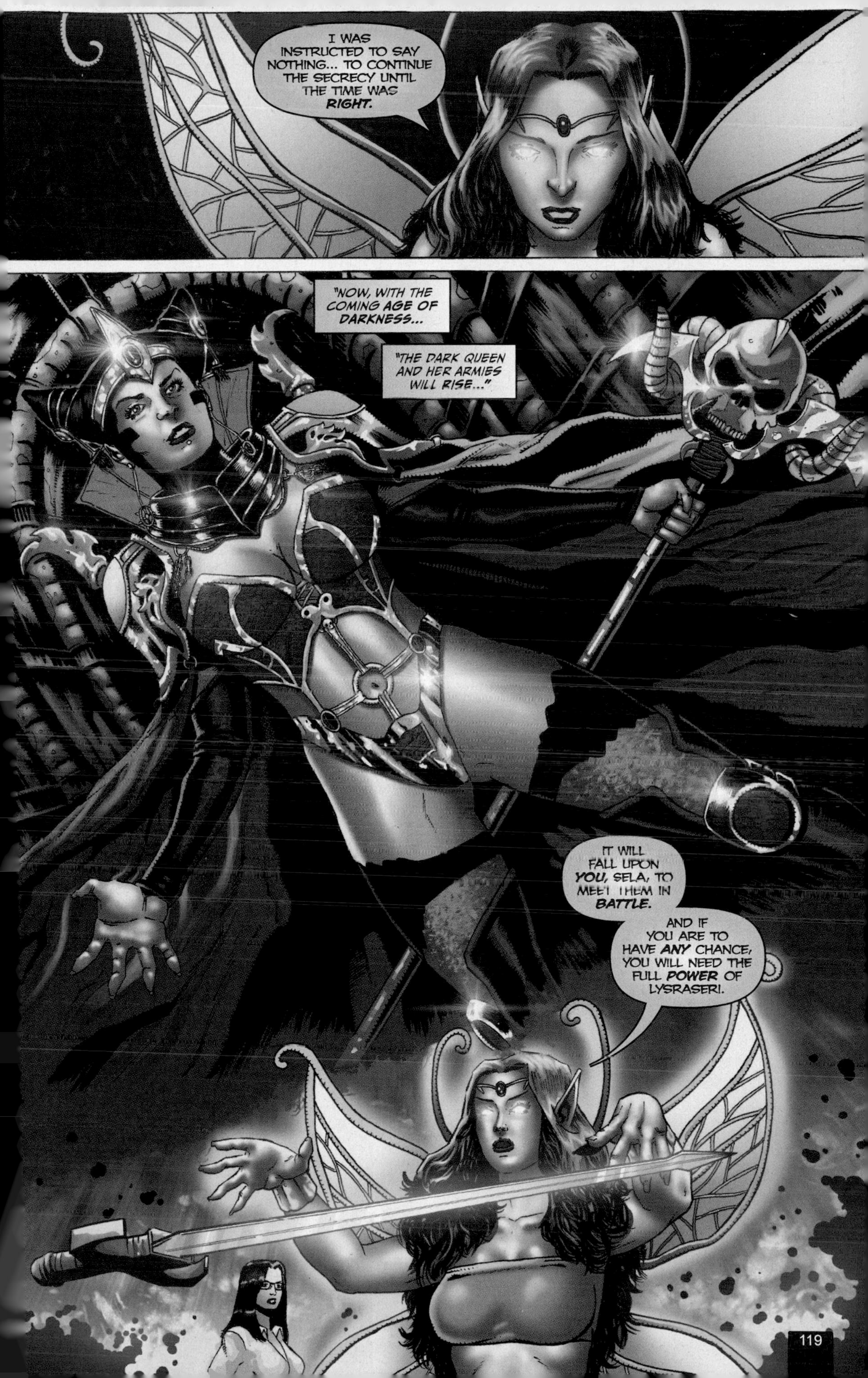
I WAS INSTRUCTED TO SAY NOTHING... TO CONTINUE THE SECRECY UNTIL THE TIME WAS RIGHT.
"NOW, WITH THE COMING AGE OF DARKNESS...
"THE DARK QUEEN AND HER ARMIES WILL RISE..."
IT WILL FALL UPON YOU, SELA, TO MEET THEM IN BATTLE.
AND IF YOU ARE TO HAVE ANY CHANCE, YOU WILL NEED THE FULL POWER OF LYSRASERI.

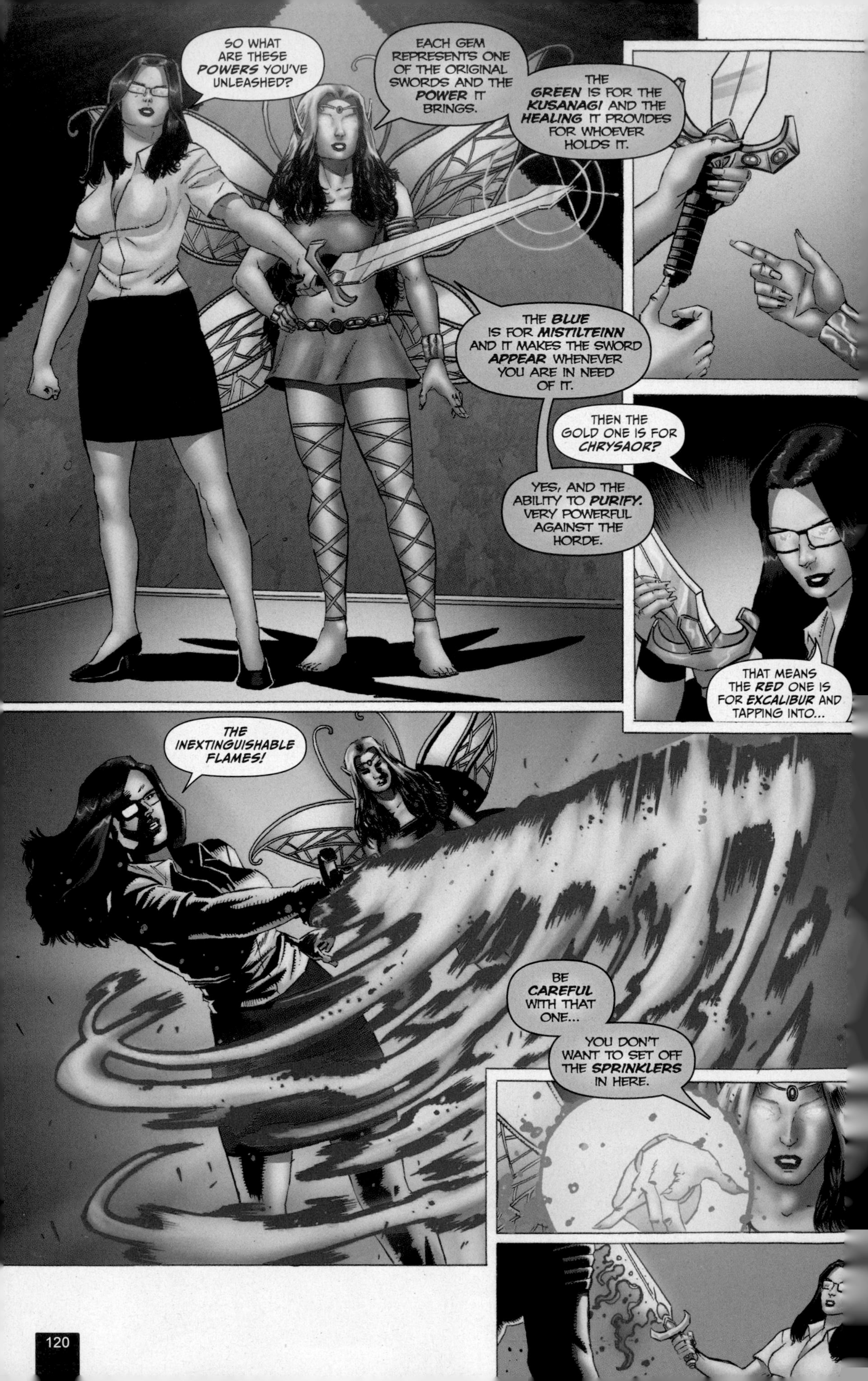
SO WHAT ARE THESE POWERS YOU'VE UNLEASHED?
EACH GEM REPRESENTS ONE OF THE ORIGINAL SWORDS AND THE POWER IT BRINGS.
THE GREEN IS FOR THE KUSANAGI AND THE HEALING IT PROVIDES FOR WHOEVER HOLDS IT.
THE BLUE IS FOR MISTILTEINN AND IT MAKES THE SWORD APPEAR WHENEVER YOU ARE IN NEED OF IT.
THEN THE GOLD ONE IS FOR CHRYSAOR?
YES, AND THE ABILITY TO PURIFY. VERY POWERFUL AGAINST THE HORDE.
THAT MEANS THE RED ONE IS FOR EXCALIBUR AND TAPPING INTO...
THE INEXTINGUISHABLE FLAMES!
BE CAREFUL WITH THAT ONE...
YOU DON'T WANT TO SET OFF THE SPRINKLERS IN HERE.

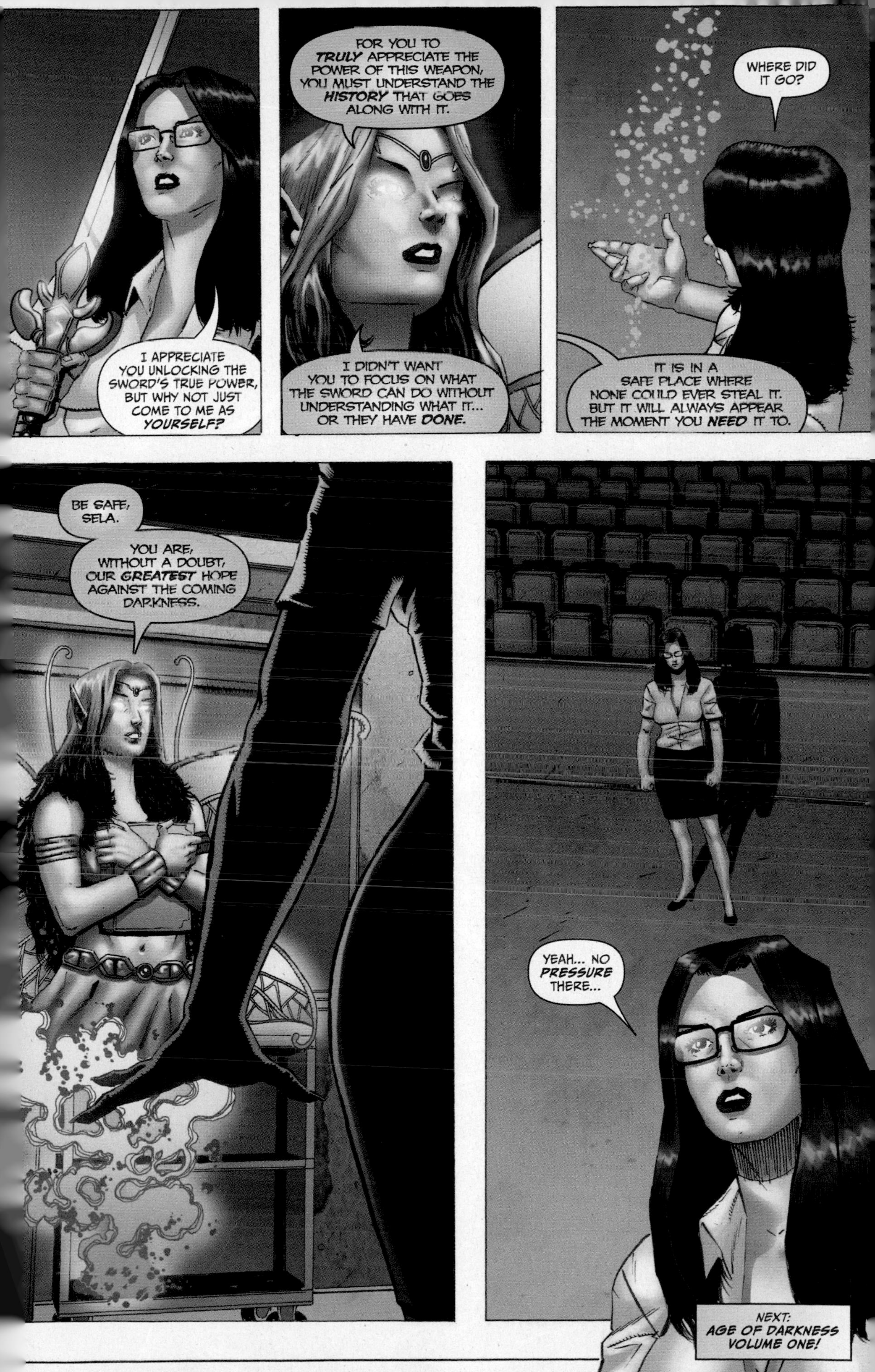
FOR YOU TO TRULY APPRECIATE THE POWER OF THIS WEAPON, YOU MUST UNDERSTAND THE HISTORY THAT GOES ALONG WITH IT.
I APPRECIATE YOU UNLOCKING THE SWORD'S TRUE POWER, BUT WHY NOT JUST COME TO ME AS YOURSELF?
I DIDN'T WANT YOU TO FOCUS ON WHAT THE SWORD CAN DO WITHOUT UNDERSTANDING WHAT IT... OR THEY HAVE DONE.
WHERE DID IT GO?
IT IS IN A SAFE PLACE WHERE NONE COULD EVER STEAL IT. BUT IT WILL ALWAYS APPEAR THE MOMENT YOU NEED IT TO.
BE SAFE, SELA.
YOU ARE, WITHOUT A DOUBT, OUR GREATEST HOPE AGAINST THE COMING DARKNESS.
YEAH... NO PRESSURE THERE...
NEXT: AGE OF DARKNESS VOLUME ONE!

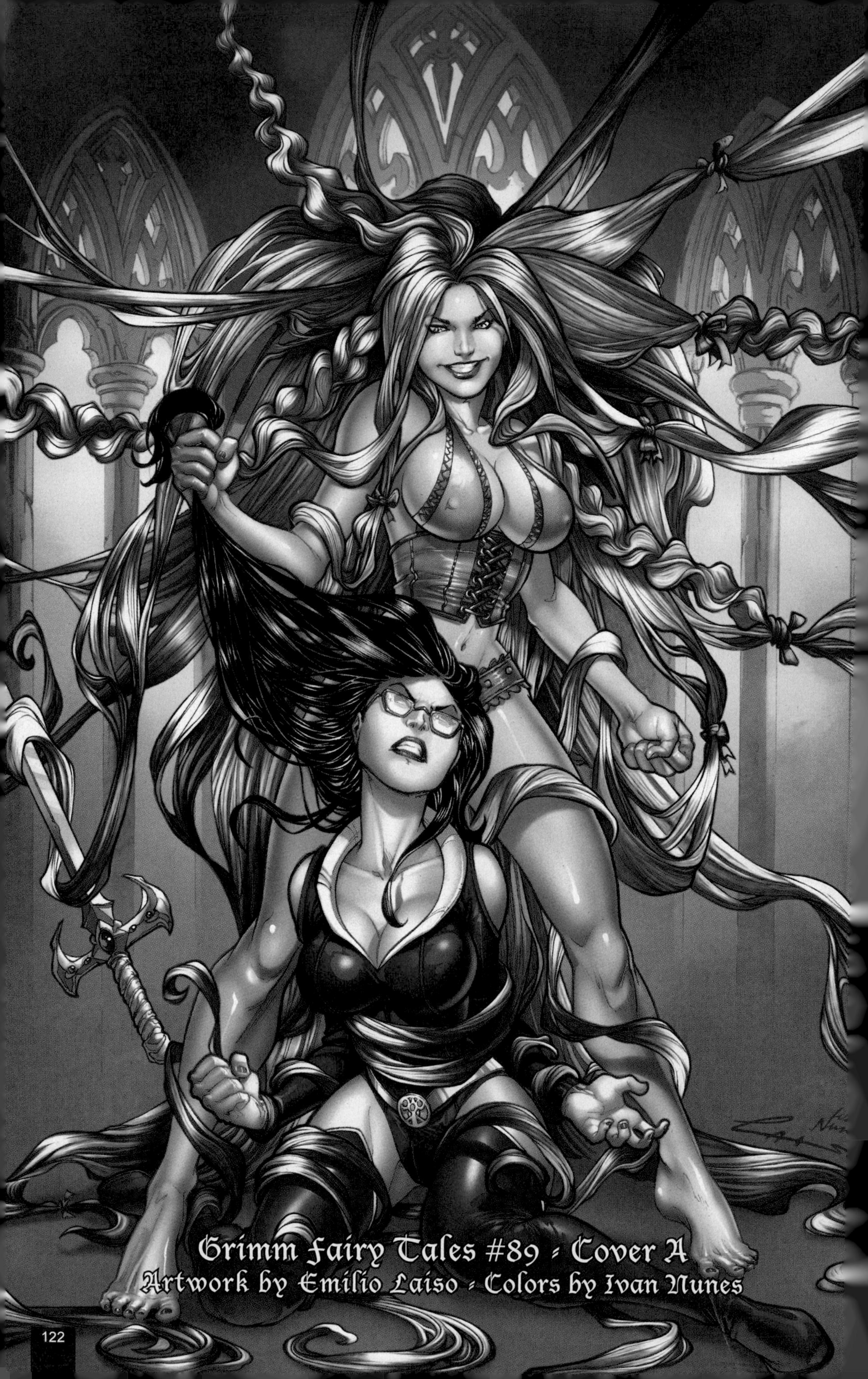

Grimm Fairy Tales #89 - Cover A
Artwork by Emilio Laiso - Colors by Ivan Nunes

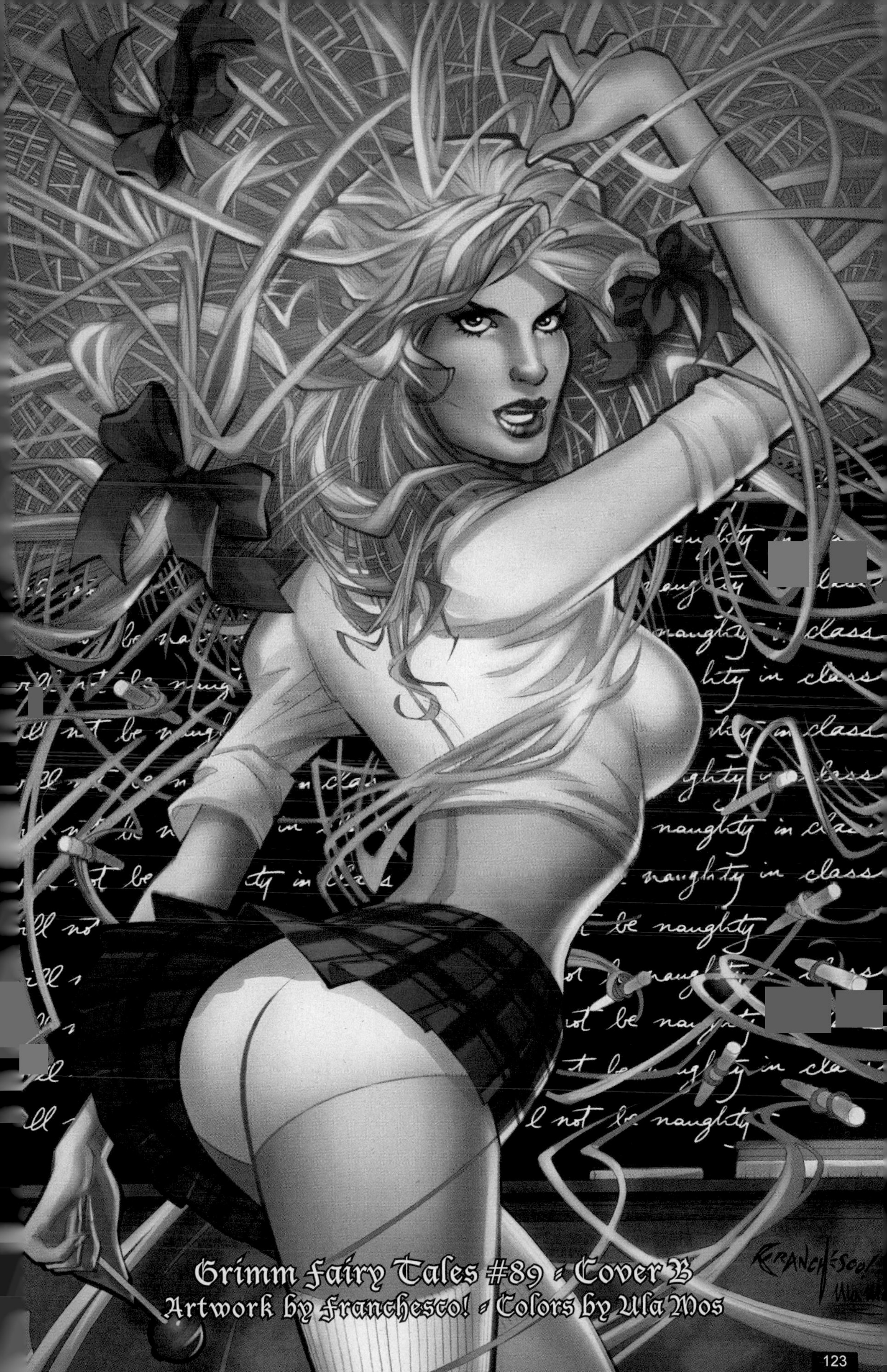

Grimm Fairy Tales #89 - Cover B
Artwork by Franchesco! - Colors by Ula Mos

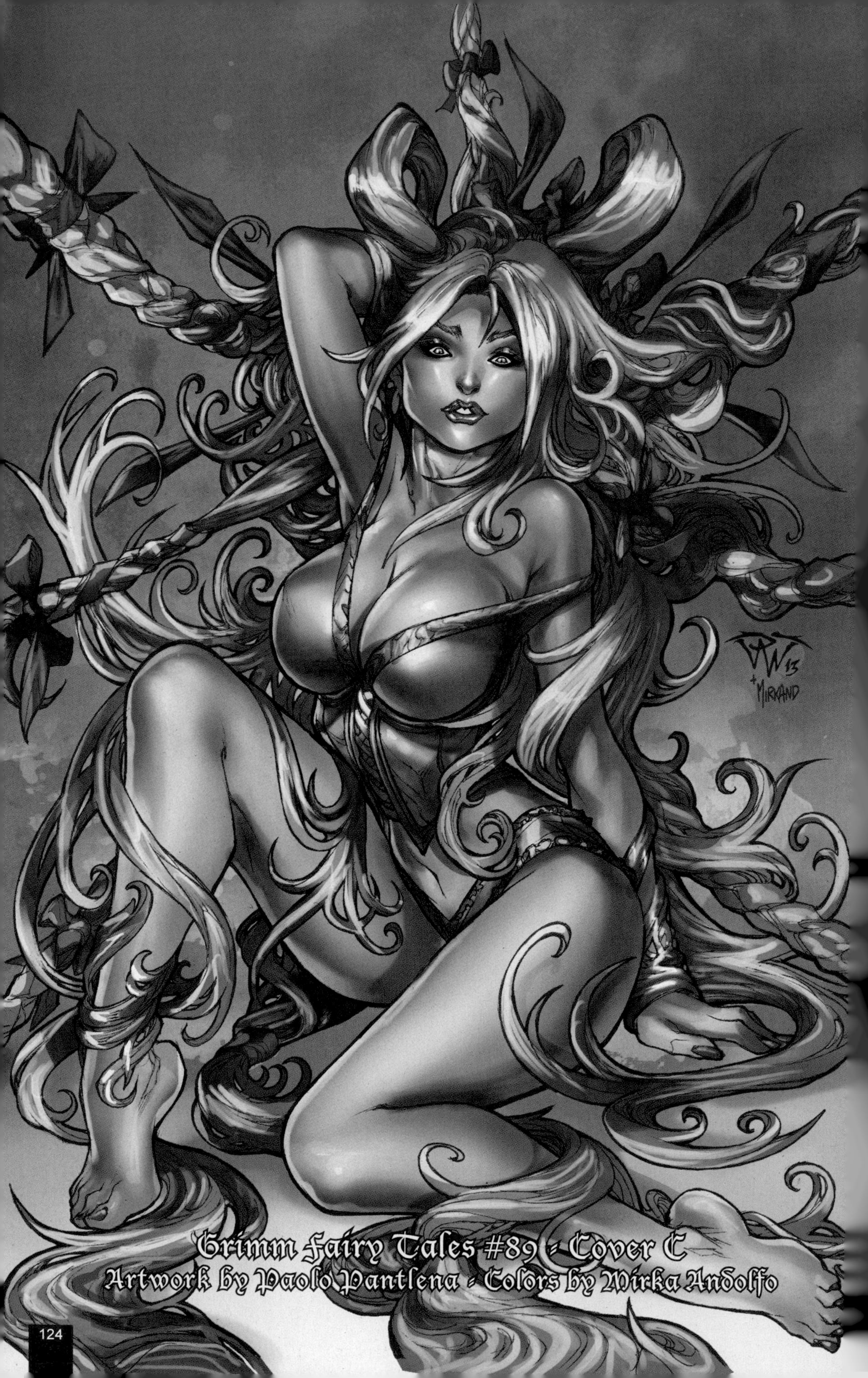

Grimm Fairy Tales #89 - Cover C
Artwork by Paolo Pantlena - Colors by Mirka Andolfo

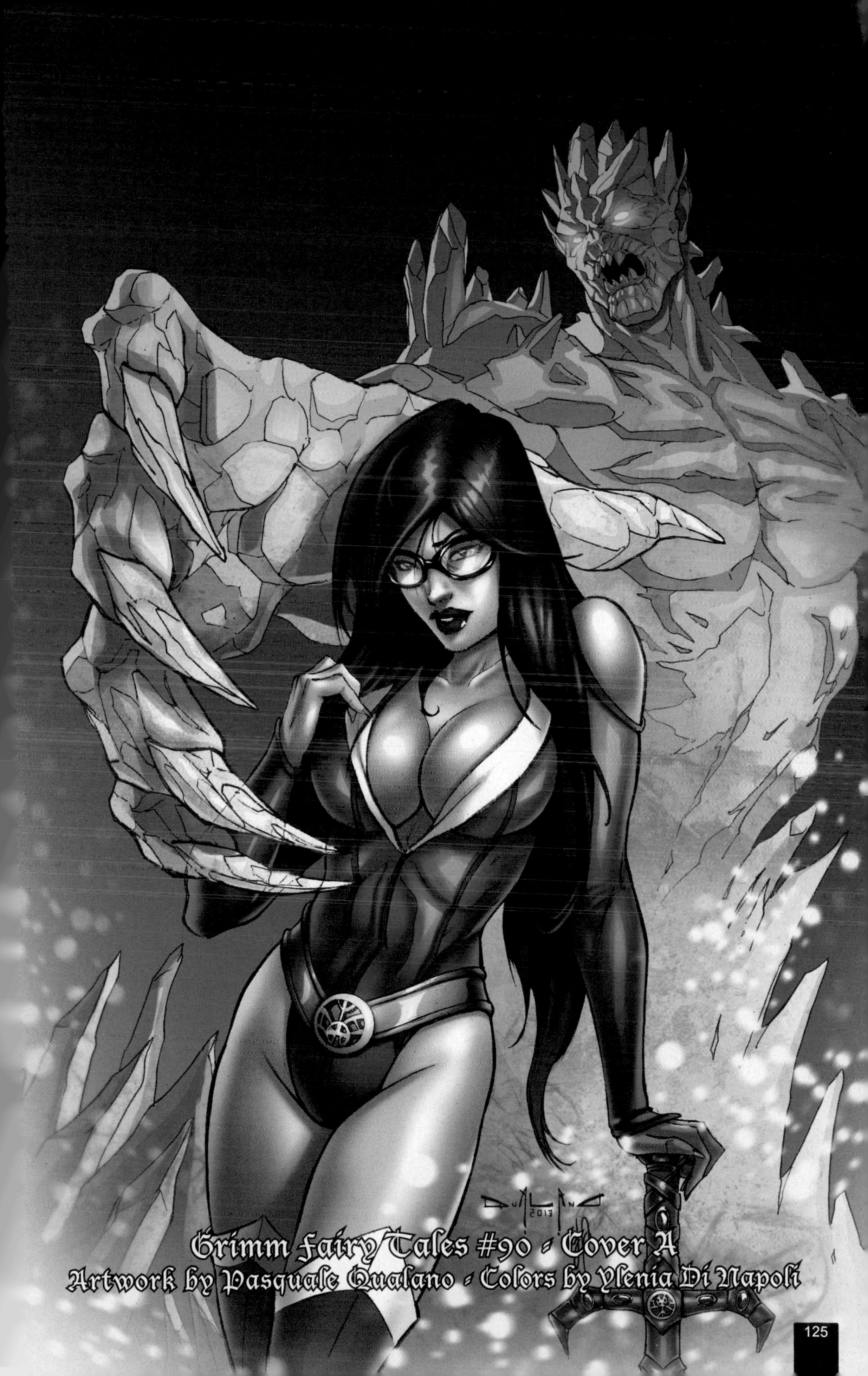

Grimm Fairy Tales #90 - Cover A
Artwork by Pasquale Qualano - Colors by Ylenia Di Napoli

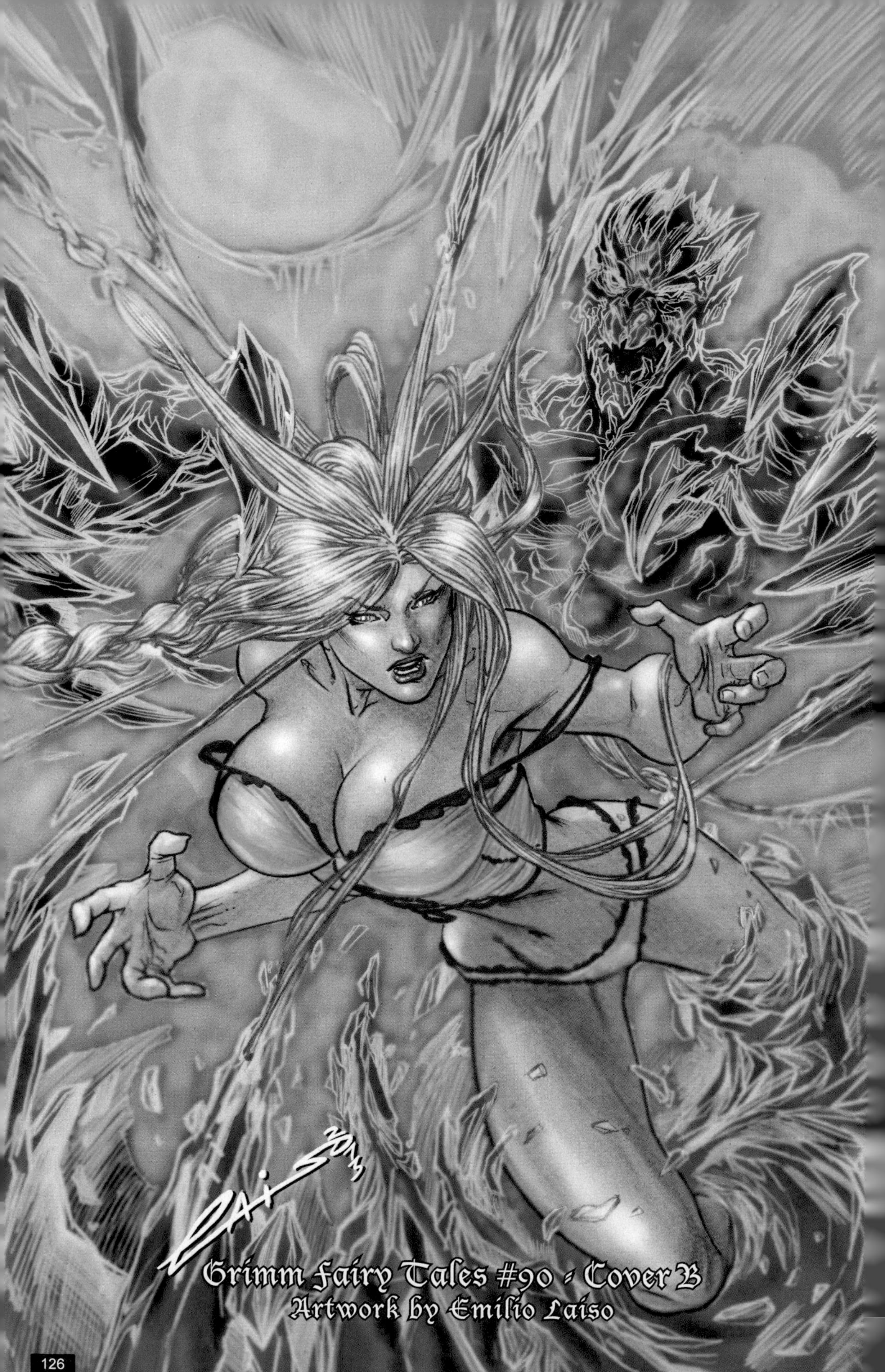

Grimm Fairy Tales #90 - Cover B
Artwork by Emilio Laiso

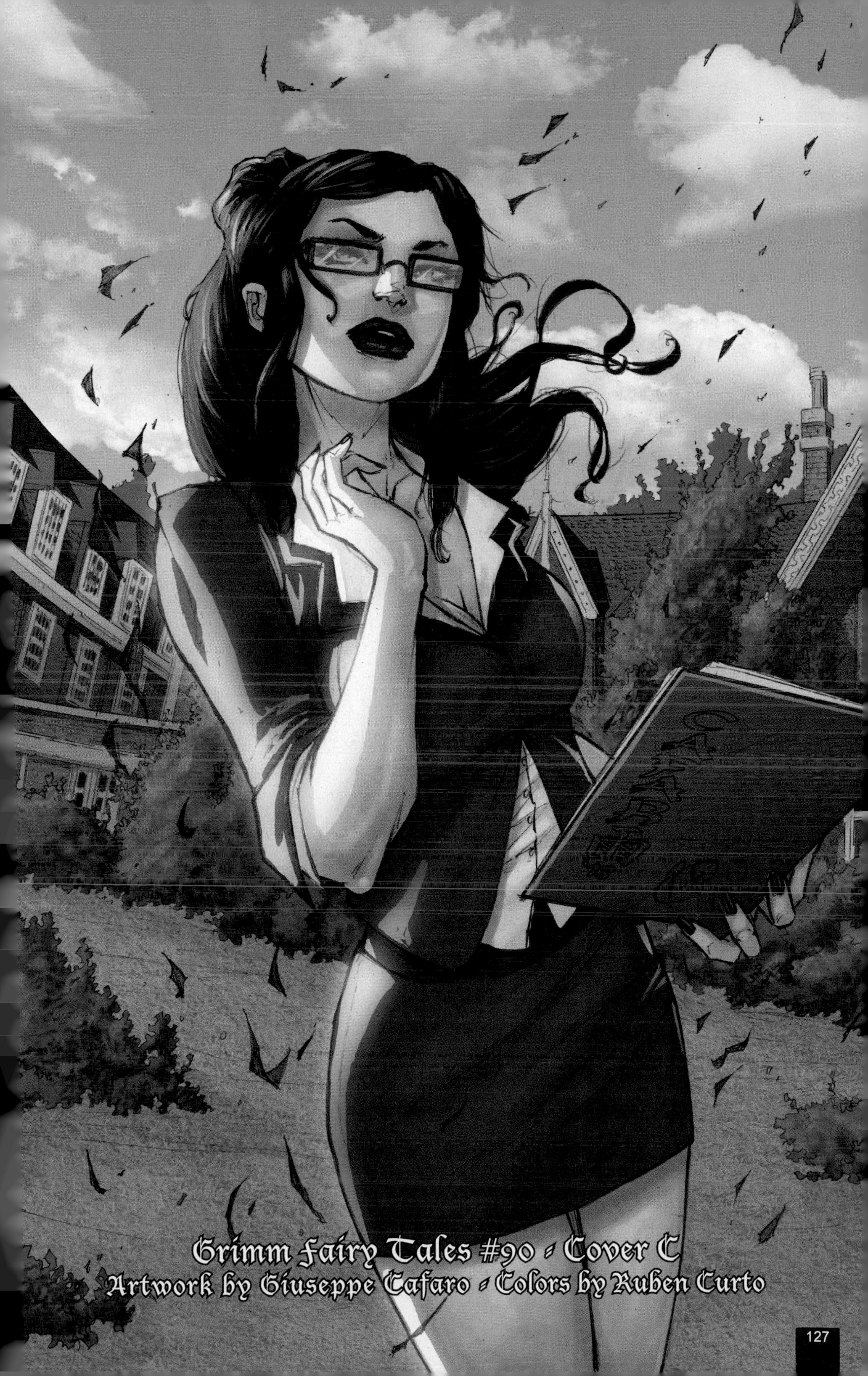

Grimm Fairy Tales #90 - Cover C
Artwork by Giuseppe Cafaro - Colors by Ruben Curto

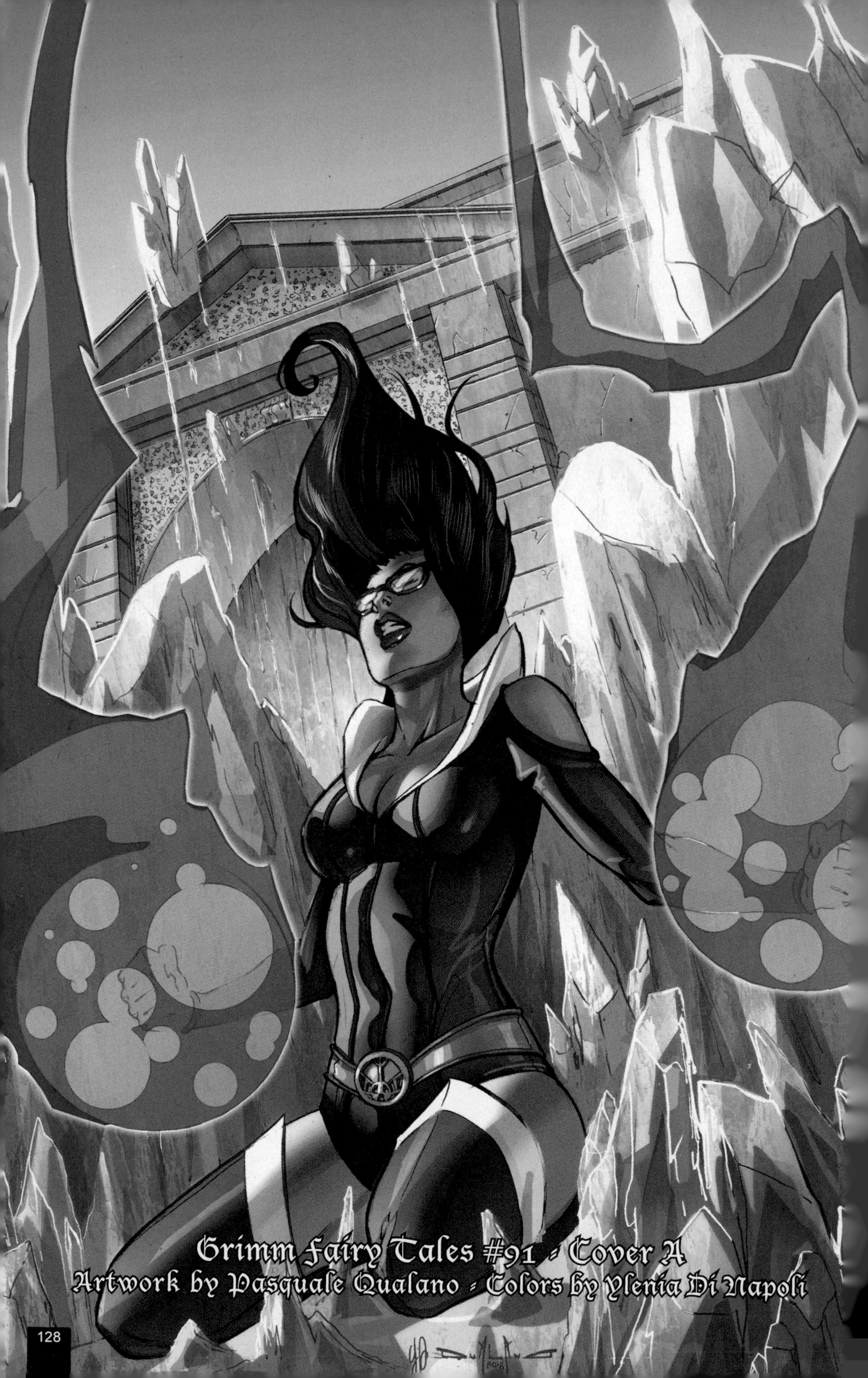

Grimm Fairy Tales #91 - Cover A
Artwork by Pasquale Qualano - Colors by Ylenia Di Napoli

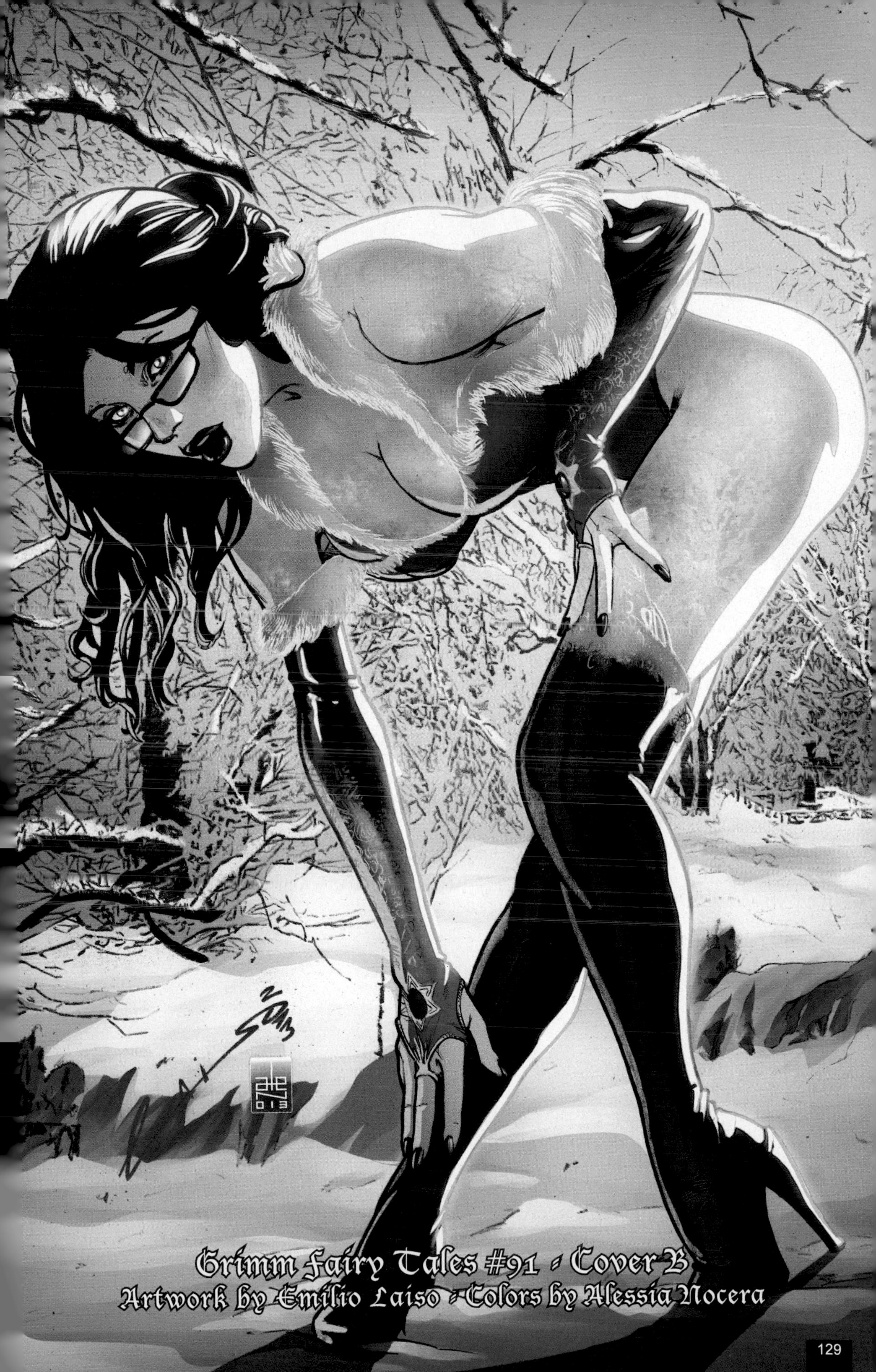

Grimm Fairy Tales #91 - Cover B
Artwork by Emilio Laiso - Colors by Alessia Nocera

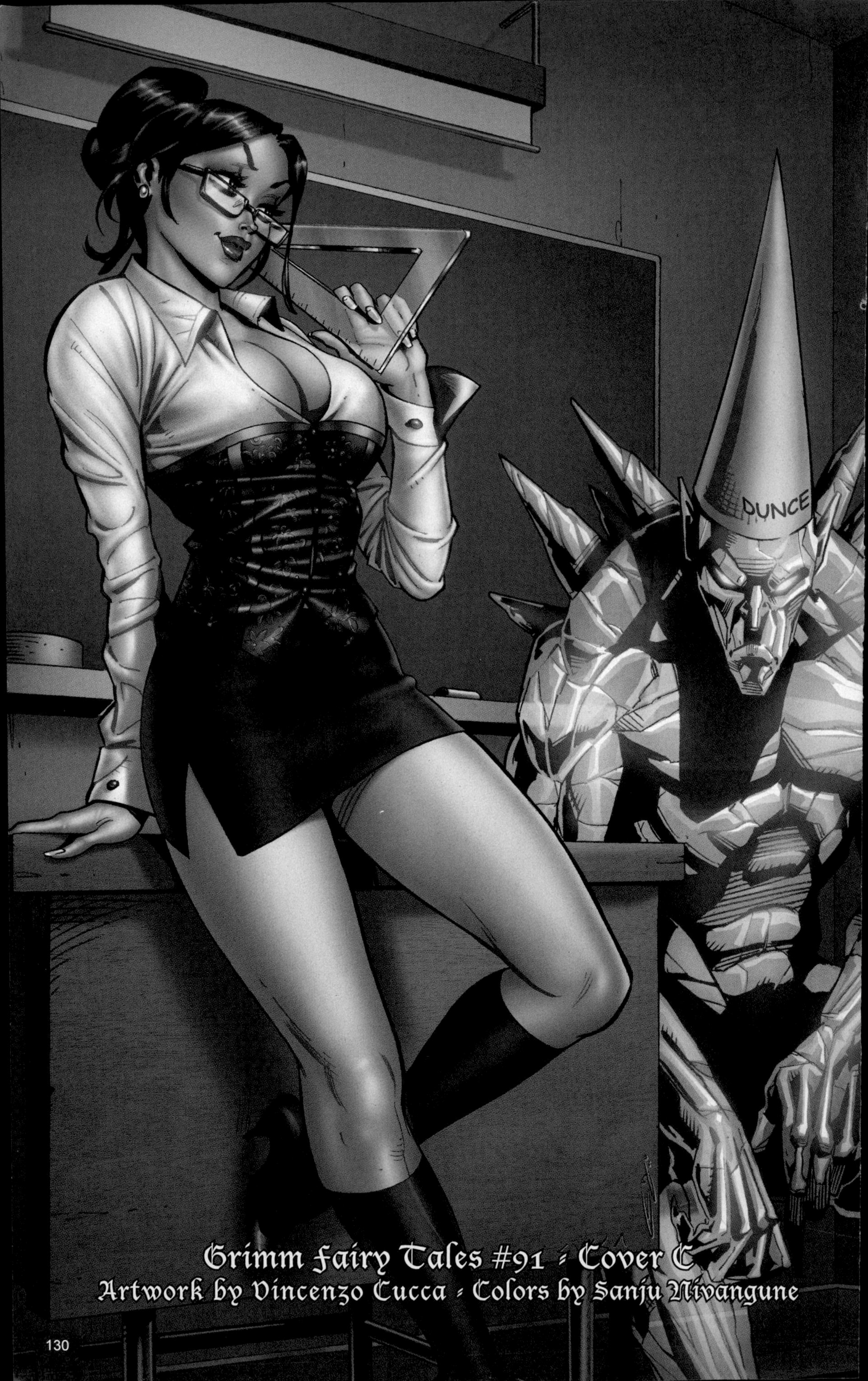
DUNCE

Grimm Fairy Tales #91 - Cover C
Artwork by Vincenzo Cucca - Colors by Sanju Nivangune

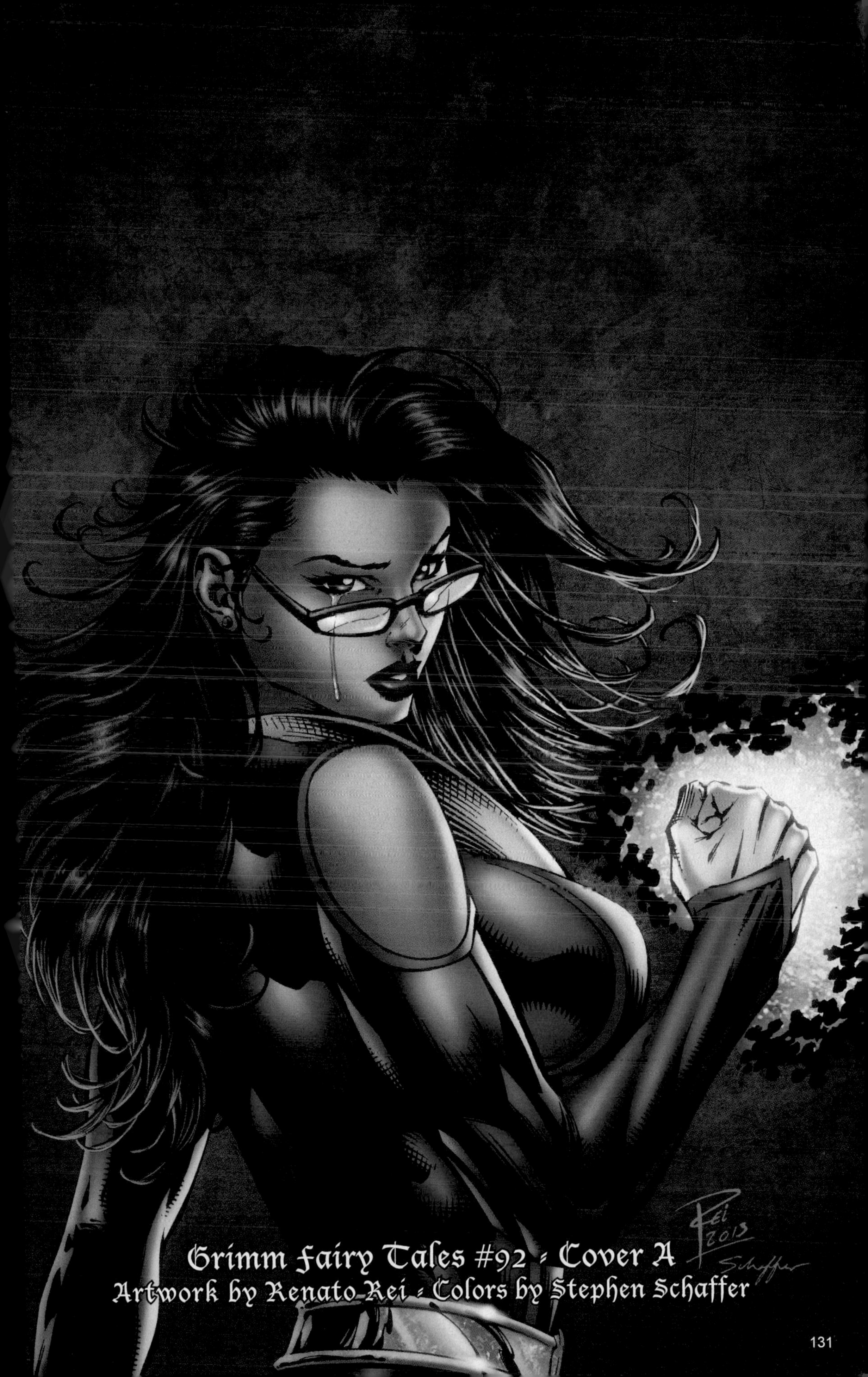
Rei
2013
Schaffer

Grimm Fairy Tales #92 - Cover A
Artwork by Renato Rei - Colors by Stephen Schaffer

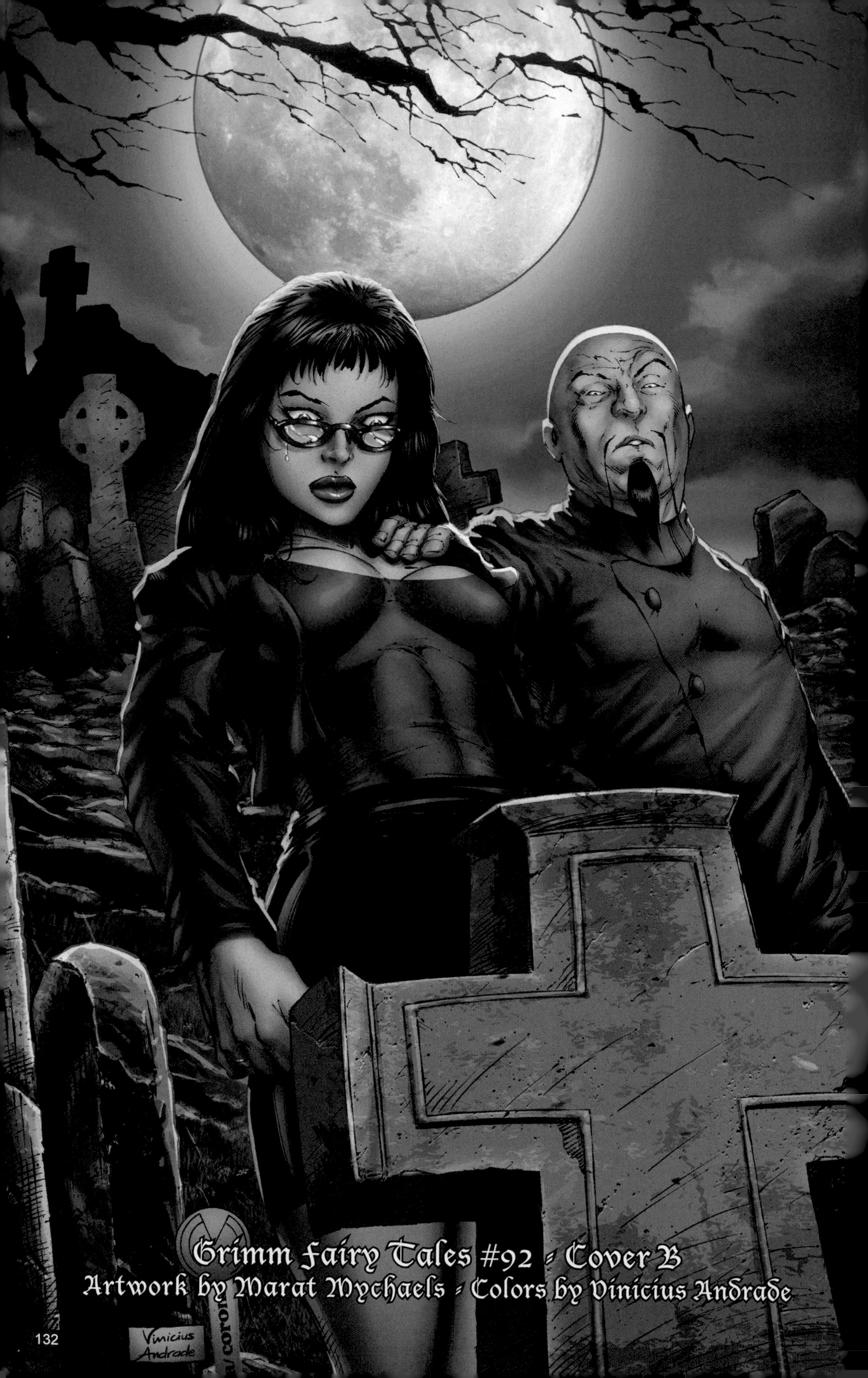
Vinicius Andrade

Grimm Fairy Tales #92 - Cover B
Artwork by Marat Mychaels - Colors by Vinicius Andrade

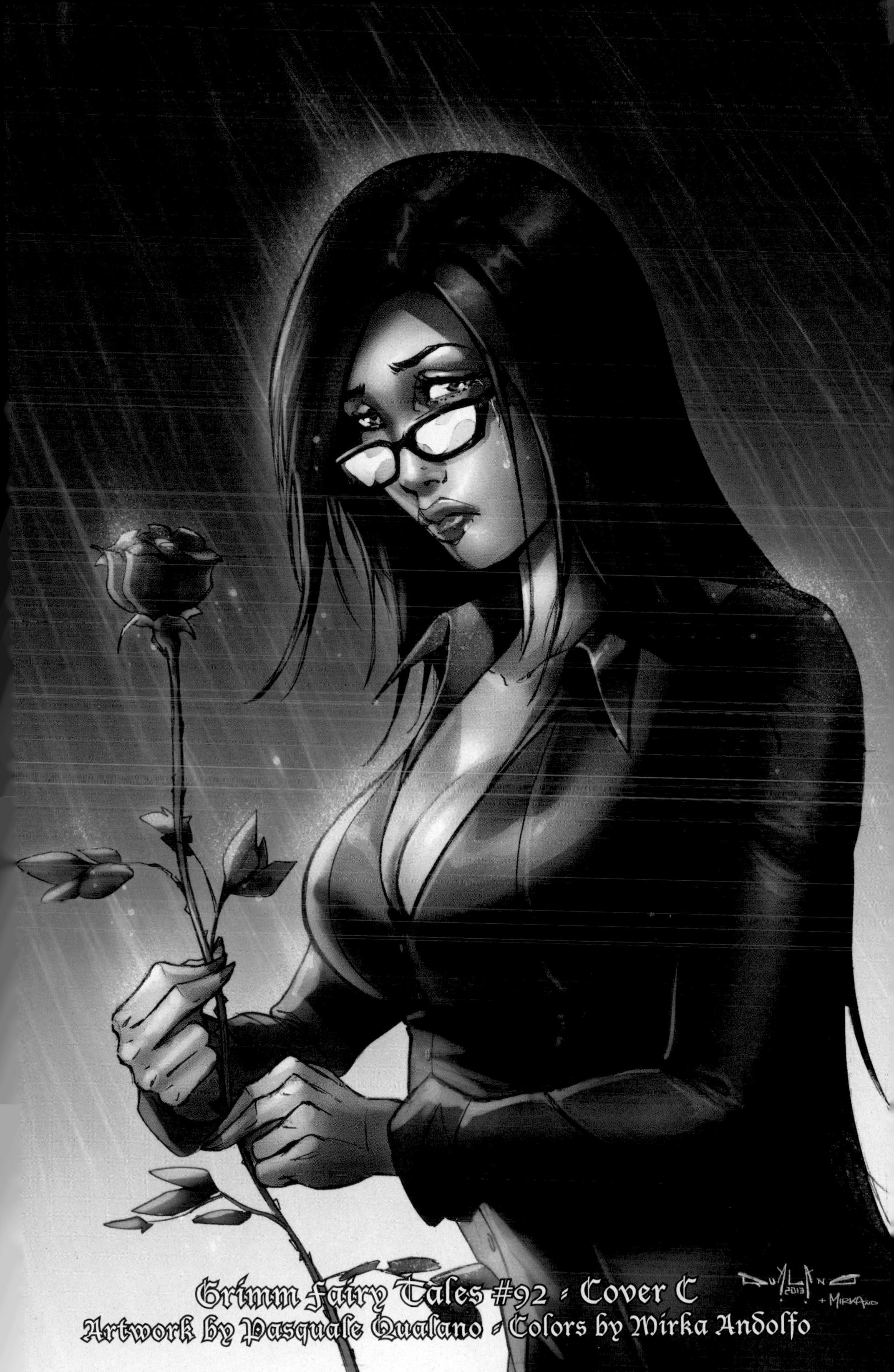

Grimm Fairy Tales #92 - Cover C
Artwork by Pasquale Qualano - Colors by Mirka Andolfo

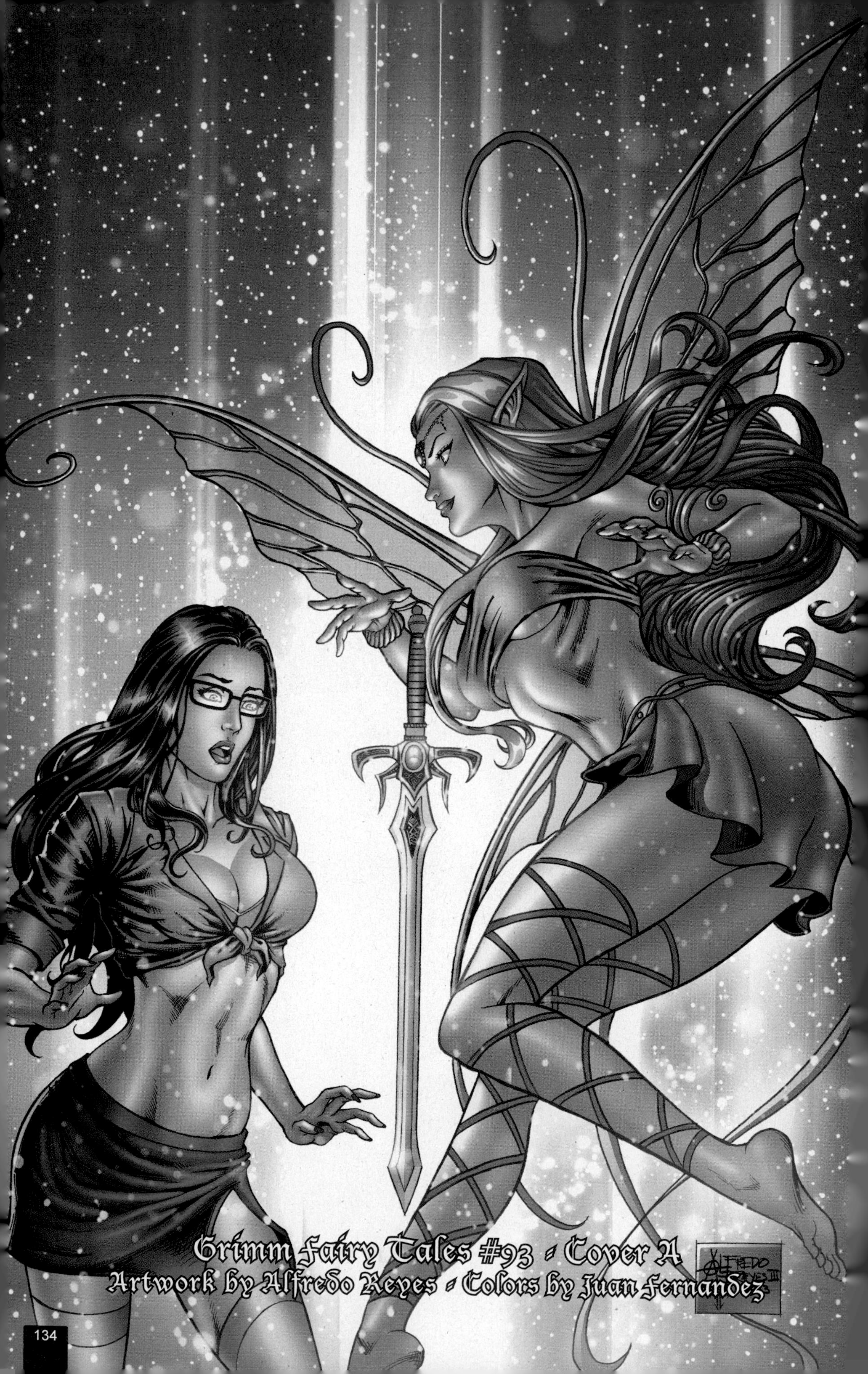
ALFREDO REYES III

Grimm Fairy Tales #93 - Cover A
Artwork by Alfredo Reyes - Colors by Juan Fernandez

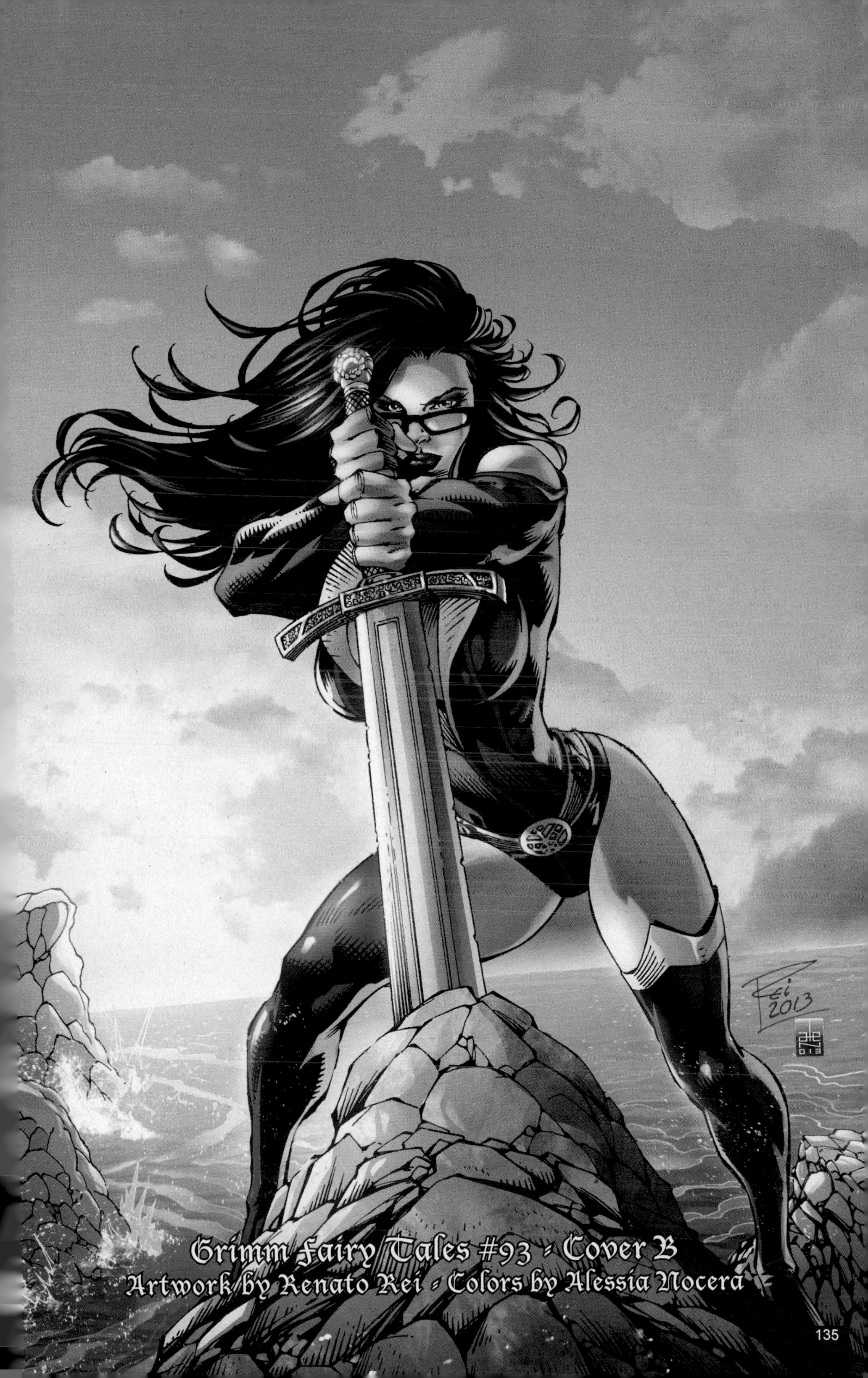
Rei
2013

Grimm Fairy Tales #93 - Cover B
Artwork by Renato Rei - Colors by Alessia Nocera

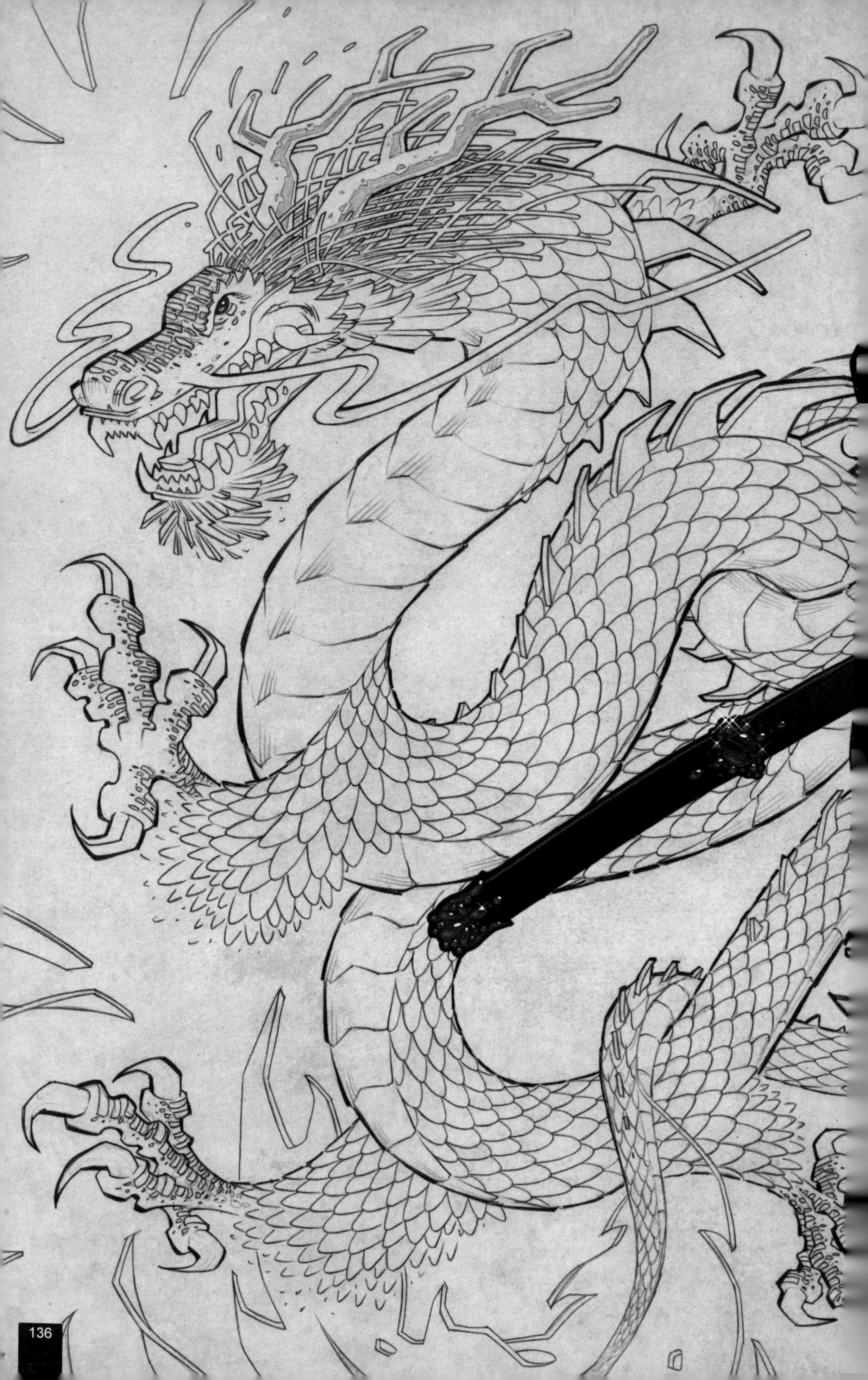

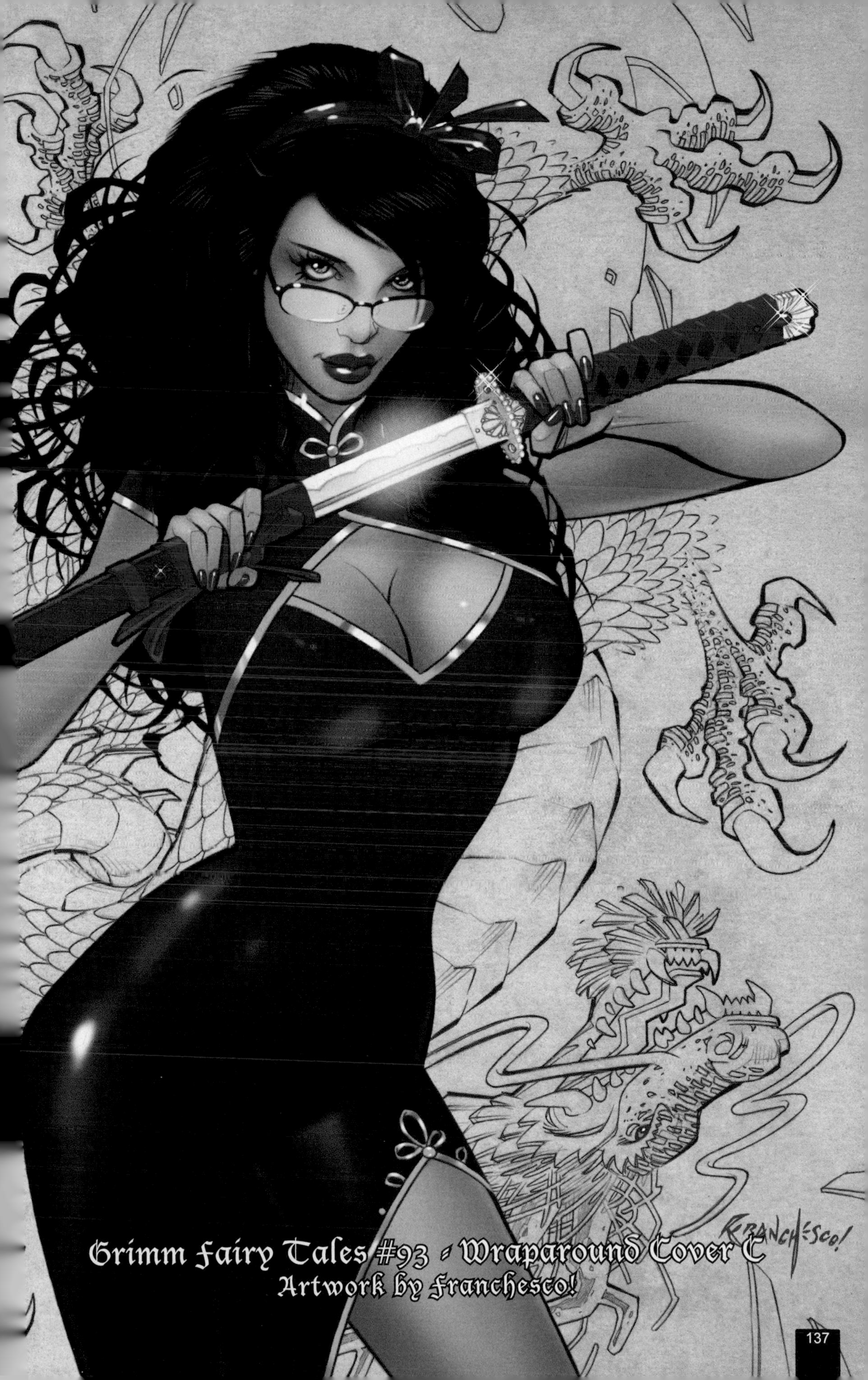
FRANCHESCO!

Grimm Fairy Tales #93 - Wraparound Cover C
Artwork by Franchesco!

An exclusive preview of...

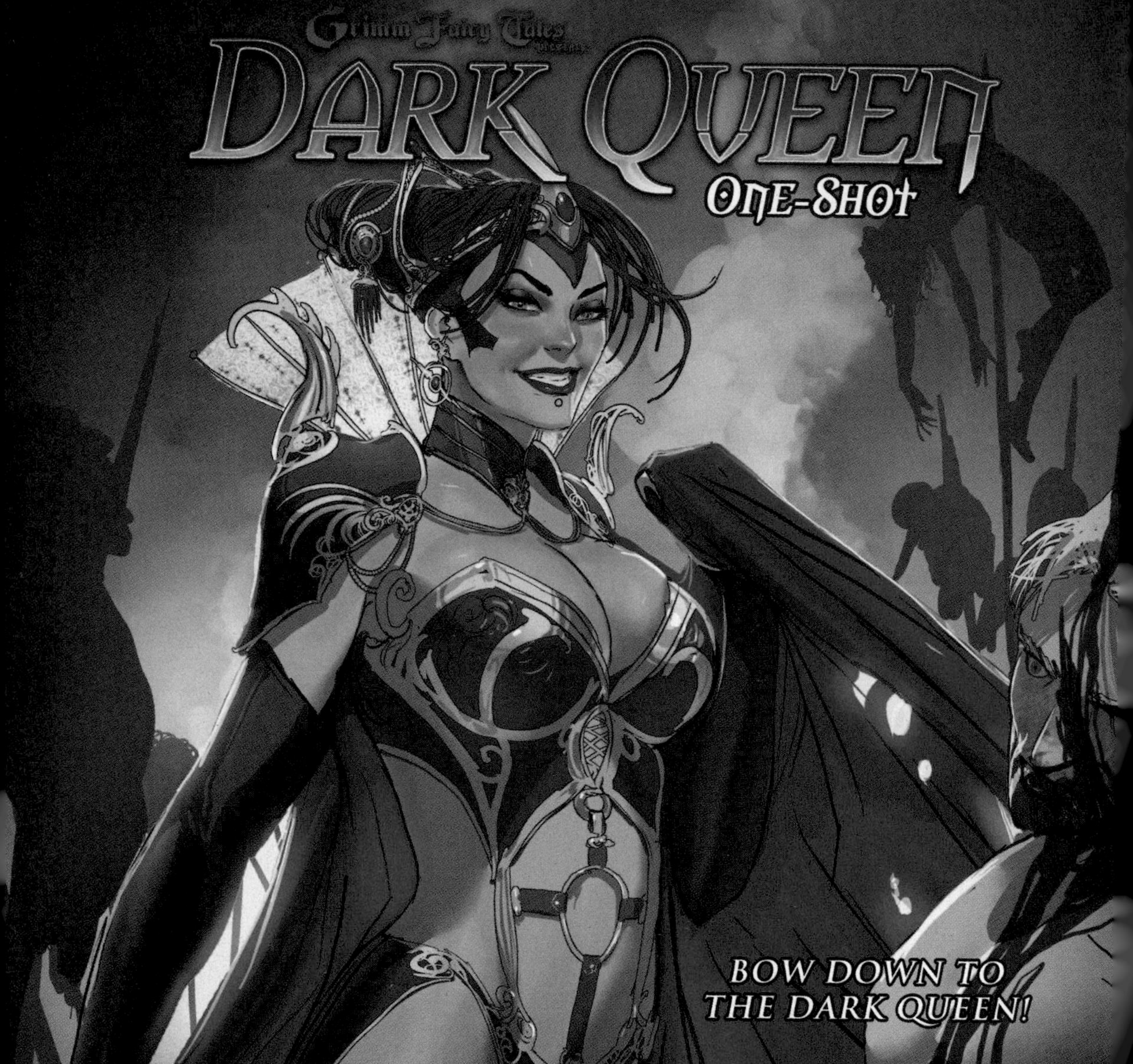
Grimm Fairy Tales
DARK QUEEN
ONE-SHOT
BOW DOWN TO THE DARK QUEEN!

Ever since her return from death, the Dark Queen has been hell-bent on restoring her evil regime, the Dark Horde, to its former glory. Armed with modern weapons and a sinister vision, the Dark Queen leads her followers against the Realm Knights as she takes the first steps toward plunging all of the realms into the Age of Darkness.

Cover art by Stjepan Sejic

Grimm Fairy Tales created by Joe Brusha and Ralph Tedesco

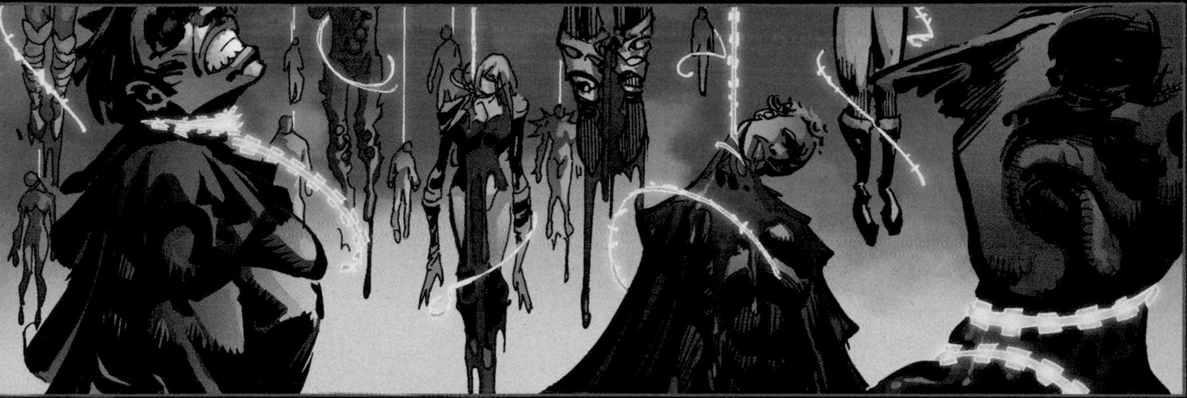

Grimm Fairy Tales presents

DARK QUEEN

One-Shot

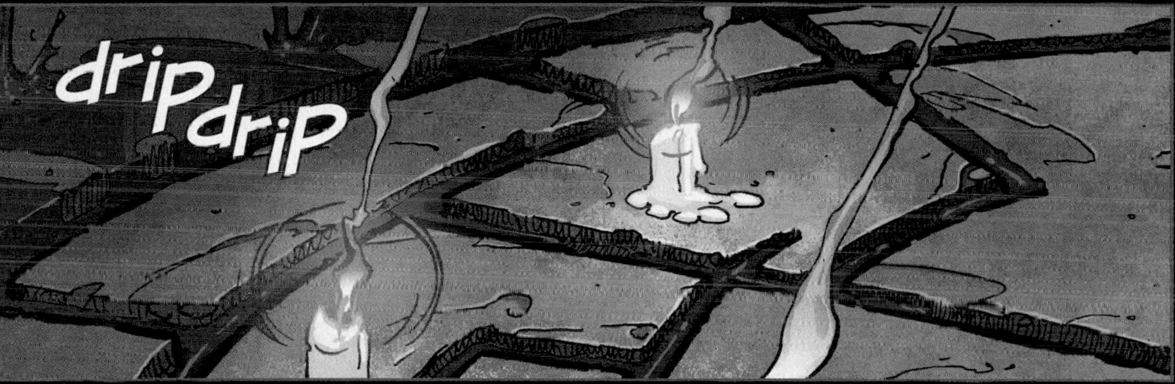
drip drip

Story	Writer	Pencils	Inks
Joe Brusha	Eric M. Esquivel	Lalit Kumar Sharma	Jagdish Kumar

Colors	Letters	Editor
Pradeep Sherawat	Jim Campbell	Pat Shand

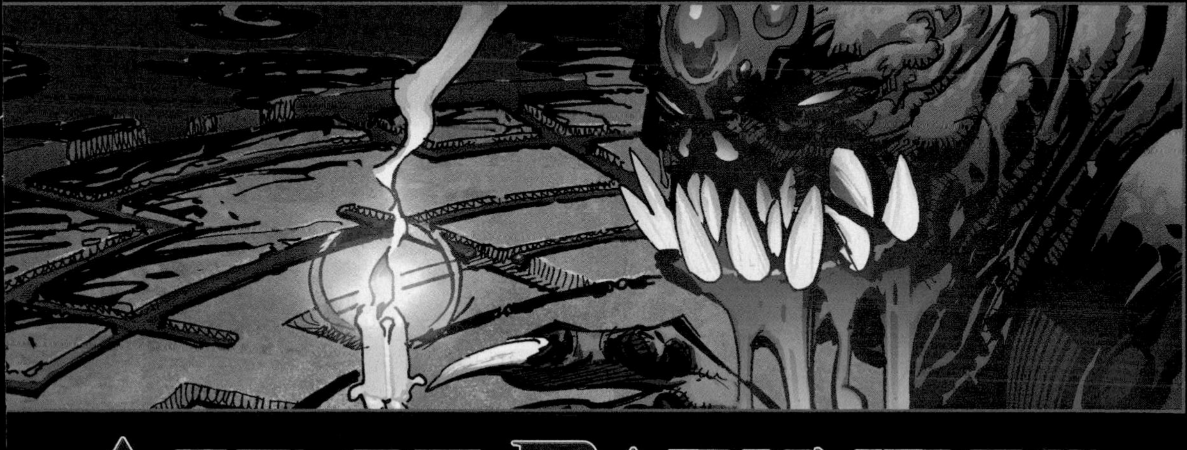

Age of Darkness

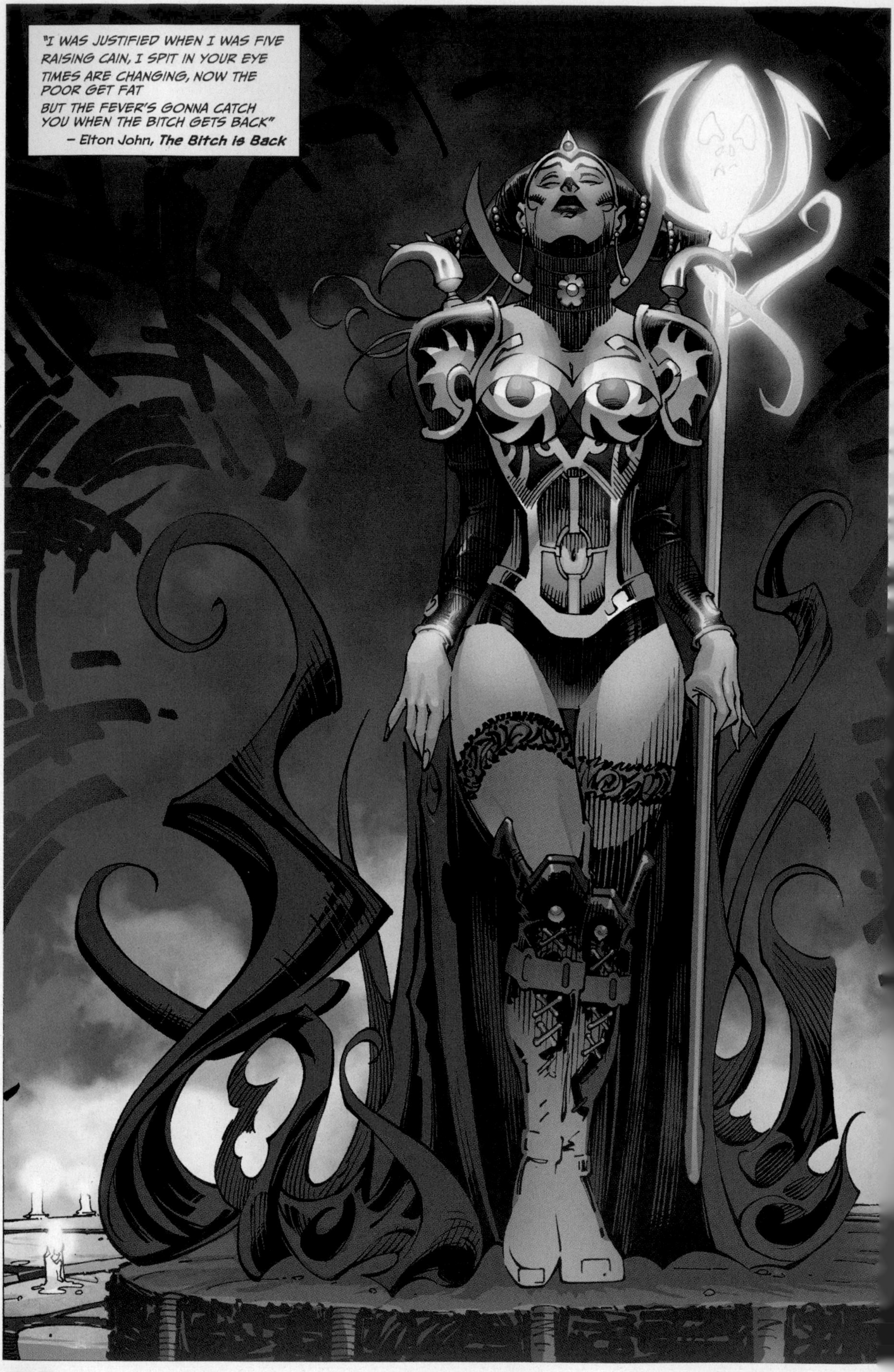
"I WAS JUSTIFIED WHEN I WAS FIVE
RAISING CAIN, I SPIT IN YOUR EYE
TIMES ARE CHANGING, NOW THE
POOR GET FAT
BUT THE FEVER'S GONNA CATCH
YOU WHEN THE BITCH GETS BACK"
– Elton John, The Bitch is Back

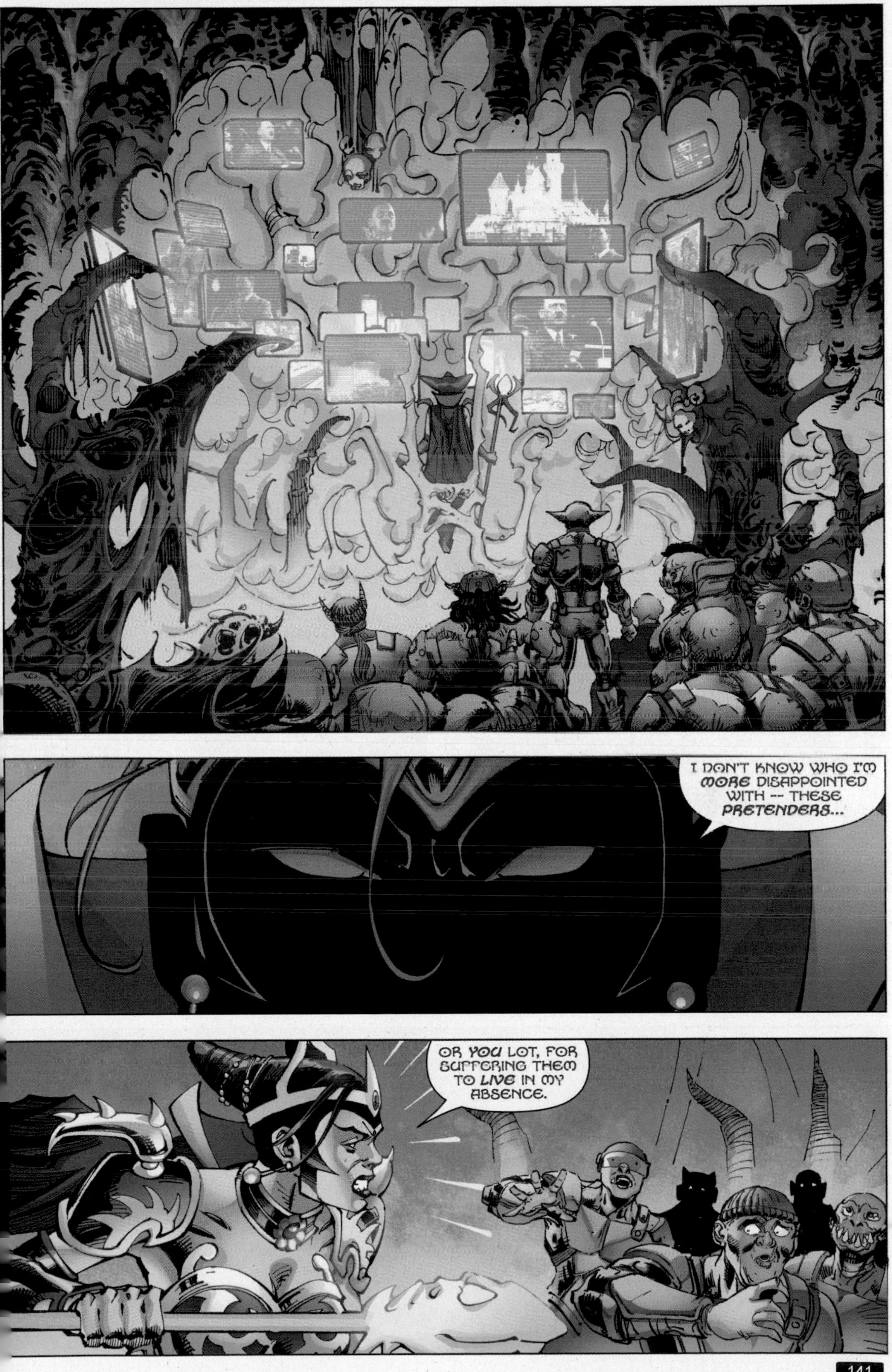
I DON'T KNOW WHO I'M MORE DISAPPOINTED WITH -- THESE PRETENDERS...
OR YOU LOT, FOR SUFFERING THEM TO LIVE IN MY ABSENCE.

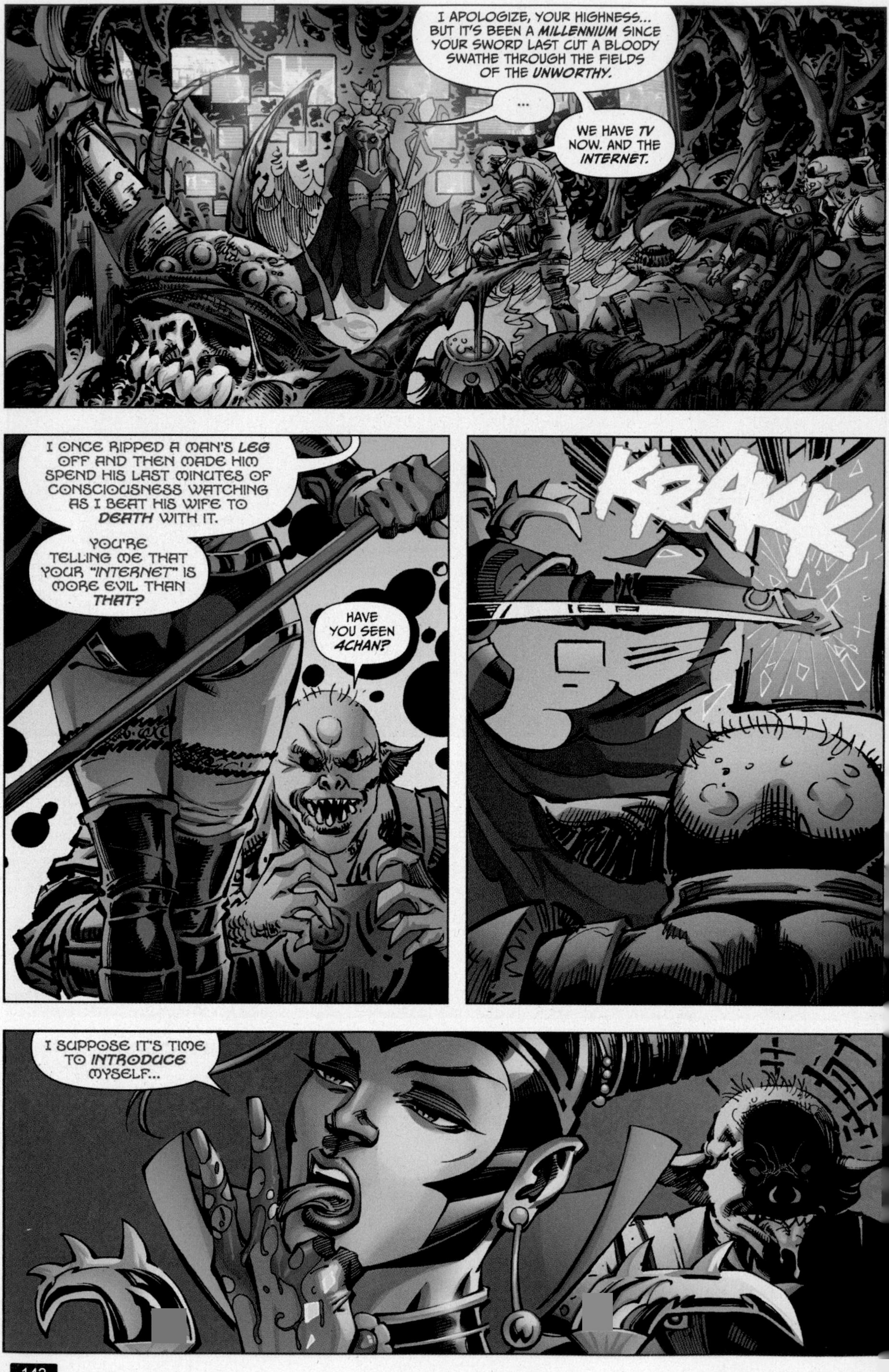
I APOLOGIZE, YOUR HIGHNESS... BUT IT'S BEEN A MILLENNIUM SINCE YOUR SWORD LAST CUT A BLOODY SWATHE THROUGH THE FIELDS OF THE UNWORTHY.
...
WE HAVE TV NOW. AND THE INTERNET.
I ONCE RIPPED A MAN'S LEG OFF AND THEN MADE HIM SPEND HIS LAST MINUTES OF CONSCIOUSNESS WATCHING AS I BEAT HIS WIFE TO DEATH WITH IT.
YOU'RE TELLING ME THAT YOUR "INTERNET" IS MORE EVIL THAN THAT?
HAVE YOU SEEN 4CHAN?
KRAKK
I SUPPOSE IT'S TIME TO INTRODUCE MYSELF...

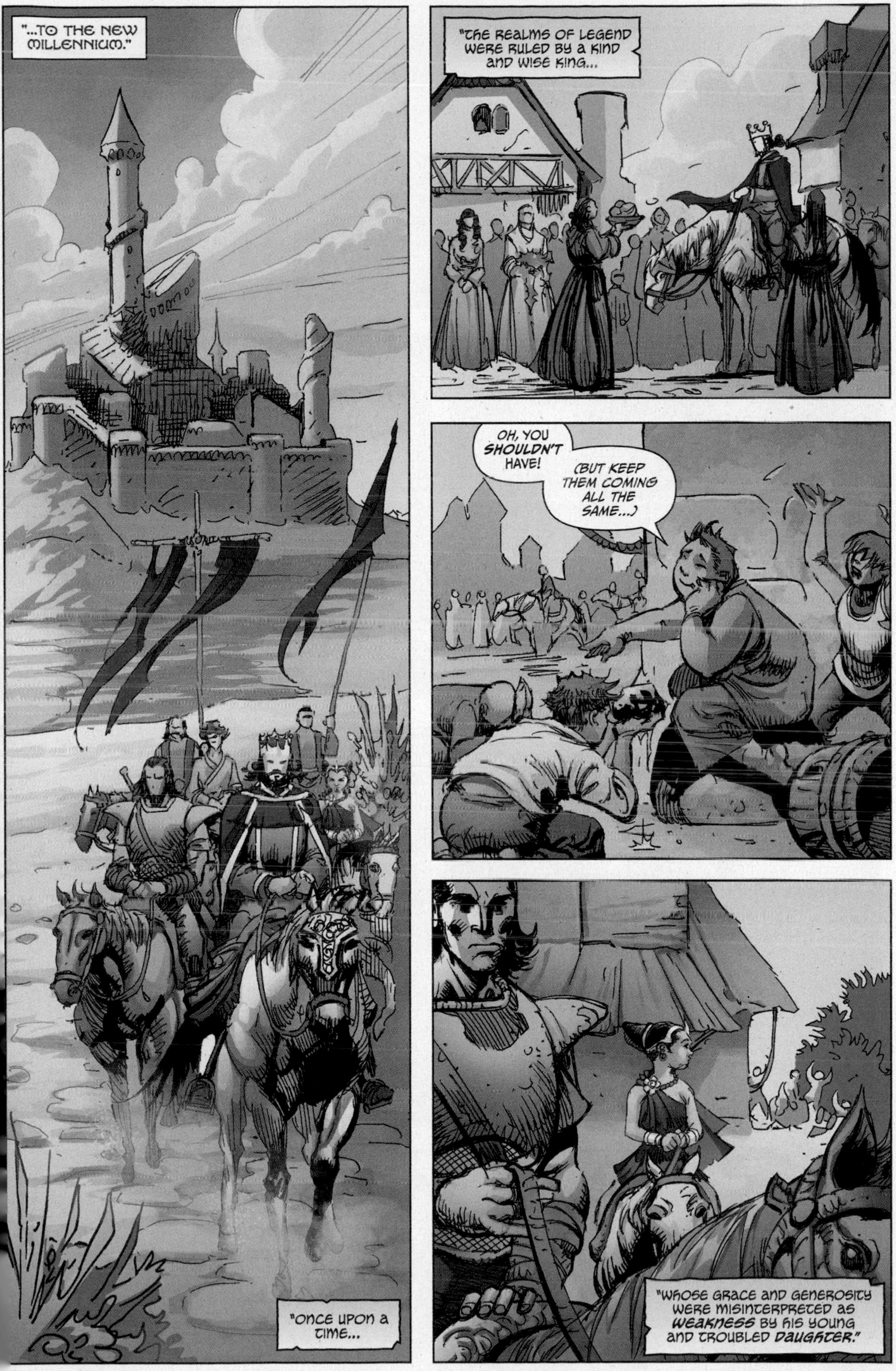
"...TO THE NEW MILLENNIUM."
"ONCE UPON A TIME...
"THE REALMS OF LEGEND WERE RULED BY A KIND AND WISE KING...
OH, YOU SHOULDN'T HAVE!
(BUT KEEP THEM COMING ALL THE SAME...)
"WHOSE GRACE AND GENEROSITY WERE MISINTERPRETED AS WEAKNESS BY HIS YOUNG AND TROUBLED DAUGHTER."

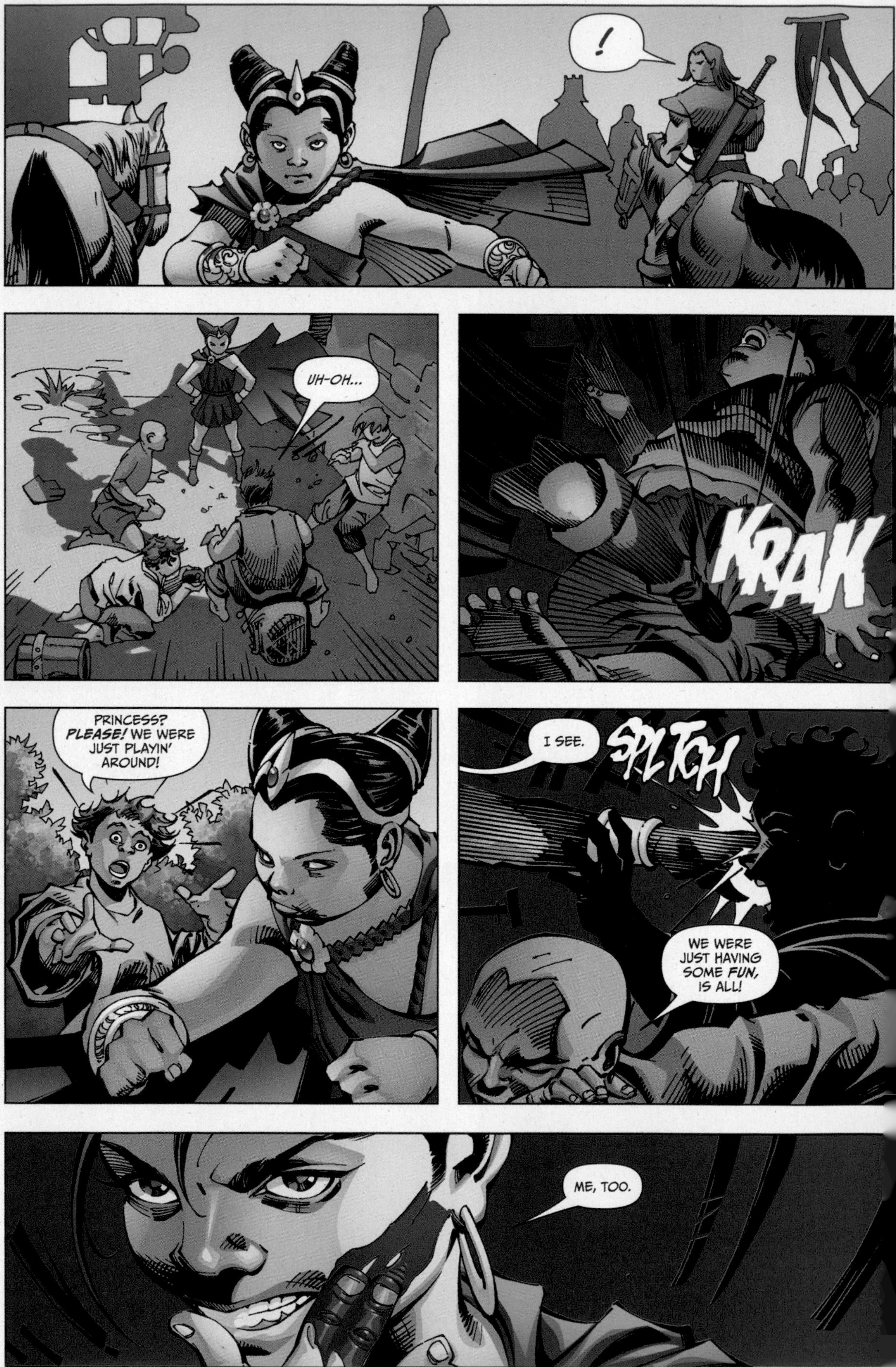
!
UH-OH...
KRAK
PRINCESS? PLEASE! WE WERE JUST PLAYIN' AROUND!
I SEE.
SPLTCH
WE WERE JUST HAVING SOME FUN, IS ALL!
ME, TOO.

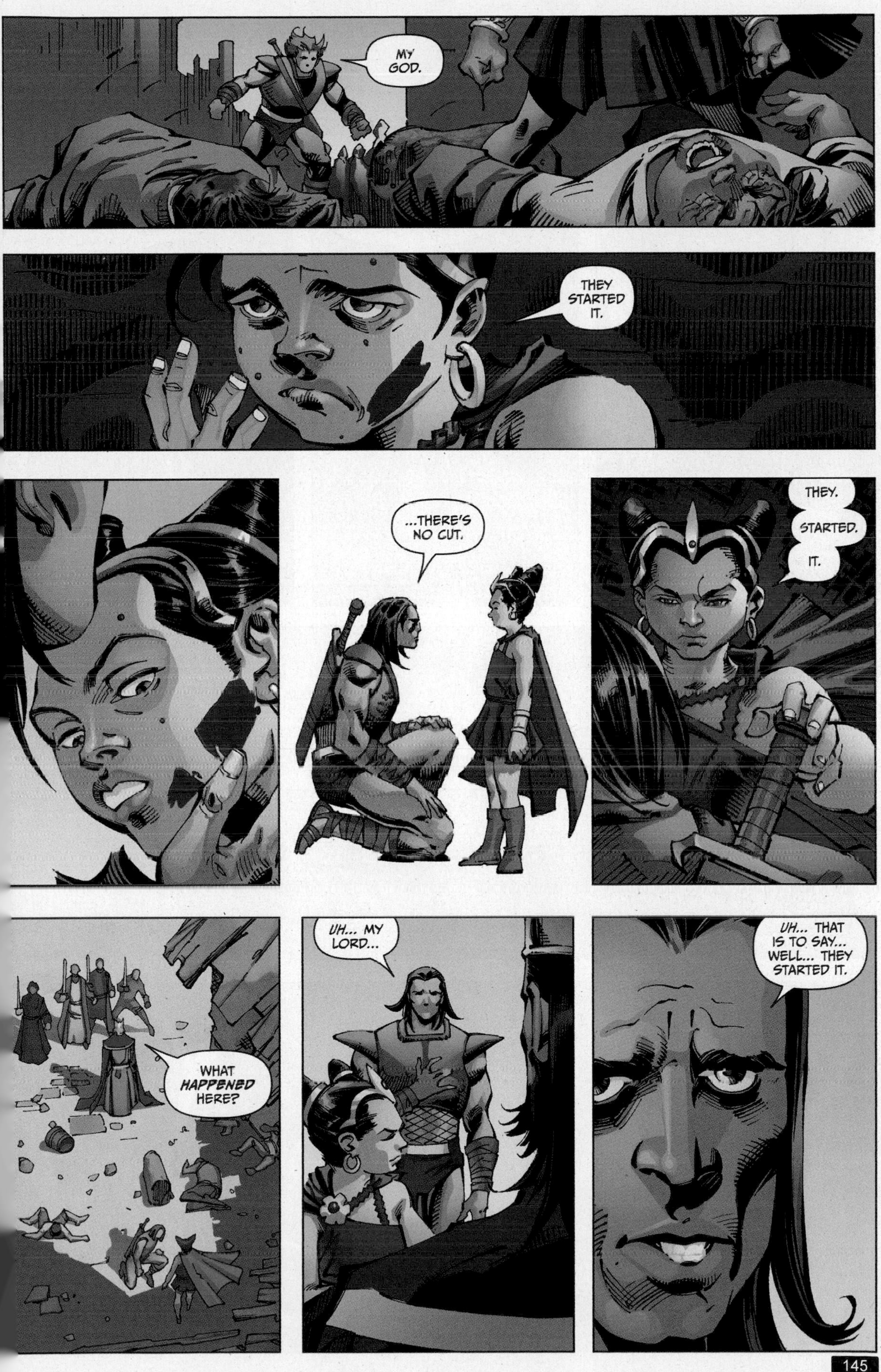
MY GOD.
THEY STARTED IT.
...THERE'S NO CUT.
THEY.
STARTED.
IT.
WHAT *HAPPENED* HERE?
UH... MY LORD...
UH... THAT IS TO SAY... WELL... THEY STARTED IT.

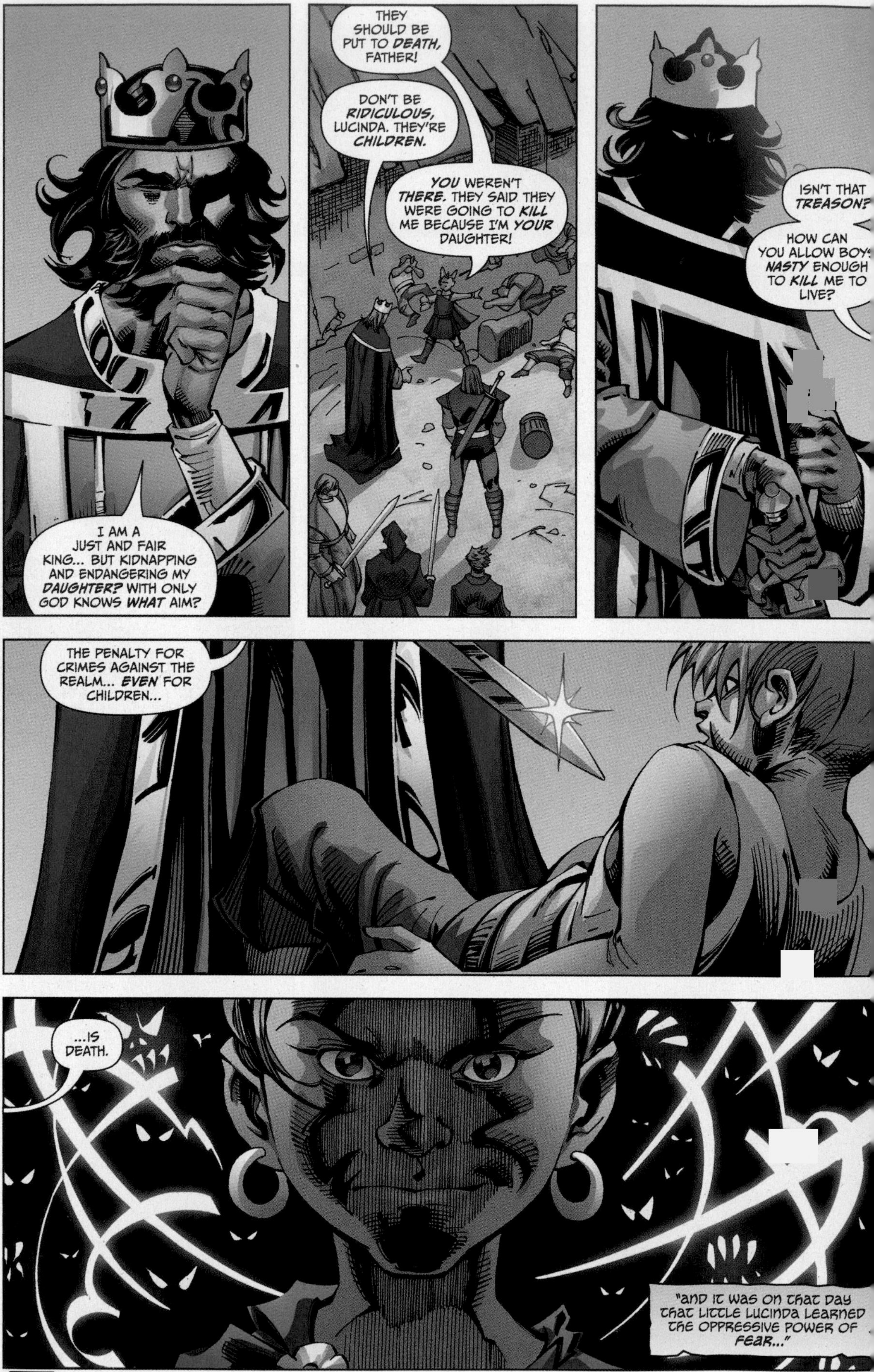

I AM A JUST AND FAIR KING... BUT KIDNAPPING AND ENDANGERING MY *DAUGHTER?* WITH ONLY GOD KNOWS *WHAT* AIM?
THEY SHOULD BE PUT TO *DEATH,* FATHER!
DON'T BE *RIDICULOUS,* LUCINDA. THEY'RE *CHILDREN.*
YOU WEREN'T *THERE.* THEY SAID THEY WERE GOING TO *KILL* ME BECAUSE I'M *YOUR* DAUGHTER!
ISN'T THAT *TREASON?*
HOW CAN YOU ALLOW BOY *NASTY* ENOUGH TO *KILL* ME TO LIVE?
THE PENALTY FOR CRIMES AGAINST THE REALM... *EVEN* FOR CHILDREN...
...IS DEATH.
"AND IT WAS ON THAT DAY THAT LITTLE LUCINDA LEARNED THE OPPRESSIVE POWER OF *FEAR...*"

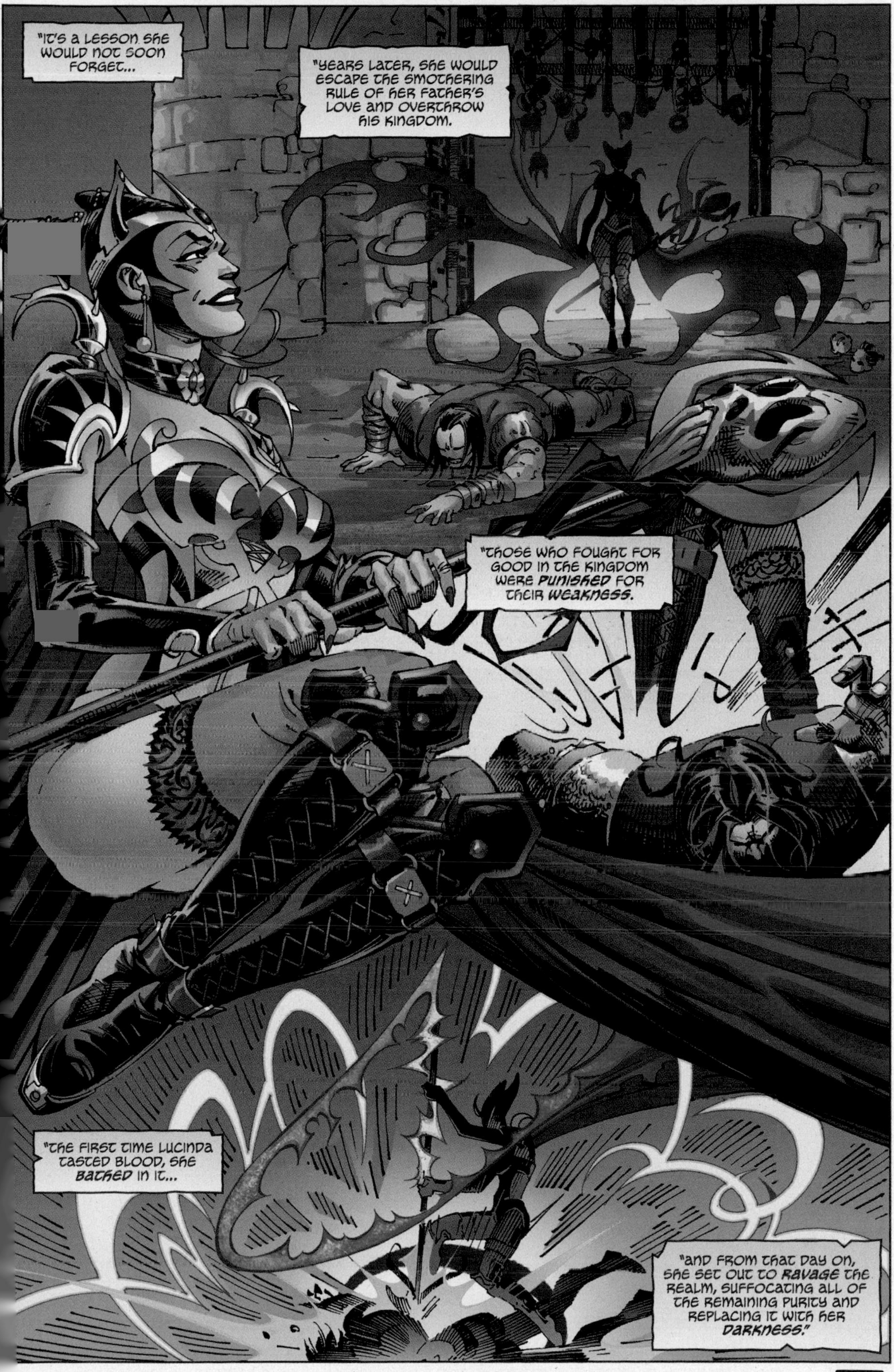
"IT'S A LESSON SHE WOULD NOT SOON FORGET...
"YEARS LATER, SHE WOULD ESCAPE THE SMOTHERING RULE OF HER FATHER'S LOVE AND OVERTHROW HIS KINGDOM.
"THOSE WHO FOUGHT FOR GOOD IN THE KINGDOM WERE PUNISHED FOR THEIR WEAKNESS.
"THE FIRST TIME LUCINDA TASTED BLOOD, SHE BATHED IN IT...
"AND FROM THAT DAY ON, SHE SET OUT TO RAVAGE THE REALM, SUFFOCATING ALL OF THE REMAINING PURITY AND REPLACING IT WITH HER DARKNESS."

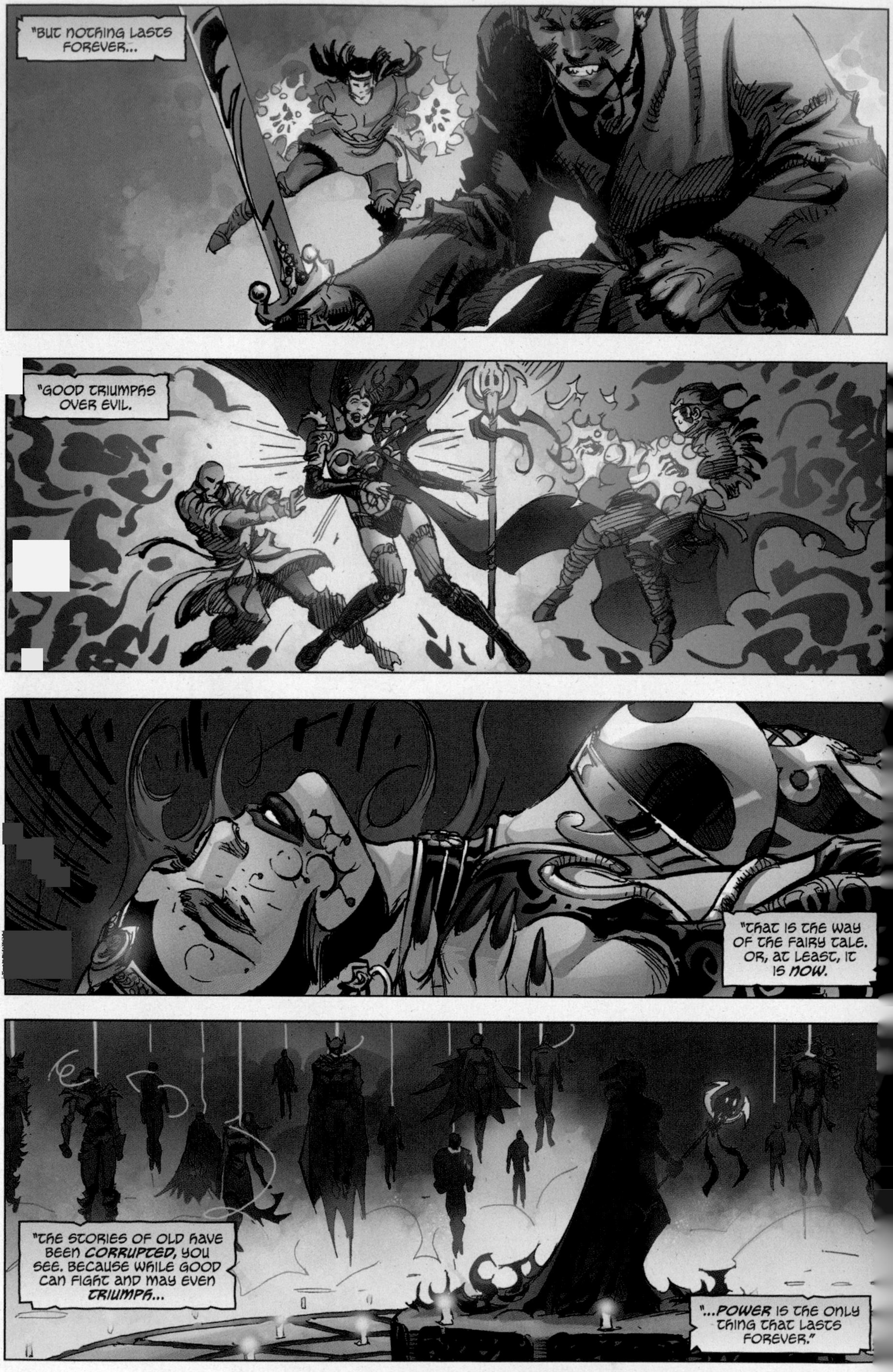
"BUT NOTHING LASTS FOREVER...
"GOOD TRIUMPHS OVER EVIL.
"THAT IS THE WAY OF THE FAIRY TALE. OR, AT LEAST, IT IS NOW.
"THE STORIES OF OLD HAVE BEEN CORRUPTED, YOU SEE. BECAUSE WHILE GOOD CAN FIGHT AND MAY EVEN TRIUMPH...
"...POWER IS THE ONLY THING THAT LASTS FOREVER."

TO BE CONTINUED IN DARK QUEEN: AGE OF DARKNESS ONE-SHOT.

Grimm Fairy Tales

Volume 15

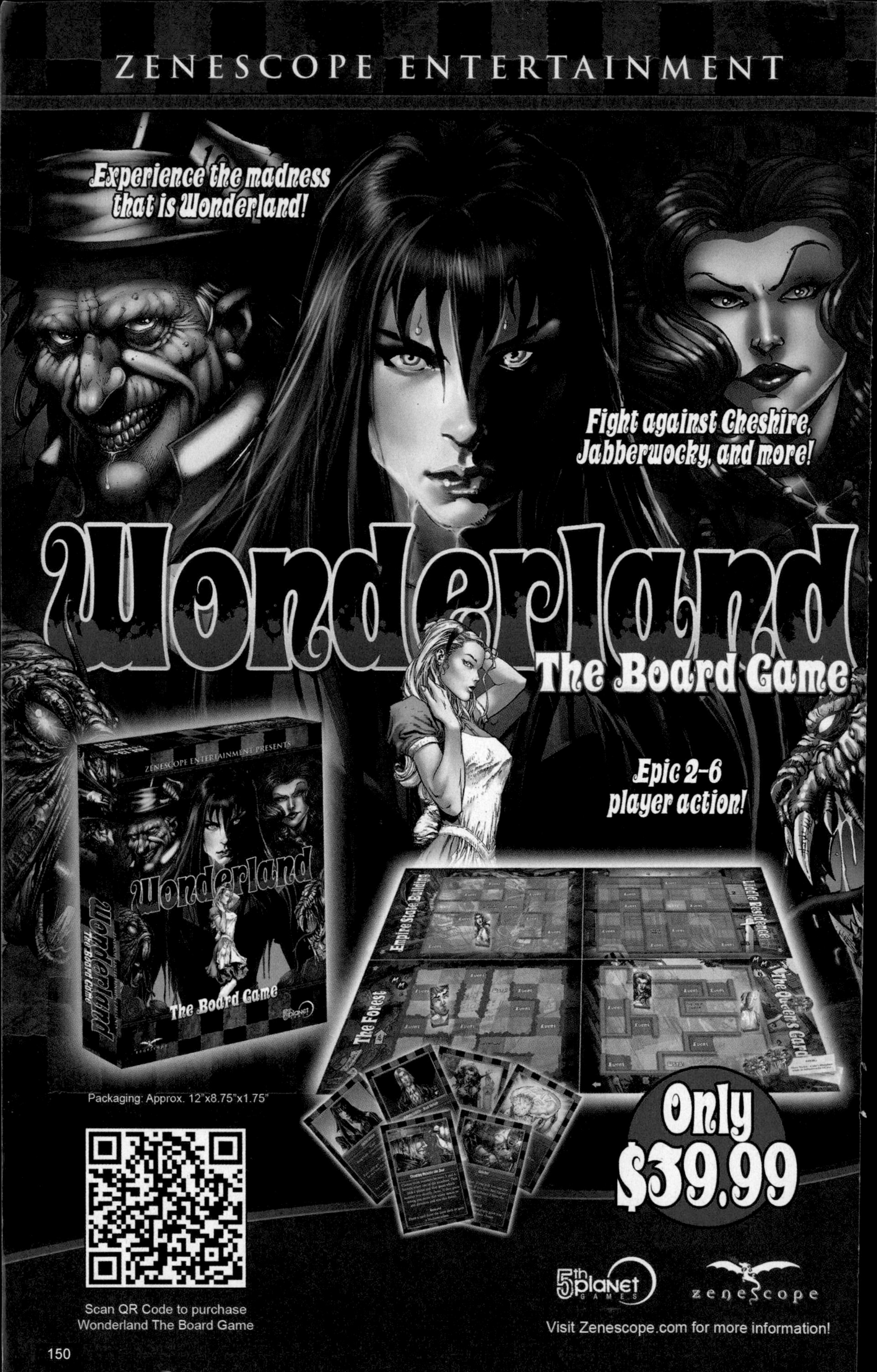
ZENESCOPE ENTERTAINMENT
Experience the madness that is Wonderland!
Fight against Cheshire, Jabberwocky, and more!
Wonderland
The Board Game
Epic 2-6 player action!
Packaging: Approx. 12"x8.75"x1.75"
Only $39.99
Scan QR Code to purchase Wonderland The Board Game
5th planet GAMES
zenescope
Visit Zenescope.com for more information!

ARE YOU READY TO PLAY?

MEGATOUCH AND ZENESCOPE ENTERTAINMENT PRESENT

Grimm Fairy Tales
Photo Hunt

only $4⁹⁹

SOLVE ALL 30 ROUNDS OF PLAY!

Available on the App Store

OVER 1,000 IMAGES FROM THE GRIMM UNIVERSE!

DOWNLOAD IT TODAY!

zenescope

megatouch

©2013 MEGATOUCH ALL RIGHTS RESERVED.
©2013 ZENESCOPE ENTERTAINMENT, INC. ALL RIGHTS RESERVED.

Grimm Fairy Tales

Volume 15